WEST-O

WEST-OVER-SEA

An account of life in the Outer
Hebrides set against the legendary
and historical background

D.D.C. POCHIN MOULD

acair

This book was first published in 1953
by Oliver and Boyd Ltd., Edinburgh,
and printed by
Robert Cunningham and Sons Ltd., Alva.

Republished by Acair Ltd.,
7 James Street, Stornoway,
Isle of Lewis, in 1999.

THIS EDITION
Cover Designed by Windfall Press.
Printed in Hong Kong
by Nordica International Ltd.

ISBN   0 86152 210 9

CONTENTS

CHAPTER		PAGE
I	WEST-OVER-SEA .	1
II	THE OLDEST ISLANDS IN THE WORLD	9
III	SAINT BARR'S ISLAND	22
IV	HEAVAL .	38
V	THE BISHOP'S ISLANDS .	44
VI	SOUTH UIST OF THE MACHAIR	64
VII	ERISKAY .	78
VIII	THE RIDGE ON THE EDGE OF THE WORLD .	91
IX	THE HILL OF THE FORDS	110
X	THE THREE HILLS	125
XI	THE COUNTRY OF THE CASTLES	132
XII	PORTRAIT OF THE MACHAIR .	153
XIII	LEWIS OF THE MOORS .	157
XIV	HARRIS OF THE HILLS .	184
XV	THE CROSS OF CALLANISH .	198
XVI	THE DUNS OF THE LONG ISLAND	211
XVII	CLISHAM TO MEALISVAL	227
XVIII	NO ROAD HOME	247
XIX	CROFT AND SHIELING .	250
XX	THE OUTPOSTS OF THE LONG ISLAND	268
XXI	CHURCH SITE AND SCULPTURED STONE	275
	BIBLIOGRAPHY .	290
	INDEX OF PLACE NAMES	294

The Viking sagas have a delightful term for their raiding and colonising visits to island Scotland. They speak of their heroes going West-over-sea. And because the Vikings went West-over-sea and settled in the Outer Isles, the Gaels of the mainland named the group Innse Gall, the Strangers' Islands.

CHAPTER I

WEST-OVER-SEA

THERE are, at the very least, three Scotlands. There is Lowland Scotland, the country of the big industrial towns and the broad farmlands. There is Highland Scotland, the mountains of the north and west, the Highlands proper; and in sharp contrast, the rolling uplands of the Border Hills. And there is Island Scotland, the Orkneys and Shetlands in the north and the Hebrides to the west.

This book is concerned with a part of Island Scotland, with the Outer Hebrides, the chain of islands which lie to the west beyond the Minch and form a breakwater against the Atlantic. The group stretches for 120 miles from the Butt of Lewis in the north to Barra Head in the south, a spatter of island shapes on the map, formed like the skeleton of some prehistoric reptile. In the north are the level moors of Lewis and the rough mountains of Harris; then come North Uist with its shapely hills, the low moor of little Benbecula and, south from it, South Uist with a fine mountain ridge; finally there is the rugged island of Barra with a string of little islands ending in the high cliffs of Barra Head. From the distance, from the mainland hills and the Inner Hebrides, the mountains of the Outer Isles, outlined on the horizon, suggest one immensely long island, and the Long Island is one of the old names of the group.

The Viking sagas have a delightful term for their raiding and colonising visits to Island Scotland. They speak of their heroes going 'West-over-Sea'. And because the Vikings went West-over-Sea and settled in the Outer Isles, the Gaels of the mainland named the group Innse Gall, the Strangers' Islands. Even to-day the old name has point, for the Gaelic speaking people of the Long Island are completely different in their habits and culture from the folk on the mainland across the Minch.

To go West-over-Sea, to the Outer Isles, one travels through the three main divisions of Scotland, from the Lowlands through the Highlands and out to the Islands. But there are a number of different roads to the Isles which may be followed, and for many people no road at all, for they will go by plane through the trackless sky. The air services operate from Renfrew and Inverness, the Inverness route going to Stornoway in Lewis and the plane from Renfrew working northward up the chain and making landings at the other two Outer Island airports, Barra and Benbecula.

At Stornoway one lands amongst flower-spangled fields just outside the town, but at Barra upon the hard sands of the Traigh Mhor (Big Beach). Yet I think that the Benbecula airport is most typical of the ways things happen in the Isles. You land upon the fine runways, constructed during World War II, in a big modern plane, and, if you are going to North Uist, find yourself very shortly afterwards splashing through the North Ford with a pony and trap. In a few minutes you can span the gap of centuries from the latest form of transport to the most ancient.

But the traditional way to go West-over-Sea is to sail across the choppy waters of the Minch, from one of the little West Highland ports. The old crossing to Lewis used to be made from Poolewe. Ullapool was another important port. Sometimes Skye formed a stepping stone to the Outer Isles: cattle for instance used to be shipped there, then made to swim the narrow kyle across to Glenelg on the mainland to begin the long trek south by the drove roads.

To-day the roads to the Isles converge upon the three railhead ports of Oban, Mallaig and Kyle of Lochalsh, having begun in the Lowlands of the Scottish Midland Valley. The road to Kyle of Lochalsh goes northward from Perth through the Grampians to Inverness and then across Scotland by the great furrow of the Dingwall-Achnasheen-Loch Carron valley to the narrow kyle between mainland and Skye. The road to Oban and to Mallaig crosses the Highland Line at Stirling or Loch Lomond and heads for Tyndrum. There the road branches, one way by the Pass of Brander and Loch Awe to Oban, the other across the wide spaces of the Moor of Rannoch, dipping down into Glencoe and then from Fort William on past Glenfinnan to Mallaig. Or one may go on from Fort William up the Great Glen and by Glen Garry and Dornie to reach Kyle of Lochalsh.

From the Lowlands through the Highlands to the Islands. At any of the three seaports you stand looking out to sea, watching the sun set behind the ragged skyline of the Hebrides. From Oban, you look to Mull; from Mallaig and Kyle to the mountains of Skye. The seabirds scream about the herring boats; all manner of cargo is being loaded on the island steamer—Glasgow-baked bread, mail, cows, sheep, a new motor van, a tractor; already there are snatches of Gaelic to be heard and you feel on the edge of Innse Gall.

I do not know which of the several routes followed by the mail steamers is the most attractive approach; each of them has its own fascination. There is the *Loch Earn* which leaves Oban and goes up the Sound of Mull to Coll and Tiree and across the open sea from these two small islands to Castlebay in Barra and Lochboisdale in South Uist. Her route is the most exposed, catching the full force of the Atlantic swell between Tiree and Barra, but the sail up the Sound of Mull in good weather is worth a lot of tossing later on. On the one hand there are the hills of Morven and Ardnamurchan, on the other those of Mull, and along the coast itself ruined castles whose names recall the great days of the Lords of the Isles: Mingary, Aros, Ardtornish and, of course, Duart, now restored and inhabited.

Mallaig and Kyle are both ports of call for the *Loch Mor*, which makes the round tour of Skye, sailing out from Kyle past Raasay and Skye and across the Minch to Tarbert in Harris. From there she coasts along the Long Island, calling at Loch Maddy in North Uist and Lochboisdale in South Uist and then returning to Mallaig and Kyle by way of Rum and Eigg. She sails close under the great mountain ridge of South Uist, and across the Minch one looks to the jagged line of the Cuillin Hills in Skye. In winter, with snow on the hills and a certain amount of mirage, you may stand on deck as the boat calls at Rodil in Harris and look across to the mainland hills, their rocks picked out in snow and every detail sharp and distinct. The fantastic mountains of Assynt—Suilven, Canisp and the rest—appear like icebergs floating on the blue Minch waters, solitary tops whose land mass is hidden below the horizon.

The ship for Lewis is the swift *Loch Seaforth*, the latest addition to the Outer Island fleet of mail boats. She runs from Mallaig, calls at Kyle of Lochalsh, and then goes direct to Stornoway. She passes within sight of the Shiant Islands, an isolated uninhabited group off the Harris coast and once a retreat of the Celtic saints.

There is a strange story told about the channel between these islands and the Lewis-Harris coast and a fabulous group of beings called the Blue Men. The Blue Men, *Na Fir Gorm*, according to Island tradition lived in the strait between the Shiants and Lewis—in Gaelic, *Sruth nam Fir Gorm*, the Current of the Blue Men or the Current of Destruction. They stirred up storms; only when they were sleeping in the caves under the sea or floating on the water was the Minch calm. If any ship dared enter the Current of Destruction, the chief of the Blue Men would challenge her in Gaelic verse and only if the ship's skipper was a better poet than the lord of the Blue Men could she hope to escape. Eventually, so the story goes, a ship sailed up *Sruth nam Fir Gorm* whose skipper was the better hand at making verses, and the Blue Men had to retire discomfited.

In the mail steamers with their radio and radar equipment, the idea of the Blue Men with their hands clutching at the planks of the ship seems very far away. But in a small boat in a rough sea, the Minch waters can indeed almost seem to be personified hostility.

Hebrideans are good sailors; you can hardly survive
the Minch seas without being highly skilled. To-day the
power-driven ship makes things somewhat easier; coast-
wise work in small sailing boats was a much harder
problem.

The story of Minch shipping is a saga all to itself. The
earliest boats, used by the first colonists, would be
curachs (coracles) and dug-out log ships. The curach,
hides stretched on wickerwork, can be built quite large
and is a very seaworthy vessel, riding lightly over the
crests of the waves. For landing on the more remote
islands, it had the immense advantage of being light and
portable so that one could haul it up out of the water
and over the rocks to lie in safety out of the reach of the
waves. Not only men, but domestic animals must have
been taken to the Hebrides in these primitive boats.

Curachs and dug-outs and some plank-built boats were
the vessels used in the days of the Celtic saints, who seem
to have managed to penetrate to the most remote and
inaccessible of the islands. The Viking inroads gave a
great upward surge to island boat-building and seamanship. It has been said, with some truth, that Hebridean
seamanship is due to a geological accident. Because
Scandinavia is a country of fiords, steep-walled and
mountain-backed, the sea had to become her highway
and the road her sons took to find richer lands to
plunder or colonise. The Northmen brought their skill
with ships to the Long Island people. Yet it is only
a half truth, for the Celtic saints in pre-Norse days must
have been very highly skilled sailors. It is the first
necessity of island life.

The Vikings did, however, introduce a fine design of

ship. The Viking galley, the 'sea ski' of the sagas, was a fast and handy ship, clinker built, with a single mast and a square sail. Additional power and manœuvrability were provided by a number of oarsmen. The typical Highland galley which is so often carved upon the medieval tombstones of West Highland churchyards is the immediate descendant of the Viking ship. It is a graceful vessel with a single mast, a square sail and a high prow and stern. Again, oars provide additional or alternative power to sail.

Highland galleys were of two types. There were the larger ones called lymphads, from the Gaelic *long fhada*, long ship, and the smaller birlinns. The name birlinn is supposed to be derived from the Norse *byroingr*, ship of burthen.

Later, the Minch saw fugitive ships from the Spanish Armada; then British men-o'-war searching for Prince Charles; in modern days, the gathering of the wartime convoys. The last of the sailing ships is still a recent memory; it is only since the First World War that the fishing boats have replaced their red and brown sails with motors.

There used to be a number of small sailing schooners which traded about amongst the Isles carrying a variety of cargoes. The last of these, the *Mary Stewart*, is yet to be seen, a rotting hulk, on the beach at Scarinish in Tiree. To-day the mail steamers carry passengers and the more perishable goods; a slower fleet of cargo steamers and the cheeky little puffers carry the rest of the Hebridean requirements.

In reverse direction, the boats take away the Hebridean exports, cattle and sheep and ponies, tweed, herrings, kippers, eggs and the famous cheeses of Coll in the Inner Hebrides. If you stand about on the piers and watch the boats loading and unloading, you will see a cross section of Hebridean life and economy displayed in front of you.

Perhaps because the islanders are good seamen, they sometimes excel themselves in understatement. Describing how a small ferry-boat had foundered close inshore (and happily without injury to her passengers), an islander told me in a soft and matter-of-fact West Highland voice that 'something went wrong with the engine. It fell through the bottom of the boat'.

CHAPTER II

THE OLDEST ISLANDS IN THE WORLD

THE story of the Outer Isles goes back to close on the beginning of things, for the rocks of which they are built are ancient gneisses of the series called Lewisian after that island itself. Everywhere about the world that these old gneisses occur they are the oldest, all the other rock formations being of later date.

And there is a tangled story within the Hebridean gneiss itself. First sands and muds and limestones were formed in the ancient sea; later, these rocks were heated and recrystallised and granite intruded into them, rising molten from the depths. And later yet, but very long ago, the rocks were thrust and crushed one against the other, till on the movement lines the gneisses were beaten out as a black, flinty crush rock.

But these were not the Isles as we know them. Ages afterward came the great volcanic eruptions and intrusions of the Inner Isles and St. Kilda. Then were formed the rocks of the Cuillin and the mountains of Rum, of St. Kilda and Mull, of Ardnamurchan and Eigg. But in the Outer Isles, bar a few minor intrusions, these Tertiary rocks are not represented. Together the old gneiss and the younger rocks formed a great mass of land which reached out to Rockall.

The rivers flowed west and north-west over the land massif in the country that is now Hebrides, cutting deeper and deeper, carrying away the land. And tensions developed in the rocks themselves so that whole blocks slowly foundered and the old continent became the new islands.

This was something of the way that the Long Island was made, first a mere district in a great land, then a real Long Island and finally a chain of islands separated from each other by drowned land valleys. Even yet this was not the Long Island as it is to-day. Lastly, there came the moulding of the ice sheets in the Ice Age, which smoothed and rounded all the rocks and hillsides bar the very highest tops.

The ice sheets moved out westward across the Minch, to where the Outer Isles rise steeply from the great hollow of the Minch. The base of the ice sheet could not ride up that steep gradient, but the cleaner, upper layers rode over the Long Island, the higher tops standing out above the bleak expanse of ice. Perhaps a few alpine plants survived amongst the frost-riven rocks of Beinn Mhor and Hecla and the Clisham, but for the most part the land was bare of life. Later, when the ice began to melt, these same high tops of the Long Island nurtured their own especial Hebridean glaciers.

This then was the beginning, the making of the land before the first Hebridean sailed northward to colonise the Islands. And always the land seems to have been growing less, for even to-day the sea is taking a little

more, here and there, of the machair land, the western
dune country.

The first Hebrideans came in primitive boats, coast-
wise, island to island. The oldest monuments that have
survived, and doubtless there were many generations in
the Isles before they were put up, are the great cairns
and the stone circles. Their builders came from the east
and knew how to grow corn and keep animals domesti-
cated.

The builders of the stone monuments, the Megalithic
people, lived at the end of the Stone Age and the beginning of the Bronze Age. But since the Isles are remote
and new cultures are slow to reach them, and the old
ways take a long time dying, the dates of these periods
may well be later than further south.

In Megalithic times, the pattern of habitation was
different from to-day. Now, roughly speaking, the east
coast of the Long Island is rocky and sterile and the main
centres of population are at the ports, where are found
deep water and shelter close inshore. The middle portions
of the Isles are mountain or peat bog, used only for rough
grazing and for sport. The west is fertile, a favoured
stretch of sandy plain called the machair (Gaelic, a
plain), and it is there that most of the people live.

But in the Megalithic period this pattern was different. Mark the cairns and circles on the map and see how
they are scattered all over the islands, all over the interior
where it is not possible to croft to-day. When a Megalithic cairn on Clettraval in North Uist was excavated, it
was found to be earlier than the peat and based upon the
rock below. Five and a half feet of peat were dug away
from the stone circle of Callernish in Lewis before the

original packing at the bases of the stones was reached.

So one can but conclude that when the Megalithic people lived in North Uist, the interior was free, or largely free, from peat, and that, for perhaps a great part of the Long Island, the bulk of peat growth probably dates from post-Megalithic times. This would similarly date the climatic changes recorded in the peat layers, in which forest and arctic periods have been found alternating with one another.

In the Outer Isles there is submarine peat, peat which the sea has overflowed in its encroachment. Peaty material sometimes comes up on the anchors of boats well out to sea off the west coast of the Long Island, and if the bulk of peat formation is post-Megalithic, this must indicate very recent and extensive subsidence. It gives point to the old story of the Princess of Harris whose hunting ground extended from Harris to St. Kilda.

After the Megalithic people, there were more incomers to the Isles: the people who built the round towers (brochs) and the other prehistoric forts (Gaelic *dun*, a fort, a knoll suitable for a fort). They were the Celtic people from Ireland who eventually became part of the new Scottish race of the kingdom of Dalriada.

It was round about 888 A.D. that the Hebrides became a part of the kingdom of Norway. The Viking raids had begun much earlier—Iona was first ravaged in 793—and these raids were followed by permanent Norse settlements. Many of the settlers left Norway because they felt they were being oppressed by their king and thought that they would find freedom West-over-Sea. But when the Norse settlements began, in their turn, to raid the mother country, Harald Fairhair took action and made a punitive expedition about the year 888. The result was the annexing of Shetland, Orkney, the Hebrides and the Isle of Man by Norway.

But the Isles have always been hard to govern from a distance. In 1089 Magnus Bareleg, so called because he adopted the kilt for his own wear after seeing it in Scotland, had to make a very large scale expedition to deal with the unruly Islanders. On this journey, Magnus got from Edgar, King of Scotland, acknowledgement of his right to all the Western Isles round which he could sail with the rudder in place. This the cunning Magnus made to include Kintyre, having his ship drawn across the narrow isthmus of Tarbert, he himself standing in the boat holding the rudder.

The Norse divided the Isles into Nordreys, the North Isles of Orkney and Shetland, and Sudreys, the South Isles of Hebrides and Man.

Toward the end of the Norse period the Lordship of the Isles arose. The Sudreys and Man were ruled by a minor king, subject to Norway, and in 1135 one Somerled appeared on the scene and laid claim to the Isles in opposition to the existing king, Olaf Bitling. Olaf compromised with Somerled by marrying his daughter Ragnhildis to him, but after Olaf was succeeded by King Godred there was open war. Eventually, about 1158, Somerled managed to drive Godred out of all the Isles and Somerled became King of the Isles.

Somerled was assassinated in 1164 when he was leading his men against Scottish forces at Renfrew. He was succeeded by his son Reginald, who styled himself Lord of Innse-Gall and King of the Isles, Lord of Argyll and Kintyre.

Although the Lords of the Isles must have been, more or less, independent kings, it was not until 1266, after the Battle of Largs, that the Western Isles were formally returned to Scotland by Norway.

The Norse left their mark in the Long Island. How far they extirpated the old Celtic inhabitants is uncertain; certainly when the Isles came back to Scotland they were Innse Gall, the Strangers' Islands, and with a population predominantly Norse. To this day Norse racial types are to be seen amongst Long Island people; and it was the Norse who gave the Hebrideans some of their skill with ships.

The Norsemen built mostly in wood and left no monuments behind them in the Isles, except the runic stone of Kilbar in Barra. They left many Norse place names, so that in a count made in the 1870's on the Harris and Lewis rental 160 holdings had Norse names and only 42 Gaelic, and these the smaller and poorer crofts. There were also 64 English names, mainly round Stornoway, and 3 others of doubtful origin. Gaelic is the spoken language of the Isles.

Some of the names are pre-Norse. Lewis and Uist are, and their original meaning is doubtful. Most of the Gaelic place names are post-Norse. Whereas on the mainland the Norse names are often coastal in their distribution, or found fingering up the big valleys but avoiding the mountainous areas to which the natives probably retreated, in the Long Island they are everywhere. Practically all the principal mountains are named in Norse, and it is the little hills that have Gaelic names —a complete reversal of the position on the mainland where the Norse raided and settled.

The Norse, in local tradition, are blamed for burning down all the Long Island woods. The islands were once well wooded, where there is now hardly a tree, and it is suggested that the Norsemen destroyed the woods so that the Islanders could not hide in them to ambush the invaders.

The tradition of the Norsemen is still vivid and to the forefront in conversation when the Long Island people speak of their past history. Everyone tells you about the burning of the woods as if it happened yesterday, and sometimes you will also get traditions stating that the Norsemen built the very much older brochs and cairns.

Under the rule of the Lord of the Isles were the different island chieftains and their clans. There were the MacLeods of Lewis and the MacLeods of Harris, the MacDonalds in the Uists and the MacNeills in Barra, the basis of the clan being Norse but becoming more and more Celtic as time went on. The MacLeods, for instance, claim descent from Leod, the son of Olave the Black, one of the kings of Man and the Sudreys.

It was in 1540 that Parliament passed the Act doing away with the Lordship of the Isles and annexing the Hebrides to the Crown. Till then, the Lords of the Isles alternated between support for and rebellion against the King of Scotland, and were not above liking the look of English gold. The position was made difficult at the start by the fact that the Government of Scotland was Lowland and English-speaking, and the Isles Gaelic-speaking and Celtic-cum-Norse in outlook. Nor could the law reach to the Isles. To catch a Hebridean chief meant a major expedition into probably hostile country. Feuds between individual clans ran their course; Edinburgh might fume about the lawless Highlands but it could do remarkably little about them.

Further, the Lowland Government was rather in the position of the fox who asked the wolf to read the inscription on the horse's shoe, and when the horse kicked and killed the wolf, remarked 'Cha'n eil mi na m'sgoileir, 's cha'n àill leam a bhi' (I'm no scholar and I don't wish to be one). The Scottish Government was not Highland and it did not wish to be. The Lowlanders disliked and feared the Highlanders and Islanders and made no attempt to understand their culture or their point of view. The Clans supported Bruce wholeheartedly at Bannockburn, but more often Lowlander and authority were in conflict with Highlander and Islander.

In 1411 the battle of Harlaw was fought. Donald of the Isles, quite rightly, laid claim to the Earldom of Ross on the strength of his marriage with Margaret the daughter of the Countess of Ross. The Countess, who had become a nun, had, however, instigated by Albany, renounced the earldom in favour of the Earl of Buchan, John Stewart. Donald arrived with force, and his invasion ended in the battle of Harlaw. This was one of the most bloody fights that Scotland has ever witnessed, and it ended with both sides exhausted and without victory for either. However, Donald was eventually forced to give up his claim to Ross.

When James I came back to Scotland after being imprisoned in England, he tried to deal with the Highland chiefs by inviting them to Inverness to a conference, and then, taking them completely by surprise, making them prisoner. Some were executed, others imprisoned— among them Alexander, Donald's son. He was released after a short interval and revenged himself by burning Inverness. On his return to the West the King managed to raise an army to intercept him and they met in Lochaber.

The Lord of the Isles was thus forced to take flight, and finally, after skulking in the hills for a while, made his way to Edinburgh and, alone, threw himself on the king's mercy on Easter Sunday at Holyrood Chapel. The king spared his life but shut him up in Tantallon Castle.

Whilst Alexander was in prison, his cousin Donald Balloch started another rebellion, in which the Islesmen defeated the Government forces at Inverlochy (1431). This affair went no further, for the Islanders merely ravaged the immediate parts of the Highlands and then went home with the spoils.

John, Alexander's son, who succeeded as Lord of the Isles, started a fresh insurrection in 1451. He managed to seize the castles of Inverness, Urquhart and Ruthven. The Great Glen formed a natural highway for the Islesmen and West Highlanders to reach and raid the fertile east coast country.

Perhaps one of the most curious acts of the Lords of the Isles was the treaty of 18th February, 1462, in which John of the Isles, Donald Balloch of Islay and the Earl of Douglas agreed to become vassals of Edward IV of England in return for money and a share-out of Scotland when that country was, by their assistance, incorporated into England. The Lord of the Isles was to get the northern part of Scotland and the Douglas the southern half.

As well as raiding on the Scottish mainland, the Islanders used to raid the Orkneys and the Shetlands. There is a tradition, perhaps adapted from the Norse one about the Long Island woods, that the Lewis men burned

c

the trees on Foula so that they should not shelter the inhabitants.

But peace did not come to the Long Island when there ceased to be a Lord of the Isles round whom the island chieftains could rally. It was James VI who conceived the idea of exterminating his unruly subjects. He had reports of the incredible richness of the Long Island fishings, and, hoping to make a vast sum of money by developing them, formed a company of gentlemen from Fife to make a beginning with the Lewis fishings.

The Fife Adventurers, who were to root out the Lewismen, develop the fishings, colonise the island and make a large profit for the king, sailed from Leith in November 1598, arriving at Stornoway four days later. The expedition failed, partly because of the inclement conditions in Lewis and partly because of the resistance of the Lewis MacLeods, who were led by some of the sons of Ruari, the last chief of MacLeod of Lewis. The Adventurers got a footing on the island, but were unable to remain there. They made two further attempts before they sold their rights in Lewis to MacKenzie of Kintail.

Kintail had been hoping to get the Lews for a long time, and had been trying to keep in with the powers-that-be and at the same time help the Lewismen to make things uncomfortable for the colonists. In 1610 Mac-Kenzie was commissioned to pacify the Lews, which he did, though Neil MacLeod, one of old Ruari MacLeod's bastards and the present leader of the Lewismen, held out on the island of Birsay on Loch Roag until 1612. Tricked out of his fortress, Neil fled to MacLeod of Harris, who calmly handed him over to authority. Neil was hanged in Edinburgh in 1613.

Elsewhere in the Isles, the treaty called the Statutes of Icomkill, drawn up by Bishop Knox and the Hebridean chiefs at Iona in July of 1609, was beginning to have effect, and the Islesmen, instead of resisting the Crown, suddenly developed their loyalty to the Stuart kings. The Statutes covered such subjects as education, the establishment of inns, maintenance of churches and ministers, disarming, restricting and reducing the numbers of idle men following the chiefs, excessive drinking and the discouragement of the bards. The bards were supposed to stir up the Islesmen to lawless deeds by their recitations of past glories and successes, and their uncritical praises of their chiefs.

In 1623 Kintail became Earl of Seaforth and Viscount Fortrose, taking the title of Seaforth from the place in Lewis on Loch Seaforth. During the Covenanting troubles the family swithered from one side to the other, but when the third earl, Kenneth Mor, succeeded, he supported the Royalists wholeheartedly against the Commonwealth. Cromwell had to garrison Stornoway against a possible Dutch invasion, for the Royalists hoped much from the war with Holland and even went to the length of suggesting that the Dutch should have the Lews in return for their help.

In the rising of 1715 all the Long Island clans supported the Jacobites—MacNeill from Barra, Sir Donald MacDonald and Allan MacDonald of Clanranald from Uist, and Seaforth from the Lews. Seaforth was again involved in the 1719 rebellion, such as it was, but came back to Scotland in 1726 and, aided by General Wade, obtained a pardon.

The '45 found only one Long Island chief ready to

join the Prince, Clanranald. Barra Head was the first sight of Scotland Charles had, Eriskay his first landing place. He was advised to return but obstinately went on to land on the mainland.

But when the Prince came back to the Isles as a fugitive he was successfully sheltered from discovery by the Islanders. Most of the population must have had a shrewd idea of Charles's movements but the troops never caught sight of him. Flora MacDonald, who got him out of the Long Island and across to Skye, was herself a native of South Uist.

Long Island fishings still attracted interest. Charles I had tried to form a fishing company but the Civil War made an end of it. Charles II tried again, inviting Dutch fishermen to settle in Stornoway, a project which failed for want of capital. Then in 1786 the British Fishery Society was formed to develop the fishings of both Islands and Highlands. It soon came to an end, but did set up one station in the Outer Isles.

The '45 meant the end of the old order in the Highlands and Islands. The pattern of mainland history of emigration, both forced and voluntary, of eviction and of changes in the ownership of the land, was paralleled in the Long Island. But the process did not go so far in the Outer Isles as in the Highland glens. The Long Island is not empty as is the case with many of the glens.

It is good to go from the mainland glens, with their rickles of stones and greens of old fields upon the hillsides, to the Outer Isles where the townships cluster thickly on the arable country.

For the moment, the Long Island is inhabited. It is still possible to live by crofting, because the weaving of

Harris tweed and fishing brings in just enough extra to make it pay. But, although the black houses are going, there is still a great deal of bad housing, overcrowded housing and, of course, a complete lack of modern amenities like piped water except in the towns at the ports. As the standards of mainland and town life go up, the pull away from the remote corners of the country grows stronger, and it is doubtful how long the Isles will be able to hold their young people.

That island life is worthwhile is undoubted. But there will have to be changes if the young people are to be kept. Mingulay, North Rona and St. Kilda are empty of people; it could happen to other islands too, not immediately but in the possible if far-distant future. 'In 300 years, there will be nobody living here,' says the young emigrant on the boat on his way to holiday in Harris. Or will there? Perhaps the little 3 h.p. tractor standing beside the loch and the ruined castle that I saw in Barra give one of the answers. The old fortress is in ruins but the new, brightly painted tractor is taking the place of the old foot plough and the spade.

But if island life is to adapt itself to compete with the attractions of the mainland towns, it must make its own adaptations for itself. Leverhume's business-like plans for Lewis and Harris were broken on the rock of crofter tradition. The Islands need the Mainland's help, but the islanders themselves must decide what to do with it.

For the Long Island is still Innse Gall, the Strangers' Islands. At Stornoway, on a fine day, they will point out Scotland to you, across the Minch. For the Minch divides more than mere masses of land one from the other.

CHAPTER III

SAINT BARR'S ISLAND

R OUND about the 1850's Colonel Gordon, the then
proprietor of Barra and South Uist, offered to sell
Barra to the Government for use as a penal settlement. The offer was refused.

Sir Donald Monro, High Dean of the Isles, writing in
1549, described Barra as 'ane fertill and fruitfull ile in
cornes, abounding in the fishing of keilling, ling, and all
uther quhyte fish'.

The real Barra is perhaps neither of these things,
neither so very fertile nor so very suitable for convicts.
Either way, the island began to seem beyond the reach
of human endeavour as we waited for the tide in Lochboisdale harbour. Behind, the day seemed to stretch
endlessly, my early start in the Highlands, Mallaig with
the sun on the white Morar sands, the ferry-boat coming
out to the mailboat from Eigg and Rum, the sun going in
and the Minch choppy and grey, Lochboisdale in the
gathering gloom and now the *Loch Ness* apparently rooted
there for the night.

There is a pattern in these things. First, we, the
Barra passengers, sat up in the lounge and chattered
about the catching of fish, about wild geese, about the

harvest on the beaches the war had brought and how to make easy money. Then, as the hours went on, and we still remained stationary, quiet except for the rattle of the crane loading, we curled ourselves up on the seats and dropped into uneasy sleep.

At last the engines started and the ship heaved to the swell crossing the Sound of Barra. Then the sea quietened, and I, sitting up, calculated that we must be almost upon Castlebay, the harbour of Barra. I got up, glanced at the huddled shapes of my fellow passengers, and slunk out into the open.

It was full moon with a cold wind blowing. The waves slipped from the bows of the steamer, white tipped, the moonlight glinting on them. The land lay dark, massive and humpy. On the one hand was the round molehill of the island Muldoanich, on the other, Barra itself, arching up to the crest of Heaval. We turned between Barra and Muldoanich, into the sound between Vatersay to the south and Barra to the north, and then, turning again, into Castlebay itself.

Upon a rock in Castlebay stood the old castle of the MacNeills of Barra, Kiessimul, its walls white like ivory. Behind was Castlebay itself, its houses ranging up the hillside, a light shining out from a window here and there. The steamer slipped past the moonlit castle to the white concrete pier, striking it a glancing blow as she came alongside. 'Bang goes Castlebay pier,' delightedly said the gentleman who had been explaining the retailing of Services' duty free tobacco earlier in the evening.

Now it was two o'clock in the morning, with the moon on the old castle and the pipes wailing from the town. Surely this island, with the white castle that seemed out of a fairy tale and the sobbing pipes, was never real? And yet, this was no mirage. The pipes were the end of a dance, and the castle, every night of the full moon, became a thing of dreams, a fortress on a rock in a shining sea.

The sea is the song of Barra. It is a compact little island, too compact for one ever to get out of sight of the sea or of some of its 2,000 inhabitants. North to south it is only 9 miles long; east to west it measures some 6½ miles. Centrally there are mountains, cut by an east-west pass; round the hills a good road links the houses. Rocky cliffs alternate with sandy beaches, lazy beds among the rocks and machair fields on the sandy flats. Northward the land narrows to a mere spit of sand dune with a broad beach upon either hand, and then widens again, buttressed by the rocky core of Ben Eoligarry, to Eoligarry itself, the northern tip of the island and the garden of Barra.

And always, the sea. 'I could not bear to live away from the sea,' one old lady told me. And even to-day Catholic Barra names the sea with reverence as a goddess not to be trifled with.

On Latha Fheill Brighde, St. Bride's Day, 1st February, when the boats are blessed and the fishing season starts, the Barra people sing a special hymn to the Trinity and the Virgin to protect them from the stormy sea.

> Athair, A Mhic, A Spioraid Naoimh,
> Biodh an Tri-aon leinn, a la's a dh-oidhche;
> 'S air chul nan tonn, no air thaobh nam beann,
> Bith'dh ar Mathair leinn 's bith'dh A lamh mu'r ceann,
> Bith'dh ar Mathair leinn 's bith'dh A lamh mu'r ceann.

Alexander Carmichael, in the *Crofters' Commission Report*, translated the verse:

> Father! Son! and Spirit's Might!
> Be the Three-in-one with us day and night,
> On the crested wave when waves run high,
> Oh! Mother! Mary! be to us nigh,
> Oh! Mother! Mary! be to us nigh.

They say that one of the Celtic saints blessed Barra, 'Toradh mara gu tir a'Cuile Mhoire', that the Virgin's treasure might be brought to the shore of the island. The sea is the Virgin's treasury. Wandering round Castlebay, I came upon a man painting the name *Ave Marie* on his boat in her honour.

When the frost turns the crotal (lichen) on the rocks red, the Barra tradition calls it *fuil nan Sluagh*, the blood of the Sluagh. The Sluagh is a curious tradition, an army fighting in the sky, a fairy host that may snatch a man up and carry him to a hilltop miles from his home. Perhaps those who have heard the Sluagh passing overhead have only heard the whooper swans on the wing, the loud-voiced hounds of heaven.

The Aurora Borealis, the *Fir Chlis* (Merry Dancers), is conceived as a battle, and the blood, falling on the earth, congeals into blood stones, for which the Hebridean name is *fuil siochaire*, fairy blood.

Whether the saint who made the Virgin's treasury the special perquisite of Barra was Barr himself I do not know. It is supposed that the island is named after him, Barr's Island, and to the north, at Eoligarry, is Cillebharra or Kilbar, the church of Barr, one of the holy places of the Outer Isles. There have been several saints of the name Barr, or in full, Findbarr, in the Celtic

Church. Barra's patron seems to have been Findbarr of Cork who died *c.* 610. His real name was Lochan, and he got the nickname of Findbarr from his fair hair, which is what the Gaelic means.

So northward I went to Cille-bharra, by the west coast, through stone-built and slate-tiled Castlebay to the townships where the black house still lingers, although here in Barra it is greatly tidied up, with a trim chimney at either end and the walls cemented. One house only in Barra keeps the old style with the fire on the floor in the middle of the house. I went past sandy beaches and rocky headlands, past the wide machair strip at Borve where the fertile level ground reaches up into the heart of the hills, past Allasdale where the blown sand is sweeping over the tarmacadamed road and Dun Cuier sits on a sharp green hillock, and on between the hills of the northern end of Barra and by the old ruined mill at Loch an Duin, with its island fort linked by stepping stones to the shore. I passed the postman, riding on a horse to deliver the letters, and a mouse-coloured pony with a couple of creels on its back, going for seaweed. And at last I turned off the main road to the rough Eoligarry track, snaking under grey rocks in front of which blazed a fire of gorse blossom, and came down to the cockle strand and the machair strip that links the rest of Barra with Eoligarry.

The Eoligarry track avoids the bumpy ride over the sand dunes by crossing the Traigh Mhor, the big beach, the Barra cockle strand. As I came down to the turn on to the sands, the little B.E.A. *Rapide* came gently down on the sand and taxied across to the small shed which stands on the grass at the edge of the beach and does duty as aerodrome offices.

There is nothing quite like the Traigh Mhor anywhere else in the Isles. The sands, which are largely broken cockle shells, have a peculiar silvery greyness, and they are left rock hard as the tide goes out, giving about a square mile of ripple-printed sand. This is the Barra airport and the road to Eoligarry, and neither the wheels of the *Rapide* nor the heavy lorries make any deep impression on the strand when they cross it. Crossing must wait on the tides, and the plane has often taken off in a shower of spray through the ebbing tide.

And, of course, there are the cockles, big succulent Barra cockles. A curious tradition surrounds their origin; you will find it in *MacFarlane's Geographical Collections* in an account dated about 1630, and in Martin Martin's *Description of the Western Islands of Scotland*, which refers to about 1695, but the earliest account seems to be Dean Monro's (1549). He writes:

In the north end of this ile of Barray ther is ane round heigh know, mayne grasse and greine round about it to the heid, on the top of quhilk ther is ane spring and fresh water well. This well treuly springs up certaine little round quhyte things, less nor the quantity of confeit corne, lykest to the shape and figure of ane little cokill, as it appearit to me. Out of this well runs ther ane little strype downwith to the sea, and quher it enters into the sea ther is ane myle braid of sands, quhilk ebbs ane myle, callit the Trayrmore of Killbaray, that is, the Grate sandes of Barray. This sand is all full of grate cokills, and alledgit be the ancient countrymen, that the cokills comes doun out of the forsaid hill throughe the said strype in the first small forme that we have spoken off, and after ther coming to the sandis growis grate cokills alwayses. There is na fairer and more profitable sands for cokills in all the warld.

When the cockles have been eaten their shells remain

and have been often used as a source of lime. The old
way was to build a heap of shells and then pile peats round
it and set it alight, the resulting lime being of very high
quality.

It would be easy to linger on the cockle strand and
look for razor-fish and cockles, or watch the patterns
made by eddies in the ripple prints, or lie in a hollow full
of primroses on the dunes behind the beach. That way,
however, would never bring one over the hill to Cille-
bharra.

The hill at the north end of the Traigh Mhor and the
dunes is Beinn Eoligarry, a rocky bluff smothered in
blown sand so that it is smooth and covered with springy
turf, the rock below only shouldering through the cover
here and there. This is Monro's 'round heigh know', I
suppose, 338 feet high and commanding a great view of
sea and islands. The road curls off the Traigh Mhor and
over the shoulder of Beinn Eoligarry. I left the track and
made my way over the crest of the hill, to look down on
Cille-bharra which is placed upon its northern flank.

After the magic of the moonlight on Kiessimul has
faded with the cold light of day, one begins to question
the charms of Barra and wonder why all the fuss over her
beauty. Her hills, after all, are lumpy and rounded, her
trees a few poor stunted things at Northbay, her streams
virtually non-existent. Her towns pitch their rubbish
and old motor cars over the side of the road toward the
sea. Her winds sting and there is no escaping them into
shelter. Somewhat in this frame of mind, I walked up
over the short turf to the top of Beinn Eoligarry on my
way to Cille-bharra and, unexpectedly, came on the
answer to the question, What is the beauty of the Isles?

For, though Beinn Eoligarry is a mere low rise, it rises alone and, like many island knolls, commands an outlook as good as any mainland mountain with thousands of feet to its height. I halted in the wind on its top and looked around.

To the south stretched the green strip of dune linking Eoligarry with the rest of Barra. To the east lay the Traigh Mhor with the tide out. The wet sand shimmered silver; the cloud shadows dappled the dune grass across which the sandy track ran like a narrow white ribbon. Beyond the beach were the Barra mountains, humpy, rocky and massive. On the other, western side of the dune spit lay the Traigh Eais, a long narrow beach of very white sand in vivid contrast to the grey Traigh Mhor. Upon this long beach the Atlantic, very bright clear blue, was riding in in long rollers, the spray blowing off the white crests as they curled over to break. Beyond I looked to Greian Head, jutting westward, and caught a glimpse of the Cliad sands.

And then I looked northward, down on the flat sandy land of Eoligarry, the garden of Barra, with its level machair fields, now in April being ploughed and planted, the strips of fresh-turned earth white with the sand that is in them. Spread out below were little brown-thatched black houses, the gaunt pile of Eoligarry House, and the more recent cottages that the islanders have built. At the extreme northern tip of Barra stood Beinn Scurival, 255 feet, a round green moleheap against the blue of the sea, which as it shallowed to the white sand beaches changed to paler blue and emerald greens. There lay the islands, the little islands off Barra: Hellisay where you may watch the grey Atlantic seals, the green sandy flats of Fiaray and Fuday, Eriskay with the Weaver's Castle squat on its rocky stack. Beyond, across the Sound of Barra, was South Uist and on it Beinn Mhor like a great table mountain with the clouds hanging low over it. As distant background across the Minch rose the ragged outline of the Cuillin and the Rum mountains.

This is the beauty of the Isles, the clear colours of a sea whose rivers bring no mud into it, the bright pale machair grass, the sands and the waves, the islands and the Cuillin spine in the distance. A pattern, not so much of form as of colour, of limpid, changing, living colour; of a light that flows upon the landscape like clear water. There is no smoke between you and the sun, no land between you and America, and the taste of the sea is in every mouthful of air.

And immediately below me, on the green flank of Beinn Eoligarry, and looking out across the Sound of Barra, was a low square wall, a cluster of headstones and a group of little roofless chapels, Cille-bharra, the most sacred spot in all Barra.

Johnson and Boswell were a little taken aback by Iona, so small and few were the ruins of the island that had once dominated Christian Scotland and the north of England. Hebridean churches are not, as I suspect Boswell expected to find, scaled-down versions of English Gothic cathedrals; they have their own styles, and by the nature of supplies of material in the Hebrides they tend to be small and simple in design. The largest of the three little buildings of rough stone at Cille-bharra is only 42 feet long. This was the church of St. Barr; the other two buildings were small chapels. When in use they would have been roofed with thatch.

I searched about in the grass to find the carved slabs and discovered three. They are very finely carved, each bearing a sword with foliage and interlacing strap-work designs round it; each slab has a slightly different pattern. There used to be more, but several seem to have disappeared fairly recently. Here too was found the only rune-inscribed stone known in the Hebrides. It bore a cross on one side and a rune on the other, and is now in the Antiquarian Museum at Edinburgh.

Assuming that the Celtic cross and the rune are of the same date, the stone is a relic of the Norsemen after they had become Christian. It is probably eleventh century work, and since carving of this sort is a Celtic and not a Norse art, it indicates some fusion of the two cultures in the Isles. The rune is obscure, but it has been suggested that it reads 'Ur and Thur erected this stone after Raskur. Christ rest his soul'.

When Martin Martin visited Barra round about 1695, there was a statue of St. Barr kept in the church. Martin tried to see this image but the people hid it, fearing that he would laugh at it. The tradition was that when the people began to build Cille-bharra, they chose a site on the south of Beinn Eoligarry, where, in fact, there was also a small chapel and graveyard once upon a time. They left the wooden image in the partly constructed church overnight. In the morning it had moved, mysteriously, to the site on the north of Beinn Eoligarry. When this had been repeated several times, it was taken as a sign from the saint that he wished his church to be built where Cille-bharra now stands.

The wooden image used to wear a linen shirt, which was renewed annually on St. Barr's Day, 27th September.

Properly St. Barr's Day was the 25th, but Barra seems to have favoured the 27th. On that day there was a great celebration, everyone coming to Cille-bharra on horse-back and taking three turns, sunwise, about the chapels. Horse races would follow on the sands. Even the minister of Barra, writing for the *New Statistical Account* in 1840, could describe as then happening this annual riding round the little kirk, 'each man on his pony with his wife or lass mounted behind him'. On St. Michael's Day, as elsewhere in the Isles, there was a further cavalcade and perambulation round the holy place.

This taking of a turn sunwise (Gaelic, *deiseil*) is a very ancient custom indeed and is presumably based upon sun worship and the movement of the sun. The tail of the Great Bear, of course, also shifts in this direction, point-ing east in spring, south in summer, west in autumn and north in winter. In Gaelic concept the seasons too move in the *deiseil* direction, the spring being considered east, the summer south, the autumn west and the winter north. Women in childbed and sick animals are kept from harm by perambulating round them sunwise carry-ing fire, and with one's torch building a fiery circle against the powers of evil. Friendly warriors approaching a fort would indicate their nature by going round it, *deiseil*; hostile parties made the circle anti-clockwise, *widdershins*.

Added to the very ancient *deiseil* idea is a Norse idea, that of horse cavalcades, which were very popular in the days when the Isles had many ponies. In Uist is the place-name Lochdar, from a Norse word, *hesta-at*, horse fight. The third element in the Barra amalgam of ideas is the veneration of a Christian saint.

There is another curious story about a well in the Cille-bharra district, mentioned in *MacFarlane's Geographical Collections* in an account probably written about 1630. It says that 'when appearance of Warrs wer to be in the Countrey of Barray That certaine drops of blood hath oftymes bein sein in this spring and fresh Water Well. The Laird and Superior of this Countrey was called Rorie McNeill being ane verie ancient man of sexscore years old or therby did report this to be true. And also did report this to be true lykewayes whensoever appearance of peace wold be in the Countrie That certain litle bitts of Peitts wold be seen'.

I went down the road past Eoligarry House, crossed the shoulder of Beinn Eoligarry and reached Dun Scurrival upon the western coast. This has probably been a galleried dun, a circular prehistoric fortress with galleries in its walls of the broch type, but little is left now but a pile of stones all covered with deep cushions of sea pinks. On the one hand is little Bagh nan Clach, the Bay of the Rocks, with some rusty wreckage flung on its shingle; on the other is the great sweep of the Traigh Eais. I clambered down between the fort and the sea, where the rocks face the waves in a sheer cliff face, with here and there ledges of turf. Here there was shelter from the wind, and a view of the sea sweeping in round the narrow channel which separates the little island of Eilean Dallaig from the cliff. This name means Mole Island for some reason or other, *dallag* being Gaelic for a mole, from *dall*, blind. Rock pigeons were squatting on the cliff ledges, and a few seagulls circled, tacking against the upcurrents of wind from the cliff face.

I went back to Castlebay by the east coast, the road

D

curling over bare, heathery uplands, with here and there a peaty loch, and the sea cliffs, low but rocky, close at hand all the way, until the road begins its steep climb over the shoulder of Heaval and descends from those heights to Castlebay. For most of the way there were houses and people. The townships have a mixture of languages in their names: there are Northbay at the road turn to Eoligarry, the Gaelic Balnabodach (the old man's township), and then the Norse ones, Ruleos, Ersary (Aefar's shieling) and Skallary (Skolli's shieling).

About these places, up amongst the rocks, everyone was busy: the women in long, full-skirted black dresses, often with brightly coloured aprons and with shawls over their heads (otherwise their hair would stand on end in the island wind), the men in blue seamen's overalls. April is a busy time in the Isles, and these people on the poorer side of the island were busy making lazy beds, or to give them their Gaelic name, *feannagan*. A feannag takes a lot of making. You mark out strips a few feet wide on the peaty moor, the line running up the slope, spread seaweed on them and then dig out the spaces between, piling the peat on the beds and leaving open drains between. In this way the peat drains sufficiently to allow the crops to grow, potatoes the first year and then a crop or two of oats, after which the beds go back to grass. This last, making a good grass park, is a major part of the lazy bed idea, for the hollows remain and keep the ground drained, whereas all around may be sodden heather ground.

On this day everyone was out, digging away at the trenches, carting seaweed in creels, and fertiliser, bashing down the hunks of peat with a special peg-toothed hand rake. Then the women, with pointed sticks and their apron pouches full of seed, would go rapidly over the beds planting potatoes. Incidentally, you cannot fork potatoes out of peat, but have to howk them up with a special hook called a crocan.

On the other side of the island, at Borve, things were very different. There the land is level and sandy, plough-able machair. On an island on Loch Sinclair is the ruin of Dun Mhic Leoid, a little square tower which, by the way, has no fireplaces. Here I saw a light 3 h.p. tractor at work, and further on everyone was out ploughing with two ponies to each plough.

'I suppose you want to know whether I'm living in 1498 or 1948?' a man asked me. I was walking up the cross-island pass from Borve, having been down to the site of St. Brendan's chapel on the machair edge by the sea. Everywhere there was the same picture—two horses, one plough, two men, one holding the stilts of the plough, the other the reins of the horses, with sometimes a miscellaneous procession of children and women and boys walking behind. The man who had spoken had but one horse to his plough and a boy to the handles and himself to the reins. He explained that each croft kept one horse, and needed two for ploughing, so they combined forces. Hence the two men to the one plough. In his case, he was teaching the boy to plough!

I went on up the west to east pass, a pleasant walk, though the path the map marks ends at the neat black house of my friend of the one horse plough.

As you come through the cleft the land falls swiftly to a wider and marshy valley, through which flows the Allt Heiker, a poor peaty rivulet. I halted at the top and looked out to the Minch and the Islands and the brown moor hills of the heart of Barra—pleasant enough hills to scramble on, though of the hollows between one cannot say so much. My descent to Ruleos on the east side of the island was marked by several sudden descents into peat hags.

As you return to Castlebay by the east coast route, and come down over the shoulder of Heaval, Kiessimul Castle is again the focal point, crouched on its rock, the mail steamer perhaps passing it on her way from Oban to Lochboisdale.

The Castle is a solid building, the largest secular building in the Outer Hebrides. It dates from about 1427, the date of the grant of the island to the MacNeills. There are, however, later additions dating from the seventeenth century, and in its later days the place was used as a herring factory. There is now talk of its restoration. On its rock it had two fresh water wells, so no doubt it served the MacNeills well as a strong place. The family were somewhat addicted at times to piracy. One Roderick MacNeill was actually captured and brought before James VI to answer for his crimes. Queen Elizabeth had complained that he was molesting her ships, and the Tutor of Kintail managed to capture the cunning chief by inviting him to a feast on board his galley and then making him prisoner, a trick that has been worked a good many times in the Hebrides. MacNeill, who was a mild-looking elderly gentleman, got himself out of trouble again by blandly telling the king that he thought he was doing his Majesty a service 'by annoying the woman who killed your mother'.

Kiessimul has some Hebridean features in its build.

Some of its slabs are bedded on edge, as is also done at Castle Calvay in Lochboisdale. The roof, which was thatched, rested on the inner side of the wall, as do the roofs of the black houses, so that the thickness of the wall provided a space along which one could walk. Kiessimul or *Cisamul* is interesting as a name, for it is Norse and means Castle holm, which would suggest that the rock was the site of a castle much earlier than the present building.

When Martin visited Barra a person called the Gockman was still employed to keep check on any would-be visitors, and, MacNeill being from home, he refused Martin admission. The MacNeill, according to an old story, used to send his trumpeter to the top of the castle wall, after he himself had dined, in order to announce to the rest of the world that they might now have their meal!

Cille-bharra is the burial ground of the MacNeills, and probably the dead would be taken there by sea, in the chieftain's lymphad. For the MacNeills the sea must have been their highroad, linking them with the other islands that were theirs, and with the rich plunder that might be taken by a bold hand. The sea must always have been the essential background to life on Barra. 'And sometimes,' as the old lady said to me in South Uist, 'you would think it was speaking to you.'

CHAPTER IV

HEAVAL

Heaval, 1,260 feet, is the highest hill in Barra, a mountain rising in a rock crested ridge from the town of Castlebay. Grassy slopes and rocky crags break up the green flanks into a series of slopes and terraces: at the top is a spine of grey rock, sheer toward the south, arching round to the north in a little ridgeway.

I walked up from the town by the main road which climbs up over Heaval's shoulder and takes the pass between that mountain and Beinn nan Carnan to the south. At the top of the road the steepest side of Heaval rises to the rocks on the summit, and that way up I went, scattering the browsing sheep on the grassy greens and scrambling up the sharp little faces of banded Lewisian gneiss: a good rock this to climb on, firm, and rough all over with holds for foot and hand. Of course you can go round the crags of Heaval, but it is better to take a handful of the stuff of the mountain itself and haul yourself up the straight way.

Heaval (high hill) is a Norse name, and for the men on the sea-ski it would be a landmark from the sea, the summit curving above the bay, the mist, often as not, floating on its top, so that it looked a mountain tremendous, mysterious. This trick of the mist on the Island mountains gives them an unreal height, so that they seem to tower above you, and coming so quickly upon their tops makes you seem a very fast climber.

But the day was clear and I lay in a hollow behind a rock on the top and looked all round at the sunlit land-scape. To the north I saw the Barra hills, the ridge of Heaval making a ridgewalk to the neighbouring Hartaval, and the flat-topped Beinn Mhartuin above the machair fields of Borve; to the west was the solitary lumpy mass of Beinn Tangaval overlooking the narrow Sound of Vatersay. These are marshy, grassy hills for the most part; only a few of the lower ones are heather covered.

Barra, unlike the islands to the north, is poor in lochs, and from Heaval only one was to be seen, Loch St. Clair with Dun Mhic Leoid on its island, a dour loch for fishing they tell me.

The sea was very blue as I looked down upon Castle-bay—the grey houses, the yellow seaweed on the rocks bared by the ebbing tide, Kiessimul grey and solid in the bay, the boats moored. As the sea shallowed toward the Vatersay shore, it changed from deep blue to a paler colour and became almost white over the bright sands. I looked down upon the Orosay of Skallary, a little rocky tidal island, and saw the white sand spit which links it to the main island through a film of water. As I watched, the clear water slid off the sands and black specks of men and beasts began to meander across to the island.

These tidal islets are very common in the Outer Isles and most of them go by the name of Orosay. There are about five Orosays in Lewis, seven in North Uist, three in Benbecula, two in South Uist, three in Barra and one in Vatersay. It is a Norse name, *Örfiris-ey*, ebb island.

Southward I looked upon the string of islands which form the thin, southern 'tail' of the Long Island. Across the Sound from Castlebay was Vatersay, twin east-west ridges linked by a machair spit, with flashing white sand beaches, perhaps the loveliest beaches in all the Isles. Muldoanich, very rocky and round, lies to the east of Vatersay, which is inhabited; Muldoanich is apparently without tradition of habitation. Southward from Vatersay is a green island with a high, rather leonine hill, Cairn Galtar, the only hill called Cairn in the Outer Isles. This is the island of Sandray. Beyond it lies Pabbay, and then Mingulay with the lift of its tremendous cliffs. Beyond Mingulay I saw Berneray with the lighthouse a white tower on its high cliffs. Round these islands are many little islands and rocks, all with their own special names in mingled Norse and Gaelic. They make a pattern of blue sounds and green islands, a pattern of a drowned landscape, of glens full of salt water and hills whose tops alone rise above the waves. It was almost incredible to realise that the cliffs of the little islands had once been inland crags.

Not very long ago the view from Heaval would have been different. The Norsemen, if they ever bothered to climb it, would not have seen the wide-mouthed bay in which Kiessimul now stands, for in 1549 Sir Donald Monro wrote, from his own seeing: 'Within the south-west end of this isle (Barra), ther enters a salt water loche, verey narrow in the entrey, and round and braide within. Into the middis of the saide loche there is ane ile, upon ane strenthey craige, callit Kiselnin, pertaining to M'Kneil of Barray'.

Now Castlebay has lost its rock barrier at its mouth and the sea between Rudha Glas and the Orosay of Castlebay, the two headlands of the bay, is a little wider than the breadth of the bay at the castle rock itself. Now the tide laps close to Kiessimul, so that the walls rise from a yellow collar of seaweed, whereas the description by the Dean of the Isles would give one the impression of a fortress set on a rock rising well above sea level.

Northward from Heaval I could look across the Sound of Barra to South Uist and the ridge of Beinn Mhor, a great bank of cumulus cloud moored over it. Across the Minch the mountains of Skye and of Rum had similar banks of cloud above them. This cumulus forming above the Hebridean mountains, and hanging like a fixed thing over them, is part of the fine-weather picture of the Isles. Above the sea the sky was cloudless.

In even clearer weather than the April day on which I climbed Heaval St. Kilda would have been visible and also the mainland hills on the other side. Mirage might bring them very close, or play odd tricks as in the case of Rorie McNeill. This young chief heard from skippers of ships and also believed tradition that there was, far out to sea, an island which belonged to him, 'which Illand is sein oftymes from the tope of the mountaines of Barray'. Rorie went to look for it and make sure of it for himself, found nothing and fetched up on the west coast of Ireland, from which he came back, disappointed, to Barra. This McNeill is said to have had 'sundrie bairns' by several noblemen's daughters; the succession being disputed among them, they came to fighting for it, and the survivor became the next chief.

Even stranger is the story of Rocabarra. This is said

to be a submerged skerry lying to the westward of Barra and on it are terrible monsters, plotting evil.

> Dà uair thainig Rocabarra am bàrr
> An treas uair bitheadh an saoghal bàth'te.
>
> (Twice has Rocabarra come to the surface,
> The third time, the world will be drowned).

Martin Martin, in his account of St. Kilda in 1697, actually locates Rocabarra as Rockall. 'Rokol, a small rock sixty leagues to the westward of St. Kilda; the inhabitants of this place (St. Kilda) call it Rokabarra.' Did perhaps a Barra man sail out in the Atlantic and see Rockall, suddenly near in mirage?

I left the top of Heaval, with its view down through the blue water of Vatersay Sound to the dark tangle beds on the sand under the sea, and returned to the road. This I crossed and climbed up over the little Beinn na Carnan, a pleasant, heathery height (500 feet) with sudden crags and gullies in the shelter of which the sun made the old heather smell as if it was in flower. From the gullies incipient streams lead down to the sea, and down to the sea I went, to follow the cliffs back to Castlebay from Rudha Charnain.

It was not particularly easy walking. There were no sandy beaches to which I could escape, and where the edge was too steep to follow, I had to detour a little inland. A cross-cut over a good spread of bare rock would bring me up against a geo and mean a trail inland to its head. These geos are very typical of the Barra coast—long, vertically walled, narrow inlets of the sea running deep into the cliffs, with primroses and celandines thick in the damp ground at their heads.

The rock of Barra has three main directions of jointing or parting: a rather faint set running horizontally, and two vertical ones along the dip and strike directions in the gneiss. This vertical jointing is the cause of the geos, for the sea works in along the planes of weakness and cuts narrow channels up them, which are sometimes roofed with natural rock arches. Inland the joint faces still affect the landscape, for the steep sides of the pass between Borve and Ersary are determined by them.

Now and again I passed old lazy beds, the ridges still marked, the turf short and green, surrounded by the unworked heather land.

I returned by Orosay—the one at the mouth of Castlebay—to the town, walking past the empty rotting sheds and decaying piers of the herring industry of Barra. Barra used to handle large quantities of fish, most of which went to the Baltic countries, and the numerous old piers of Castlebay are a relic of the trade. They give the place an air of slight decay, though in the height of the season I believe the place was unbearable. It was only in the latter part of the time that the guts and other rubbish were taken out to sea and dumped. Before then, Castlebay in the herring season had busy piers and packing sheds and smelt strongly and continuously of bad fish.

CHAPTER V

THE BISHOP'S ISLANDS

SOUTHWARD from Barra it was sailing that I would go, to the little islands where the Atlantic swell rides, crested, back from the high cliffs, and the little beaches lie white and solitary. Vatersay alone is inhabited now, but there are cattle and sheep upon Mingulay, Pabbay, Sandray and Flodday, and men go at times to tend them. Upon the southernmost, Berneray, commonly called Barra Head, there is a lighthouse.

These islands are called the Bishop's Isles, for, as Dean Monro stated, they all 'perteined to the bishope of the iles'. He tells us too that 'All thir nine iles forsaid had a chappell in every ile' (Wattersay, Sanderay, Scarpnamut (Muldoanich), Fladay, Pabay, Megaly, Berneray, Gigarun and Lingay). Vatersay, Sandray, Pabbay, Mingulay and Berneray also have ruined duns or forts, and these are said to be in sight of one another so that signals might be exchanged from island to island and on to Barra and the Isles to the northward.

To Vatersay I crossed upon a choppy day, to the annoyance of Allan MacDonald, ferryman and coxwain of the Castlebay lifeboat. He said that he did not like taking people out and bringing them back 'like drowned

rats'. There is perhaps a mile and a half of water between
Castlebay and the landing place at Uidh on Vatersay, but
the tide through the sound between the islands can be
exceedingly rough. That day the little ferry-boat put
her nose into the waves, and now and again one came
over the bows and I shut my eyes with the sting of the salt
water. We crossed the deep blue water of Castlebay,
and then, for the first time, I looked over the side of the
boat, and saw suddenly paler blue as we came to the shallows off Uidh. There were the seaweed beds, dark and
mysterious, the true origin perhaps of the legend of the
Land under the Waves. There was the clean white sand,
ridged with the to-and-fro of the tides.

Vatersay—the name is Norse like those of all the
Bishop's Isles (*ey*, island; *vater*, water)—is H-shaped. The
two legs of the H are the two rocky ridges which run
east-west, the high northern one of Heishival More and
the Uidh peninsula, and the lower southern one of Ben
Rulibreck and Am Meall. The cross-piece of the H,
linking the two ridges, is a strip of sand dune, with a long
white beach upon either side of it.

Island life on Vatersay has followed a pattern familiar
in the Isles, the ousting of the people to make the one
big farm, and, latterly, the breaking up of the big farm
into crofts. Vatersay houses are neat and new looking;
I saw no black houses among them, and the comparatively recent dividing of the land is perhaps the reason.
Her men go out to catch lobsters among the rocks of the
Bishop's Isles, and these, packed in tea chests, eventually
find their way south to the London markets.

I scrambled ashore at Uidh, with the realisation that
Allan MacDonald was taking the lifeboat out on an

exercise later in the day; he had firmly said that he could
not bring me back to Barra himself and that everyone
else in the island would probably be busy on their crofts.
Vatersay has no road; there is a sort of track over the
rocky ground at Uidh, past the little Roman Catholic
chapel and along the flank of the northern ridge above
the sea. There was a pile of wreckage by the path where
a plane had crashed during the War, and further on the
new school building looked down upon the wide sweep
of Vatersay Bay.

Facing the east, backed by the dunes and a broad
white sand beach, with to the north the rocky ridge of
Uidh and to the south the round lump of a hill called Am
Meall, Vatersay Bay is one of the loveliest in all the Isles.
It has, as Dean Monro recorded, 'ane excellent raid for
shippes that comes ther to fische', and there the Vatersay
boats are moored. There too the lobsters are kept
sunk till sufficient are caught to make up a box for the
market. Now that artificial pools are organised, the
lobsters can be sent to them first and kept back for the
high winter prices.

Across the dunes to the west is another white beach,
the Bágh Siar, which in the winter storms sometimes
encroaches deep into the dunes, so that Vatersay is in
danger of being cut in two.

To the south is Vatersay village, a cluster of houses
set upon the machair green and the pleasantest village
that ever was. For this little township of Vatersay has
no roads between its houses and no streets, only the
short turf of the machair, with the cattle, and the shaggy
Highland bull, roaming loose on it. There are little fences
around the houses to keep the animals away from their

immediate vicinity; light wooden harrows lie heaped here and there ready for the sandy potato ground; the township is vaguely untidy, redeemed by the green sward about the buildings. Now, in April, the primroses and daisies were just beginning to show on the machair land, the primroses that bloom all summer in the Barra isles.

It was to Bágh a'Deas, southward from the village, over the white sandy fields, that I was directed to go, for they told me that Bágh a'Deas, South Bay, was the finest beach in Vatersay, the island of fine beaches. With its clean sand swept between two rocky bluffs, the machair behind it just tinged with primroses, and the Sound of Sandray in front, I believe that they are right about Bágh a'Deas. It is a small beach as island beaches go, but perfect in shape and proportion and colour. The island of Sandray lies just across the water from it, while Flodday out in the Atlantic is glimpsed through the sound.

Vatersay is a good island for crofting, with fairly level fields, grazing for the cows upon the lower land and for the sheep among the rocks of her hills, the highest—Heishival More—being 625 feet. The island had three old duns: one near Vatersay village, one, a broch of which a certain amount remains, at Coalis (Dun a'Chaolais, the fort of the strait, the Sound of Vatersay) and one at Biruaslum. This last is a high and inaccessible rock off the coast to the west of Heishival More.

Where the Uidh promontory tails out to the east, in the skerries of Snuasimul and Sgeir na Muic, is the tidal island of Uinessan. Upon this islet is an ancient burial ground and a ruined church, Cille Bhrianain. The chapel is commonly called Caibeal Moire nan Ceann, the Chapel of Mary of the Heads. Mary was a Coll woman who married a MacNeill of Barra. She had the attractive habit of having anyone beheaded that she took a dislike to, hence her by-name, Moire nan Ceann. She asked to be buried in sight of her native Coll, and with that intent her body was carried to Cille Bhrianain. But when they got there Muldoanich blocked the view of Coll. The men were tired, however, and they could not be bothered to go any further, so they buried Moire nan Ceann there, with a splendid view of Muldoanich!

How I got back to Barra from Vatersay, Allan Mac-Donald having a lifeboat exercise and the men busy at their crofts, is typical of the way things are done in the Outer Isles. Mrs. Campbell of the Post Office in Vatersay village directed me round beyond Uidh, to Coalis, on the narrowest part of the Sound of Vatersay. There I was to ask at a particular house to be taken across to Barra.

When I had followed the path round, two men were busy with a boat, and I went down to enquire of them for the person I was seeking. But as I began my explanation they cut me short, for Mrs. Campbell had already rung them up on the telephone and told them to expect me. But, alas, they were fitting a new engine to their boat and it could not go. Still, if I asked at the house I would next come to, there would be a boat.

This I did, but the woman who came to the door looked suspicious till I mentioned Mrs. Campbell and whence I came. Then action was immediate; the men went down to the little slipway among the rocks, a passing Barra boat was shouted at and brought in, and I stepped into it.

She was a small boat, this *Ocean Spray*, manned by a party of smiling young fishermen. They lent me an oilskin and instructed me to lie on the bottom of the boat as we caught the rough stuff in the middle of the sound, the little ship striking the waves in a series of violent bumps and the spray dashing over her bows. 'I hope you're not seasick,' said one of the men as we bounced across, for all the world like a car taking potholes at speed. But a moment later we passed into smoother water and cautiously drew up to seaweed-covered rocks on which I somehow or other made a landing. 'Will I be owing you something for this?' I asked, balancing on the wet seaweed. But they smilingly refused any suggestion of payment for the ferry and were off again into the Sound, while I climbed over a rocky ridge back to Castlebay. It had been a grey morning. Now the sun suddenly came out, the sea became a deep blue flecked with white and the mist slowly cleared off the broad shoulder of Heaval.

It was a very low tide, and when Mrs. Campbell of Vatersay's husband, Neil, brought his little lobster boat up to Castlebay pier, her deck was well below the floor of the alley way down which they drive the cattle into the holds of the boats to take them to the mainland. Furthermore, the only means of getting to the small boat seemed to be by some gymnastic work with an end of rope. When I looked down, the slight swell rocked the boat sickeningly, the green shadows under the pier shivered and gleamed, and the gap between boat and pier changed with every ripple. To a landsman with a half-mended sprained ankle the position called for strong language, and only the presence of two Catholic priests restrained it.

E

But at last the moment came, and I grabbed the rope and slithered down into space and, surprisingly, on to the deck of the lobster boat. On this Sunday afternoon, a perfect April day, we were to go to Mingulay and Berneray to land supplies. The priest of Castlebay and I were making our first visit to Mingulay.

So away we sailed from Castlebay, the town that was once called Baile Mhicneill, MacNeill's town, past Kiessimul Castle on its rock and out into Vatersay Sound while Heaval rose green at the back of the town behind us and the glossy straps of the tangle were bared by the ebb tide. Someone watched intently for the lobster pot buoys that we might not foul them as we passed between the skerries which reach out from Uinessan to Muldoanich. One group of rocks is pleasantly called Sgeirean Fiaclach, tooth skerry, from the jagged edges of rock.

Muldoanich itself is round and humpy with steep craggy cliffs. Dean Monro says there was a chapel on it, that there was 'a hake nest in it' and that it was 'full of pastures, and verey guid for fishing'. He called it Scarpnamutt, and this, or Scarp, was its old name; Duncan's island, Muldoanich, is its present name. Martin Martin (1695) calls it Muldonish and says that it 'is the only forest here for maintaining the deer, being commonly about seventy or eighty in number'. Toward the Barra side a low rock off the coast is called An Laogh, the Calf; Muldoanich is presumably regarded as its dam.

Then we headed southward, past the white sweep of Vatersay Bay and the rocky heap of Am Meall, past Ben Cuier, green with the shell sand blown up against its rocks, past little Bágh a'Deas as we turned westward into the Sound of Sandray.

Sandray, Sandy Island, abounding in rabbits, is an island of two hills, Cairn Galtar (678 feet) to the one hand and a lower ridge to the east, the big valley Gleann Mor making a trench between them. There is a dun high up on Cairn Galtar overlooking the Atlantic, and the traces of an old chapel, Cille Bhride. The chapel site, now partly occupied by a sheep fank, is to the south-east of Bágh Ban—the white bay so called for its sand—which faces across the Sound of Sandray to Bágh a'Deas in Vatersay. There are several little white beaches among the Sandray cliffs, and backing them we saw the greens of old cultivations and the traces of ruined houses. The cliffs rise sheer and high. To the west is Knock Noddimull and then, leading from it to the south, a great craggy tail of rock edges out into the sea like a break-water; it is Ard Pabback, the Priest's Point. On the east side, curving out from a white sand bay, is Meanish, another rough little point, off which flounders are to be caught, and round which we watched sharks gliding, their dorsal fins jutting through the water.

As we went southward upon the west coast of Sandray, out to sea was Flodday, sheltering us from the full force of the Atlantic swell. The name perhaps means Floating Island, and it seems to float upon the sea, a low, green-topped mound, or rather two mounds. The green turf of the islands ends in steep little cliffs, and the two parts are joined by a narrow neck of rock, through which the sea has cut a natural arch. This cut has been made by the sea working along one of the vertical joint faces in the gneiss, the same joints that cause the geos of the Barra cliffs.

Between Sandray and Pabbay is a further sound, the

Sound of Pabbay, wider than that between Sandray and
Vatersay. In it is the low moundy islet of Lingay, heather
island, and the rock of Greanamul. Next is Pabbay,
the Priest's island.

The several Pabbays of the Islands, the name being
Norse, are generally supposed to mean that there were
priests of the Celtic Church on them when the Norsemen
came to the Isles. And yet, of course, the name may not
be as old as that; the priests of the Pabbays may have
come there when the Northmen had been, more or less,
converted to Christianity.

It is a pleasant island, this Pabbay of the Bishop's Isles.
To the east are sandy greens, and another white-sanded
Bágh Ban, sheltered by a rough, rocky point called Rosinish, Horse Headland. At Rosinish is the red fort, Dunan
Ruadh, a broch which looks across the Sound of Pabbay
to the other dun, also a broch, in Sandray. At Bágh Ban
in Pabbay are the faint remains of another ancient chapel,
and as the sand drifts human bones often appear in the
old burying ground. Three cross-marked stones are to be
seen, and a very interesting and ancient symbol stone,
marked with a crescent, a cross and a lily. These symbols
are of quite a different culture and tradition from the
interlacing patterns of the tombstones at Cille Bharra,
and indicate a distinct influence from the eastern
'Pictish' parts of Scotland.

The shell sand of Pabbay is so rich in lime that with
the frequent rain it has dissolved and been redeposited
to form beds of impure limestone. To the west the island
ends in cliffs. The Hoe is 560 feet high, and its Atlantic
face is for the most part a great sheer cliff. Here there is
no Flodday to break the Atlantic swell; it comes in straight

for the high cliffs and piles against them, the wave crests arching back on the heave behind them and charging forth again to merge in the incoming surge. It had been calm in Castlebay that morning, and it was smooth enough until we had got upon the Atlantic side of the Bishop's Isles. Now we were in the swell, a long Atlantic swell, and, keeping close under the cliffs for my benefit, were into the trough and crest of this back-and-fro off the cliffs. For the first time I realised how the sea can have topography like the land, hills and glens, valleys blue and sudden, the bases of the islands suddenly out of sight as we plunged into the troughs. I waited for the crests to photograph the cliffs and thought that the dinghy, which we were towing, might provide a more exciting ride. It pranced on its rope behind us on the tossing sea whose blue was hard and dazzling to the eyes.

The Sound of Mingulay between Pabbay and Mingulay is marked by two groups of rocky skerries, the Inner and Outer Heiskers, a Norse name that may mean Flagstone islands. The Inner ones, low, dark, lean rocks, jutting into the swell, seemed to me like hounds straining at the leash to be away to the westward. Behind us was Pabbay and someone began to tell the story that has been told more than once in the Hebrides. On Pabbay one day the women and the children and the old men looked in vain for the return of their menfolk who had gone fishing in the one boat. They never came, and no one knows what rock or what sea was their ending.

It has often been said that if the people had stayed a little longer on these islands with their swift seas and sudden storms the coming of the power-driven boat would have revolutionised life there. It is a very different thing to face the seas with a petrol engine. Even so, everyone was pointing out the rocks where ships of the wartime convoys had run ashore. The Mingulay man who was steering stood very straight against the shifting sea, looking into the distance as he brought the boat round the rocks of Mingulay Sound. Ahead rose the great western cliffs, the second highest in Britain (St. Kilda has the highest, some 1,300 feet). Off them stand sheer rock stacks, some with English names, the Red Boy and the Barnacle Rock, some Norse and Gaelic mixed, Sgeir nan Uibhean, Solon More and Solon Beg.

We came into the shelter of the island, coming across to the east side where the cliffs are lower, and the rocking of the boat steadied. Running close in the shelter of the land, someone suggested that the men tending the sheep on the island would be taken by surprise and not able to damp down the still in time! Maybe it was not mere idle talk, for Barra had once upon a time been a great place for the distilling.

Mingulay is shaped like a broken saucer, sloping to the east from the high cliffs on the west side, where Biulacraig, the second highest cliff in Britain, drops sheer nearly 700 feet to the Atlantic; to the east there is a little white sand beach with rocky cliffs on either side. A stream runs through the sands; its source is nearly at the sea edge to the west at Biulacraig, and is a token of the great sea erosion that has gone on in the Outer Isles.

In May and June the birds come to the Mingulay cliffs in their thousands, sitting there packed nest to nest. How they remember whose nest is whose is something of a mystery. Most fascinating of all are the sea galleries of Mingulay, the long tunnels, the arcades and arches where the Atlantic has eaten in along the gneiss joints.

'There is,' wrote Alexander Carmichael in the *Crofters' Commission Report* (1884), 'probably no more interesting island in Britain than this island of Miuley, with its wonderful precipices, long narrow sea galleries, several hundred feet high in the perpendicular sides, and marine arcades, winding their gloomy subterraneous ways under the precipitous island. To boat through these galleries and arcades needs a calm sea, a good crew, and a steady nerve. The writer was the first to discover, and the first and the last to go through much the longest, largest, and gloomiest of these wonderful sinuous sea arcades.'

The landing on Mingulay requires calmish water (this very morning would have been too rough). I believe the people used to rush the surf on the sands, but the present routine is to land on the rocks at either side of the bay. Already we had been seen by the men camping at the old schoolhouse; they all came trooping down the track to the cliff edge and then festooned themselves down a rock face. The dinghy was pulled alongside, loaded with meal and petrol and what-not and rowed off to the rock edge. As the swell brought her close up, a tin went out and was passed hand to hand up the cliff to a safe stance. We came afterwards, jumping for the wet rock and scrambling up the cliff to the top. To switch from the pitch and toss of the lobster boat to the more or less stable business of climbing up rock is a peculiar sensation. But the reverse proceeding is rather worse, since the object you are trying to reach is itself shifting upon the sea, and at one time I considered whether it might not be better to remain permanently upon Mingulay.

After the breeze on the sea, the cup-shape of Mingulay was stiflingly hot. We passed the old schoolhouse where the men managing the sheep stay, and went on to the old village at the head of the bay, with its drifts of sand and little round graveyard standing on a knoll. The old black houses are ruined and roofless. Behind them is the fairly modern chapel house, with an outside flight of stairs leading up to the chapel over the living rooms, which now house the shepherd's potatoes. We climbed up the stairs and pushed open the door into the empty room that had once been Mingulay chapel. The priest took off his hat as we stood on the bare boards with the sunlight filtering in through the dirty glass of the windows; it was even more desolate than the roofless houses of the old village.

Mingulay potatoes are claimed to be the best in the Long Island, and the neat fields, each fenced with stones, lead up almost to the western crags. The sheep were cropping them now, but down by the old village was a piece of ploughing ready to grow a crop for the shepherd's use. An Iron Horse 6 h.p. tractor, gay in its yellow paint, was at work there. They brought it ashore in pieces and reassembled it on the island, and when we landed little heaps of parts were still scattered along the cliff edges.

To the north is Macphee's Hill (735 feet), to the south Hecla and Carnan (891 feet), both green and grassy heights. Hecla (Norse-named, 'hooded shroud') is one of two so-called in the Outer Isles. The other is in South Uist. We made our way up by the stream-side, across the old fields to the cliff edge, Biulacraig, and looked down sheer to the sea, some 700 feet below. From that height the sea looked still and calm, and there was nothing to give scale to the crag until one picked out an odd white speck of a bird here and there. Roseroot and royal ferns, clumps of primrose and celandine grow on the Mingulay rocks. Looking back down to the bay, we could see, across the Minch, the tops of the Cuillin and of Rum.

How did the Mingulay people live? T. S. Muir, writing in 1866, describes the village as 'a picturesque huddle of rude dusky huts, inhabited by eighteen families, supporting themselves by their fishings, and the potatoes, small oats, rye, and barley, grown on their little farms. The rents of these, I was told, range from £2 10s. to £3 10s. each'. He goes on to say that each crofter kept two or three cows and at least one pony, and that they had plenty of peats. The people of Berneray, on the other hand, had to come to Mingulay to get their peats, there being none on their island.

The seabirds provided the Mingulay people with a supply of food. Incidentally, seabirds are still relished in the Isles. The chief point to note in preparing them is to extract as much of the oil as possible first. If, for instance, you make a broth of them, with oatmeal, the oil should be skimmed off as it rises.

Mingulay people, unlike the St. Kildans who habitually used ropes, went after the birds and their eggs by scrambling up the rocks like goats. The gneiss is a good firm rock for climbing but a man slipping would have little chance in the surf swirling round the bases of the cliffs. In Martin's time (1695) the Mingulay people had a star climber called Gingich. This man, when they went after birds on the stack of Lianamul, used to jump first out of the boat, scramble up and let down a horse-hair rope for the rest. Coming back, he again took the chief risk by jumping first back into the boat.

Entirely without ropes, however, the Mingulay people went up Greanamul after fachaich. Fachaich (fatlings) are the young of the shearwater, and in the old days were a kind of currency in which Mingulay rents were paid. MacNeill would arrive in his galley from Barra a fortnight before Lammas and stay at Mingulay for four weeks. Until he came the Mingulay people were not allowed to go after the shearwaters. MacNeill used to get at least 20 barrels of birds each year. The crofts were of different sizes, Peighinn (penny) ones paying 2 barrels of fachaich rent, Leth-Pheighinn paying 1 barrel, Feoirlig (farthing) paying a half barrel and Clitig (half farthing) a quarter barrel.

The rock of Biulacraig was both the war-cry and the crest of the MacNeills of Barra. Martin relates that if any Mingulay man lost his wife he used to ask MacNeill to choose him another. A widow, in like fashion, could apply for the choice of another husband! MacNeill also made up to his tenants any milk-cows that might be lost in bad weather or by accident.

Another old custom once observed in Mingulay was that of dividing up any party of strangers, one to each house in the village, separating even husband and wife. On arrival, the islanders used to insist on the stranger having a meal immediately. This meal was called Ocean Meat and they said it was essential because the sea air gave one a sharp appetite.

At the time when the old *Statistical Account* of Mingulay and the other Barra isles was written (1794), the Mingulay people used to take their sheep to the stack of

Lianamul, the same which Gingich used to climb. The men got up first and then pulled the wedders up after them on ropes, leaving them to fatten on the rich grass on the top of the rock.

The name itself, Mingulay, is spelt by Dean Monro Megaly (much the way they say it still in Barra); MacFarlane spells it Mewla. The Gaelic is *Miulaidh*. It is a Norse name, *Mikil*, big, or big island. The 'g' is soft, the way it is still in some parts of Norway, where they pronounce it *Migil*.

The people left Mingulay about 1908 and most of them settled in Vatersay. In 1901, 135 people lived on Mingulay, and 11 on Pabbay. At the time of the old *Statistical Account* (1794) Mingulay had 8 families, Pabbay 3, Berneray 3 and Sandray 9.

Mingulay must have been settled very early in Hebridean history, for at the south-west corner of the bay is Crois an t-Suidheachain, a stone setting resembling a part of a short stone cist, and making a link with the Bronze Age, whose so-called Beaker people buried their dead singly in little stone cairns. Crois an t-Suidheachain, Mingulay cross, seems to have had associations of some sanctity for the people, for here, in the time between the ruination of their old chapel and the making of the present one, open air mass used to be celebrated. Martin, in his account, confuses Mingulay with Berneray; perhaps it is to the Mingulay cross that he refers when he says: 'There is in this island an altar dedicated to St. Christopher, at which the natives perform their devotion. There is a stone set up here, about seven feet high, and when the inhabitants come near it they take a religious turn round it'. Such a turn would be in the *deiseil* direction, sunwise. The stone would probably be a Megalithic standing stone.

Mingulay had a church dedicated to St. Columba at the north-west corner of the bay, but there is now nothing left of it. Columba himself never visited the Outer Hebrides, though there are several churches dedicated to him there. Mingulay is said to have had another old chapel on the rock of Geirum More to the south of Hecla, a place very hard to reach. This same rock also had a dun upon it, and there was another dun on the main island, on the point of the fort, Sròn an Dùin, looking out Atlantic-wards.

To see Mingulay in the sun is to see an island friendly and snug, an island where the ill beasts of Highland legend surely have no place. And yet Mingulay has its story of the water horse, the *each uisge*. This was the way of it:

A Mingulay girl met a young man on the hill. He was attractive and they met often; then she noticed the water weed in his hair and knew him to be a water horse in human form. However, he persuaded her to marry him in a year and a day, and agreed not to visit her till then. As the time passed, the girl was ill with fear of the return of the water horse, and eventually decided to tell her father of the affair. When the day came, the people formed a circle round the house to guard her, but the stranger passed through them unhindered and snatched the girl away. Together they plunged into a well, in which were later found shreds of the girl's clothing, and the water was all reddened with blood. Ever since, the well has been Tobar na Fala, the well of blood.

This story is not peculiar to Mingulay but is, with variations, the stock *each uisge* incident of the Highlands and Islands. Once the compact has been made with the water spirit, no human agency can prevent it being fulfilled. The victim's heart or lungs are usually found floating on the loch or stream into which the water horse plunges. In one version the story is told the other way round, the girl only finding out that the husband she has married is a water horse after her baby has been born. In this story the girl leaves the *each uisge*, who laments for her return and tries to soothe the baby and hush its crying:

Eisd a bhobain! Eisd a bhobain!
A Mhor! a Mhor! till ri d'machan

(Hush baby, hush baby. O Marian, Marian, come back to your son).

Round the fire in the Mingulay houses, the surf beating on the sands, the Mingulay people would pass the long dark evenings with these stories and with songs. Perhaps they spoke of mermaids or of the King of Lochlann's Three Daughters, for these stories were the common heritage of the Western Isles and Highlands, and many more there were than have ever been collected for print.

Beyond Mingulay is Berneray, Bjorn's Island, Bearnaraidh an Easpaig, Berneray of the Bishop. On it is the lighthouse, for Berneray is the most southerly of the Long Island group. More usually, the island is called Barra Head, the name of its most southerly headland.

The lighthouse is to the west, linked to its landing place by a steep little road on which runs a lorry. The road is such that the lorry is stated to have never been out of first gear! The lighthouse itself is placed beside an ancient dun, a promontory fort called Dun Stron Duin ('the fort of the point of the fort'). The fort has turned the headland into a natural defensive enclosure by making

a strong wall across the neck of the point. The wall itself
is built in the style of the brochs, a thick drystone structure with galleries running in its thickness. The lighthouse was built beside it in 1833.

A second fort on Berneray is a little to the north of
the lighthouse one, and is called Dun Briste. This second
dun is also a promontory fort. By building a wall across
a headland in these cliffy islands one obtained a very
strong defensive position, for the sheer cliffs around are
unclimbable, and only the short length of wall required
defence.

I visit these promontory forts in some trepidation
when there is a wind blowing, and in a gale they can
hardly have been snug places. In the big storms, surf and
fish are blown on to Berneray (highest point, 628 feet);
and in January 1836, a block of gneiss weighing 42 tons
was moved five feet by the wind. The force of the waves
on the Mingulay and Berneray cliffs has never been
measured, but the wave pressure was recorded on the
Skerryvore, 36 miles to the south-east of Barra Head, in
1845. It was 6,083 lbs per square foot.

Beside the lighthouse is a geo, whose walls are 600
feet high. The open part of the geo is 100 yards long and
it leads into a cave whose extent is not known; a similar
state of affairs exists in the galleries and geos of the
Mingulay cliffs.

Down at MacLean's Point on Berneray is the site of
an old chapel and burying ground. Nothing is left of the
chapel, but a slab with an incised cross is still to be seen.

The island is 54 miles from the most westerly point of
Scotland, Ardnamurchan, and 95 miles from the nearest
part of Ireland. The lighthouse light is visible for 35

miles, and the island itself can be seen, if the weather is suitable, from the top of Ben Nevis, 100 miles away.

For Prince Charles Edward, Barra Head was his first sight of Scottish land when he came northward in 1745. *La Doutelle*, or as the ship's log spells it, *Dutillet*, was a frigate commanded by a man called Durbé. Durbé's log records their landfall:

Monday 2 (August) noon to Tuesday 3. I set a course N.E., so as to try to pick up the island of Bernera, which is the most southerly point of the island of Wice. [Durbé called the whole Long Island Wice—Uist.] At 6 pm sighted Bernera, bearing E., distant about 9 leagues. These islands are very high, and are studded with small ones between. At daybreak, I bore away to the E. of these small islands of the island of Wice. On my starboard there were several islands, 5 or 6 leagues off, which are marked on the charts, and I found myself abreast of a big lump of an island [this would be Muldoanich], very high, deeply scored, and very perpendicular on all sides, behind which on the main island [Barra] there are houses.

We, too, were coming back past Muldoanich into Castlebay harbour, a cooler wind blowing as the evening drew on. Between the little islands, through the sounds, we looked westward to a sunset of gold and green with long streaky clouds. The fine weather was ending.

CHAPTER VI

SOUTH UIST OF THE MACHAIR

THE good Scots tongue has never been bettered for descriptive writing and Sir Donald Monro's word picture of the island of Uist in 1549 is still as vivid as the country the good Dean traversed. He wrote:

The grate ile of Ywst, 34 myles lange from south-west to the northeist, sex myle braid, ane fertile countrey and maine laiche land, full of heigh hills and forests on the eist cost, ore southeist and all plenisht laiche land in the northwest, with five paroche kirkes. Within this south part of Ywst, on the east cost of the same, layes ane salt water loche callit Vayhastill [Boisdale]. This countrey is bruiked by sundrey captains; to witt, the south southwest end of it, callit Bayhastill [Boisdale], be M'Neill of Barray, the rest of the ile, namit Peiter's parochin, the parochin of Howes, and the mayne land of the mid countrey callit Mac kermeanache perteins to Clanronald, halding of the Clandonald. At the end heirof the sea enters, and cuts the countrey be ebbing and flowing through it: and in the north syde of this there is ane parochin callit Buchagla [Benbecula], perteining to the said Clandonald. At the north end thereof the sea cuts the countrey againe, and that cutting of the sea is called Careynesse, and benorth this countrey is called Kenehnache of Ywst, that is in Englishe, the north head of Ywst, whilk termis twa paroche kirks, and is mare of profit than the rest of the haill of Ywst, perteining to Donald Gormesone.

At ebb tide the strands link the three isles, South

Uist to Benbecula, Benbecula to North Uist, and make the one country of Uist. The tide rises, and there are three islands again. This way perhaps the sounds between the Barra islets were first formed, and eventually, as the land sinks further, there will always be sea between the Uist divisions.

South Uist itself is the country of machair and mountain, the mountains to the east and to the west, and the machair over against the clear waters of the Atlantic. There are some twenty miles of it down the west coast, long white sandy beaches with here and there a rocky skerry or a shingle strand; behind the beaches lie the dunes, and behind the dunes is the machair. Beyond the machair is a string of fresh-water lochs and further east are the moors at the foot of the mountain.

The machair, the plain, is the wealth of Uist. Upon it are the villages, with rough yellow tracks running down to them from the tarred main road that runs north-south from Pollachar to Benbecula. Some are of old black houses, some of new crofter cottages; sleek Highland cattle come walking out in the morning to pasture, the calves tripping behind the cows and the bull walking solemnly beside them. The children go running barefoot along the sandy paths to school. The crotal (lichen) is golden on the stones of the ruined chapels. The people are friendly, Catholic, and mad keen on the pipes. For of all the Outer Isles, South Uist is the one for pipers.

Upon the machair sand grows a hard springy grass, in summer bright with primrose and daisy, with eggs-and-bacon, silverweed (whose roots were used for food before the potato was introduced), clover and bedstraw.

F

Upon it the herds of cattle roam, and there, between the villages, are the croft fields.

Machair is easy land to work but it needs constant rain. A dry spell browns it and burns it dead, for the sand cannot hold moisture for any time. The plough turns it up white with the sand, speckled with a little peaty earth. To the beaches the islanders go with ponies and creels, or with coup carts, or with lorries, according to their circumstances and the access to the beach, and fetch up quantities of seaweed for manure. Sometimes it is put straight away on the land, sometimes heaped and allowed to rot first. With it, to-day, go artificial fertilisers. The machair grows fine potatoes, and these are followed next year by oats. After a while the field is allowed to grass over again, and a fresh piece of machair is broken up with the plough. So the cultivated areas move about on the machair.

MacCulloch, the geologist, who visited the Isles at the beginning of the nineteenth century, saw the Uist people do a peculiar trick with the seaweed. They spread it on the shingle above the high water mark and sowed barley on it. By harvest time, when the seaweed had all decayed, the crop appeared to be growing on nothing but pebbles of gneiss and quartz!

Upon the broad Uist sands and the machair the people used to hold their horse races and cavalcades. Martin Martin, as he left South Uist, saw a party of some 60 horsemen crossing the sands, 'being between me and the sun, they made a great figure on the plain sands'.

St. Michael's Day saw a great festival of horse racing. It was lawful to steal a neighbour's horse for the racing, provided you returned it unharmed at the end of the day. A piece of dried tangle served as a whip for the riders. After the racing, the day ended with the eating of the special St. Michael's cake, baked for the occasion. Now there are not many horses left in South Uist, though a good many are bred in North Uist and roam in herds over the machair there. In South Uist I saw big herds of Highland cattle on the machair, but only a few horses.

The original island cow was a sleek little black animal, the old Highland breed. In the 1840's, when the *New Statistical Account* was compiled, there were two trysts or sales of black cattle, one in July and the other in September. They still have two sales each year, but the breed has changed to Highlanders and Shorthorn crosses. The sales are held at a number of different stances on the same day, the buyers going by bus from one to the other, so that nobody has to go very far to get his beast to market.

I joined the buyers and auctioneer in their special bus, and we drove first northward from Lochboisdale to a stance near Carnan Iochdar on the ford across to Benbecula. The bus pulled into a passing bay, and we all began to pick a route over the bog to a dilapidated drystone fank a little way off on the moor. Round it a few people and cattle were already grouped; in the distance was the hard blue line of the Atlantic and, behind us were the South Uist mountains, Hecla and Beinn Mhor.

At first there seemed more people about than cattle, but they soon began to come in, here a string of shaggy young Highlanders, every colour from black to pale honey or near-white, here a stirk on a rope held by an old lady. One or two lads came up with ponies and held them tethered away from the main crowd round the cattle.

This was the old scene that the Islands know well, for cattle have been an important export from the Isles for some 300 years. They used to be taken across to Skye, made to swim the narrow strait to the mainland and driven south along the drove roads. Down to England some of them went then, and down to England some of them go now. The 'Sassenachs' were waiting to get on the bus at Daliburgh and the Scots buyers moved up in the bus to make room for them. Some of them had come out to the Isles by air; now they stood in the open by the fank in the old island fashion.

Outside the fank they formed a ring, the auctioneer with his back toward the entrance of the enclosure. The first beast came into the ring of men, the bids followed one another rapidly, the sold animal was pushed into the fank and marked with an ear-clip or paint. The pace was fast, and soon the moor was empty of cattle and the fank crowded. Little island collies scampered about. The Gaelic flowed outside the sale ring, and the English within it. Gaelic for one's feelings about the price and English for the naming of the actual amount seemed to be the formula!

As the cattle trampled round, the grass and the heather

and yellow irises were crushed down and the smell of trampled grass lay heavy on the air, so that I had only to shut my eyes to see a vision, disconcertingly out of place, of an English country fair ground.

When all the cattle had been sold, the sale ring walked across the bog back to the road and reformed there, so that the few ponies could be trotted up and down on a firm surface. This done, the buyers, feeling for their sandwiches, climbed back into the waiting buses to move on to the next stance for the second sale of the day. Meantime, the cattle were let out of the fank, and the big drove down to Lochboisdale began.

It was twenty miles from Carnan Iochdar to the boats at Lochboisdale. A big herd of shaggy beasts went slowly down the road, gathering, snowball-like, additions from each stance on the way. Traffic pushed its noisy way through the slow moving, close packed animals. One broke away and galloped over the peat banks, the collies yapping foolishly at its heels. Now and again an escaping beast bogged in the soft peaty soil and had to be pulled out by the drovers. Once this was the way of it right across the Highlands, now the drove only walk as far as Lochboisdale.

There, with much chasing round and shouting of men and barking of dogs, they were loaded into the boats, for Oban if they were going south, and for Kyle of Lochalsh if they were intended for the Dingwall-Inverness district. Meanwhile, Lochboisdale hotel bar hummed with activity, and there was more than one who walked unsteadily down the road, singing in Gaelic at the top of his voice.

I walked barefoot over the ripple-patterned sands of

the South Ford between Benbecula and South Uist. The
new road bridge across the ford, built to link the aerodrome in Benbecula with the port of Lochboisdale during
the war years, stood on its stilt-like concrete piers above
the cockle gatherers. Where you see a spout hole, there
you dig, probably with an old spoon, and with any sort
of luck or skill at all, you finish with a pail of large
cockles. Now and again you may secure a cockle lying
free on the surface of the sand, but the vast majority are
buried.

Here and there on the broad spread of sand were
shallow pools of warm water, for the sun was very hot.
Peculiar track-like markings on the sand I followed up to
a tuft of tangle growing on a stone; it had made them
as the stone rolled in the backwash of the ebbing tide.

I crossed to the sand spit of Gualann, which almost
closes the gap of the South Ford to the Atlantic, and
walked upon the wiry bent grass and the thistles, and
then out on the open sea beach upon the other side.
The sea had incredible colours: white or gold where it
shallowed over the sand, merging outward to the deeper
water through shades of apple green and emerald, pale
blue and the hard gentian of the open sea.

Across the bay, at Hornish Point, the tangle for the
seaweed plant at Boisdale was drying, the stems laid on
long mounds of earth or stone, or baulks of driftwood.
The dark ridges on the machair edge are a familiar sight
now in the Isles, and the air near them acrid with an
iodine smell.

I went inland a little to Liniquie, where a small loch
upon the outskirts of the great Loch Bee once held an
island dun. Most of the duns of the Outer Isles have been

reconstructed into houses and dykes, and the dun of Liniquie has been replaced by a pleasantly styled black house and outbuildings, placed upon the promontory in the loch where the original fort was. The water was deep blue; tall green rushes fringed it, and cattle stood in it to keep cool, while a mare and a fluffy foal lazed in a neighbouring field. Marsh marigolds were golden beside the water edge. Liniquie rushes are never cut, though they would be useful, for the people hold them sacred, thinking that it was on this variety of reed that the sponge of vinegar was handed to Christ.

In the little level plot of land between Loch Bee and Carnan, hardly more than a mile square, the Ordnance map marks five duns. Liniquie's is quite gone, but I explored another on the roadside to the north of Clachan. It consists of a collapsed circular wall in drystone with a suggestion of collapsed galleries in the thickness of the walls. Originally it stood on an island in a loch, but the loch is now mostly silted up and one easily picks a way across. The fort is called the yellow dun, Dun Buidhe.

Another ruined dun, with a stone causeway leading out to it, its walls a pile of stones overgrown with fern, stands on an island at the edge of another silting loch between Ardnamonie and Ollag.

The sandy roads and paths were blinding in the glare of the sun. When I came back to Carnan the tide was in, the sand entirely covered where I had walked that morning, the waves rippling about the piers of the bridge. Beyond the bridge was the island of Benbecula, its solitary hill of Rueval rising like a molehill from the level moors. Eastward, through the gap of the ford, the very clear blue sea was lapping on the shores of green islets and

headlands, and across the Minch rose the Cuillin Hills of
Skye. Peat cuttings were dark against the green-brown
moor, the turf all spangled with daisies by the roadside.

The sea has encroached much on the sandy west coast
of the Uists and Benbecula. At Carnan Iochdar the peat
extends below high tide mark and the seaweed grows on
it—a sign of recent subsidence. There too is a Megalithic
cairn, now largely demolished, which is now entered by
the tide. Another cairn in a similar state is at Geirisclett
in North Uist. These cairns would have been built out
of reach of the tide.

Twice the rental of North Uist has been reduced by
the sea's incomings. In 1542 it was reduced by 2 or 3
marks; and in 1721 there was an appeal for a further
reduction because of murrain amongst the cattle and the
encroachment of the sea.

MacFarlane's Collections include an account written
about 1630 which describes the encroachment in North
Uist:

There was ane Ancient man in a toune in Wist called Killpettill
and this old man said that he was sex or sevinscoir of years old and he
did sie another church with the lands of the Parish wherein that
church did stand. And these lands were more profitable fertill and
pleasant than those that are in Wist now. And that his father and
mother, his grandfather and Grandmother did see another parish
Church which was destroyed with the sea long agoe. And that they
did call that Church Kilmarchirmore. The next was called Killpettill.
And this church wherein he doth dwell now into, was called Killmony
which is now Killpettill that is to say the Mure church, because it
lyeth next the Mures, Mosses and Mountains. And this Church is
below the sands except foure or fyve foot length of the pinnacle of
that church . . . . And the countrie people will take lobsters out of
the windowes of the Pinnacle of that which was first called Killpettill
before it was destroyed with the sea.

Killmony of course has nothing to do with the Scots word Muir. It is Gaelic, either the church of Mary (the Virgin) or of St. Maelrubha. Kilmarchirmore is perhaps the church of the great machair.

There runs the length of the west coast of South Uist a grassy track across the machair, close beside the sea. I followed it southward from the pleasant little village of Howmore, with its black houses and its group of little ruined chapels. Here are the remains of two churches, with dedications to St. Mary and to St. Columba. The bigger one usually goes by the name of Teampull Mor (big church) and the smaller one is Caibeal Dhiarmaid (Diarmaid's chapel). There were also two chapels, the smallest of which is Caibeal nan Sagairt, the priest's chapel. Inside the ruins of one of the four buildings is a very fine armorial panel upon which are carved a lion, a bird, a thistle, a lymphad and a castle.

The grassy track, the day I walked it, seemed to lead endlessly southward. The sun was harsh and hot and the wind was violent from the south. Skylarks sang continuously and lapwings wheeled and cried. Tractors were busy on the machair fields, for it was May, and seaweed carting was in full swing.

I went out to Rudh'Ard-mhicheil (St. Michael's Point), where there are two burying grounds but no trace of the old church. The older burying ground is further out towards the sea, full of unnamed and unhewn boulders marking the lairs.

It is pleasant country, the sea upon the one hand, the Uist mountains upon the other. Yellow pansies and little pink geraniums mingled with the daisies on the machair, there were marsh marigolds and bogbeans round the lochs, and later there would be white waterlilies. From the reeds of the marshes the corncrake croaked mechanically. No streams link these machair lakes with the sea half a mile from them, but there will, of course, be seepage through the porous sand.

Beside a farm is Ormaclett Castle, a gaunt ruin. It is an island version of a late 'Scotch house', built by Clanranald in 1701 and burned in 1715. The panel over the door shows a helm, mantling and shield. The bearings on the shield are those of the Howmore carving but reversed. The shield is parted per pale and charged in the upper dexter corner with a lion rampant above a hand grasping a cross. The charge in the upper sinister corner is obliterated but may be a burning mountain or a castle. Below is a lymphad. The house was roofed with the green schistose tiles quarried on Stuley Island off the east coast of South Uist.

I went past Rudha Ardvule, on which headland was a broch, Dun Vulan, and past Loch Bornish (Loch of the Fort headland) and a standing stone to Loch Kildonan. There, on a little green headland, is the site of Cille Donnain, Donnan's chapel. Donnan, one of the Celtic missionaries of the sixth century, seems to have followed a route across Scotland from Candida Casa, taking the line which Ninian took on the trail of the invading Roman legions. This route, as indicated by the churches Donnan founded, turns about the Grampians by the East Coast and then reaches the West Coast and the Outer Isles by the trans-Scotland passes of the Great Glen district. Donnan founded two churches in the Outer Isles, one here in South Uist and the other on Little Bernera off Lewis.

Southward from Loch Kildonan is Loch Eilean an Staoir

with a very green little island on it, that looks as though it may be a crannog. Beyond lie the marsh and the rushes about Loch Hallan, and the big Hallan graveyard on the slope of the machair overlooking the sea. Here there is a grey tombstone with a carved foliaceous design probably filched from Howmore. There is also a block of gneiss with a cross roughly carved on it. I sat on the top of the hill and looked along the sandy coast and beyond to Barra.

A little beyond Hallan burial ground is the site of Cladh Pheadair. No traces remain of the chapel there dedicated to St. Peter, or of that dedicated to Bride at Cille Bhride in the extreme south of the island. Kilpeter church is first mentioned in the records in 1309. Originally there were two parishes in South Uist: Kilpeter, which extended from Eriskay to Loch Eynort on the east and Ardmichael on the west, and Howmore, which comprised South Uist north of Kilpeter.

Inland through the heart of South Uist runs the main road from Pollachar to Carnan Iochdar, with the important branch down to the steamer port of Lochboisdale. This latter road from Daliburgh to Lochboisdale was first constructed as a relief measure in the years of the potato famine, 1846-48. The work was suggested by the local Catholic priest, a Chisholm.

Boisdale was the scene of a violent religious persecution in the latter half of the eighteenth century. The MacNeills of Barra lost their rights in the Boisdale district after the affair of the piracy on Queen Elizabeth's shipping and Clanranald got hold of them. At the time of the persecution one of this clan, Alasdair Mor MacDonald, was laird. The Catholic priest held him up to public

censure for making his people work on St. Michael's
Day, which was a holiday of obligation and the day of
the horse races. Alasdair Mor (Big Alasdair) was so
enraged by the insult that he turned Protestant and
began to try to persecute all Boisdale into becoming
Protestant as well. He went to the length of telling
his tenants to renounce Catholicism or quit, but they,
stubborn as Alasdair Mor himself, refused to give way.
Public funds were raised to help the worst affected, and
100 people were so helped to leave Uist for America in
1772.

Boisdale, in due course, had to moderate his demands,
and on his deathbed is said to have recanted and called
for a priest. His son, however, brought up a good Protestant, refused to have one brought to his father.

In the mouth of the sea loch Boisdale is an island,
Calvay, and on it the ruin of an old castle. Its date of
construction is uncertain, but, though smaller, it rather
resembles Kiessimul in Barra and has the same method
of bedding some of the slabs on edge. It was in this ruin
that Prince Charles and his companions skulked during
the latter part of their time in South Uist.

Another South Uist fort of which a considerable part
remains is Caisteal Bheagram on an island in the fresh
water Loch an Eilein. The rugged little ruin still stands
12 feet high, and originally had at least two stories. The
New Statistical Account spells it Caisteal Eilen bheag rum
and says that it means the 'Castle on the island of small
dimensions' and that it was Clanranald's ancient place of
refuge. There is a Ronald Alansoun of Yland Bagrim or
Ylanebigorn recorded in 1505 and again in 1508.

Of the later duns in South Uist, Dun Raouill on Loch

Drudibeg is an interesting specimen. Some 6 to 8 feet of wall still remain and the wall itself is up to 8 feet 4 inches thick. It is a rectangular building, entirely in drystone work. Outside is a harbour used by the boats of the fort.

The only trees in South Uist are on an island in Loch an Eilein at Askernish (not the loch where Caisteal Bheagram is), and the planting includes a couple of monkey puzzles.

Another island, or promontory rather, into Loch a'Bharp by Lochboisdale is occupied by a small and neat black house. The building puzzled me to the extent of my shouting questions at an elderly and rather deaf Uist man, who mildly replied, 'Oh, that is the house for the bull. There will be nobody there but himself.'

CHAPTER VII

ERISKAY

It is some five miles across the Sound of Barra from Pollachar in South Uist to Eoligarry in Barra, and a wild enough crossing if the mood is on it. Neil Campbell, the Saltavik ferryman, told me it had once taken him over four hours to get his little motor fishing boat across. But this May morning it took under the hour.

We glided over an unruffled sea, down through whose clear depths we could look to the white sand flooring the sound, to the seaweed beds and the occasional rocks. Once we swung close inshore after a small bottle-nosed shark whose every detail was clearly discerned through the golden water of the shallows. Eider ducks bobbed beside the tangle-fringed skerries; gannets dropped, stone-like, into the sea after fish. Now and again the seals' heads peered at us, as they slipped off the rocks into the sea. King's daughters under a spell the island legend names the seals, and the Hebridean clan of Mac-Codrum claims descent from them—Clann 'ic Codrum nan Ron, the MacCodrums of the seals.

We skirted around Fuday, one of the many islets of the Sound of Barra, a pleasant sandy island, all its turf yellowed with primroses. Beside Fuday's beautiful western sandy beach is the ruin of a broch, Dùnan Ruadh or the red fort. And there, according to tradition, the last of the Norsemen were slain. A bastard son of MacNeill of Barra fell in love with a Norse girl. She told him that the Norsemen on Fuday were defenceless at night. So young MacNeill made his way over there and killed them all, throwing the heads of the last three into a well which has ever after been called the Well of the Heads.

We turned back from the landing place at Eoligarry and headed for Eriskay, Eric's Island, the principal islet in the Sound of Barra. It is a little island, barely three miles long and only two across at its widest, edged by rocky cliffs except for the sands in the north-west corner. For these sands we headed now, the ferryboat coming into the rocks of the Sloc Dallaig beside the strand of Coilleag a'Phrionnsa.

'If you get hungry, ask at any house for tea,' urged Neil Campbell as I scrambled on to the rocks, not without reason, for it was hot enough on the sea and treeless Eriskay was like a furnace.

I climbed up on the grass beside Coilleag a'Phrionnsa, the Prince's Strand. Here, according to the tradition, Prince Charles landed in 1745. It was the first Scottish soil upon which he set foot, and this was the way of it:

Le Dutillet, after sighting Barra Head, came into Barra to pick up a pilot and get news. There the party was told that their coming was known and that the whole plot was revealed. However, they decided to run for Canna. But, on leaving, they saw a ship which they were convinced was a man o' war, and a hasty council was summoned to decide what to do. On local advice they headed for 'a harbour which is between the island of Bara and the island of Uyst, and is very large, though one cannot get out by the west side. One can recognise this harbour by a square tower which in old days served as a light-house: its top is now in ruins, and it is on the N. side of the entrance' (Durbé's log). This anchorage is the An-t-Acarsaid Mhor between Gighay and Fuday, and the old tower is the Weaver's Castle on the Stack Islands south of Eriskay.

The other ship saw them and gave chase, and it was then decided that the principal passengers, the Prince and his company, should be landed on Eriskay to be out of harm's way. Durbé gives the date as 3rd August, the 'Lyon in Mourning' as 23rd July.

The party landed at Coilleag a'Phrionnsa, and one of them is said to have had a pocketful of the seeds of a pink, fleshy-leaved *convolvulus major*, which he scattered. They have grown there ever since and Eriskay calls them the Prince's Flower.

On Eriskay the Prince first experienced the acrid peat reek of an old style Hebridean house. Angus MacDonald, with whom they stayed, was quite exasper-ated with Charles for continually going out for a breath of fresh air. 'What the plague is the matter with that fellow,' he exclaimed, 'that he can neither sit nor stand still, and neither keep within nor without doors?'

Messages were sent off to MacNeill of Barra and Alexander MacDonald of Boisdale and some others to come and meet the Prince. MacNeill was away from home, but Boisdale came. MacDonald condemned the whole venture, tried to persuade them to go straight back to France, refused to join in himself and went back to Uist to caution everyone else to keep clear of the rising. He succeeded in restraining some hundreds and had a letter sent him by Lord Loudon thanking him for his work.

Next day, in the pouring rain, the party returned to *Le Dutillet*, wet to the skin. The first British ship, together with another, a frigate which had joined her, tried to approach, but the wind was so much against them that they could not get into the Sound at all. *Le Dutillet* slipped out when darkness came and arrived at Loch nan Uamh, Arisaig, on the Scottish mainland, the following afternoon.

Rock dominates Eriskay, smooth, ice-rounded grey gneiss. It is a curious landscape of green and grey with the shimmering sea encircling it; between the rocks all the lazy beds must be dug by hand. In the north of the island the crags rise to Ben Scrien (609 ft.), in the south to Ben Stack (403 ft.). Between these two hills the sea nearly cuts the island in two in a fiord cut deeply in from the east.

A path, for there are no roads on Eriskay, links the houses at Rosinish in the north with the main village on the sandy north-west shore, and then, by the low bealach (pass) between the two hills, leads across to Na Pairceanan and the houses beside the fiord loch, Acairseid Mhor ('big harbour', but not to be confused with that in which *Le Duttilet* anchored).

Most of the houses are modern ones, though there are still a few black houses left, and black houses also serve as byres for the animals. I followed the little path, dazzled by the sun on its white surface, across to Na Pairceanan, where the marsh marigolds blazed yellow

G

beside the cas bheag ('little foot') heaps of drying peats, and the fiord glinted and sparkled. I walked on, past lazy beds, narrow ones where the potatoes were sprouting, broader ones pale green with young oats, and past a loch that would later be speckled with white waterlilies, to Rudha Liath (the grey headland) under Ben Stack.

Beside the water-lily lochs there was a peat cutting, and a fire burning briskly in a stone setting, with a big black pot over it. I had seen these fires and boiling pots outside the houses further back, but this fire was a long way from the nearest house. I went down for a gossip with the woman who was superintending operations. The dry spell had dried up all the local wells and they had come this far for water for washing. A man was coming over the brae with a large sack of washing on his back. Soon the clothes and blankets were spread out on the ground to dry, held down by stones. At Rosinish I saw clothes-washing taking place in the salty pools left by the spray on the headland rocks.

Beyond the water-lily loch I found a narrow gut, a broadened geo, leading down to a tiny beach of shingle with high cliffs upon either side. Sheep were huddled out of the sun under the one ledge of the cliff, and I went on down to the shingle itself, where one rock overhung sufficiently to give some sort of relief from the glare and the heat. Roseroot, celandine and primrose grew in the crevices of this cliff; the sea sloshed coolly in the narrow entry. As a comfortable place to eat one's lunch I could not commend it, for the shingle was exceedingly hard to sit upon, but at least it was out of the sun.

I scrambled up the turf from the beach and looked northward, across a very blue sea to the grey smooth rocks of Ru Melvick, the southernmost corner of South Uist. It was a dead calm, not a breeze stirring to relieve the dazzle from the water and the metallic blaze from the cloudless sky.

Eriskay is a strange little kingdom on its own. Its path is too narrow for the smallest coup cart and the island is devoid of both carts and cars. The temporary presence of a lorry brought over by a firm of engineers was a major occasion. Nor are there any ploughs, for the croft fields are all lazy beds between the rocks and are dug by hand.

That day Eriskay seemed deserted, for most of the folk were away up to the big peat cutting on top of Ben Scrien. A white pony, with a creel on either flank, was going slowly up the hillside, a girl perched on top of it reading a magazine.

'The good time, when there was plenty money, was when the fishing was on,' a crofter told me at Rosinish, leaning on a pile of herring nets. Eriskay still fishes a bit, for lobsters and herrings, but the two World Wars killed the main industry. In the old days Eriskay men, backed by their crofts, made a good thing out of the fishings. Now life is not so good.

But life was fine in 1941 when the *Politician* went aground between South Uist and Eriskay. One cannot go to Eriskay and remain indifferent to the *Politician*, a theme which Compton MacKenzie has made into a book. She carried, amongst other good things, a big cargo of export whisky intended for the American market. She lay conveniently and officialdom was slow to move.

The Eriskay man pointed out the exact spot. 'It was just like a town out there, at nights, with the lights of the boats. Some of them came from the East Coast and went back through the Caledonian Canal with the cases of whisky hidden under the herring nets.' The whisky was great stuff—'mild as milk. You never were sick or had a head, just in a good mood all the time. I never thought of taking tea to the croft in those days.'

Hiding places were all quickly filled; much was lost when the metal caps corroded in the peaty earth. Many people were so drunk that they forgot where they had hidden their share. Fortunately, no one was hurt unloading the wreck, in spite of the fact that they all drank as they worked. Men counted their haul in dozens of cases.

A man in Barra, passing a black house where an old lady lived, heard howls of mirth coming from it. He went in to find the old lady lying on her bed shaking with laughter while the kettle boiled vigorously on the hook (the hook on the chain which hangs down the chimney over the open fire). 'Take it off,' she sobbed, 'I can't get up.'

'I was coming home,' she explained, 'when someone called me into his cowhouse to give me a cup of whisky. I went on a bit and someone else made me have another cup. Then I couldn't refuse the offer of a glass outby. When I got in, I put the kettle on for tea and thought I would lie down, and now I can't get up!'

Good days! You could afford to take a sip at a bottle and if you didn't like the particular brand, throw it away and try another. 'It's spoilt us for the stuff they sell in the Bar.' Some *Politician* stories are apocryphal, for obviously it cannot be true that Eriskay could not plough its fields next spring for bottles, when Eriskay has no ploughs.

The War, of course, brought many other cargoes to the beaches, from cooking fat to lubricating oil and grapefruit. Islanders beachcombed with much profit. It was no new idea to them, as shown by this old story which was first collected in the early 1800's:

A certain covetous man in South Uist was continually searching the beaches, despite the reproaches of his neighbours who thought he already had sufficient to live upon, and should not be continually watching for more. One day his nephew reproached him in this manner, whereupon the man said that for all his working the beaches he got much less than the rest of them. Looking at his nephew's shoes, he then asked him where he had got such a good pair. The boy, who actually had bought them, said he had got them off a corpse that he had found on the beach. The uncle again bewailed his ill-luck on the beaches, and the crafty nephew went off laughing to himself.

When night came, the nephew went down to the beach and tunnelled himself into a bank of seaweed washed up by the tide, leaving his two feet sticking out. Soon his uncle came along and seeing what he supposed was a dead man with a good pair of shoes, began to remove them for himself. The nephew, choosing the moment, gave him a hearty kick. The poor man fell over backwards on the sand and then crawled off home much alarmed.

Next morning the nephew called at the uncle's house, to find him ill in bed. 'What is the matter with him?' 'He has fallen and hurt his face.' In went the nephew to see for himself and the uncle told him everything. Was it not wonderful that a dead man should be allowed to hurt him? 'Aha,' said the nephew, 'don't you know that it is a great sin to rob a dead man?' Rubbing in his advantage, he went on to tell his uncle that the experience ought to be a lesson to him.

The uncle was ill for about three months, after which he returned to his beachcombing. The nephew tried another trick, again without permanent cure. He managed to secure an old chest of the uncle's, filled it with seaweed, stones and a broken quern, lashed it with ropes and left it on the strand. The uncle duly found it with great glee and not till he had laboriously carted it back to his home did he recognise his own old chest.

The Gulf Stream, which warms these shores, brings with it many odd things out of the Tropics to fling them on the beaches of the Outer Isles. A turtle arrived in North Uist in 1900, for instance; and it is usual enough to get various West Indian seeds, beans, shells and even cocoanuts appearing from time to time. The cocoanuts have sometimes been in bunches. Sargasso weed has also been thrown up.

Of the nuts the most famous is the Molucca bean, the fruit of *Guilandina bonducella*. There is an account of these nuts in the 'Description of the Lewis by John Morisone Indweller there' in *MacFarlane's Geographical Collections*. John Morisone probably wrote between 1678 and 1688. He says:

The sea casteth on shore sometimes a sort of nutts growing upon tangles round and flat. sad broun or black coullored, of the bread of a dollor some more, some less. The kernell of it being taken out of the shell, is ane excellent and experienced remedie for the bloodie flux. They ordinarlie make use of the shell for keeping ther snuff. Ane other sort of Nutt is formed in the same maner of a less syze of a broun collour, flatt and round with a black circle about it, quilk in old tymes women wore about ther necks both for ornament and holding that it had the vertue to make fortunate in catle and upon this account, they were at pains to bind them in silver, brass or tinn, according to their abilitie. There are other lesser yett, of a whitish coulour and round, which they call Sanct Marie's Nutt quhilk they did wear in the same maner, holding it to have the vertue to preserve woemen in child bearing.

In Harris, Martin Martin, some years later, saw these 'molluka beans' and was told how they were used as amulets against witchcraft and the evil eye. Children wore them round their necks and if evil was intended the bean was supposed to change from black to white.

Malcolm Campbell, the steward or factor of Harris, told Martin that a few weeks before the latter's arrival he had been troubled by his cows' giving blood instead of milk. A neighbour told his wife that this was caused by witchcraft and told her to put St. Mary's Nut into the pail at the next milking. Mrs. Campbell did so. Again blood came, and the nut, rather obviously, changed from white to dark brown. Mrs. Campbell tried the experiment again and the cows began to give milk, which change was duly ascribed to the virtue of the nut.

In Gaelic the Virgin Nut is called Airne Moire, literally Mary's sloe. The most prized variety has the cross indented on it. It was supposed to preserve one from sudden death and nearly every sort of misfortune, though its particular use was in childbirth. Here follows the Uist tradition:

Mary and Jesus were travelling one stormy night and asked for shelter at a house. The husband wanted to turn them away, but his wife let them in and gave them somewhere to rest. A little later, the wife was seized with labour pains and her condition seemed critical.

Jesus said to Mary (they both apparently had the Gaelic), 'Seall, a Mhoire, a'bhean, 's i air fòd a'bhais' (Mary, behold the woman, in the throes of death). Mary answered, 'Seall fheinn oirre, a Mhic, 's ann orra (air do) chomas a tha' (Son, succour her Thyself, for thou hast the power).

Jesus turned to the woman and told her to make the sign of the cross three times and 'A'choinneal a lasadh, an leanabh a bhaisteadh, 's a'bhean a bhi slan' (to light the candle, to baptise the child, and that she (the wife) might recover).

In the Uist rite the midwife gave the Airne Moire to the mother, who held it in her hand and repeated the Ave Maria three times. Then the midwife took the nut, made the sign of the cross with it over the patient and recited the dialogue between Mary and Jesus. At the least, these prayers would be effective in raising the morale of the patient; to-day the islanders also look for help to the ambulance plane and the hospitals of Glasgow or Inverness.

Eriskay itself has a curious little rune to recite when putting the cattle out to graze:

> Gu'm bu duinte gach slochd
> 'S gu'm bu reidh gach cnoc—
> Buachailleachd Chalum-Chille oirbh
> Gus an tig sibh dhachaidh.

(May each pit be closed, And each hillock be plain—The herding of Columba be on you, Until you return home.)

In the Outer Isles Columba is regarded as the patron saint of cattle. I failed to find out the reason for this: his memory may have become entangled with some far older idea, as that of St. Maelrubha of Applecross was confused with a pagan ceremony of sacrificing bulls.

South from Eriskay is a little group of rocky islets, the Stack Islands, on the most southern of which is the fortress of Caisteal a'Bhreabadair, commonly called the Weaver's Castle. This is the 'square tower' of Durbé of *Le Dutillet*. It is a very prominent landmark which once belonged to a piratical MacNeill of the MacNeills of Barra. There is only one way up to the castle and that is difficult. It is a small building, some $12\frac{1}{4}$ feet by $9\frac{3}{4}$ feet, with walls $4\frac{1}{4}$ to $4\frac{1}{2}$ feet thick. For ease in transport, the walls were made of very small stones, and the cementing mortar was prepared with lime made from the shell sands of neighbouring beaches. The remains of walling where a crane or small hoist was once placed can be traced.

The Weaver's Castle must have been a wild place when the storms were on in the Sound of Barra, and the Atlantic swell raced between the islands to meet the tides of the Minch, when the breakers crashed all day on the rocks of the island and the spray flew over it. Yet MacNeill doubtless felt like another Highland gentleman who remarked that he did not want a fair road to his home, because if his friends really wanted to see him they would find some sort of way, and as for the others, he would rather they stayed away!

The little Vernal Squill, a sweet-scented, deep blue scilla, was flowering vividly upon the Rosinish cliffs when I traversed them and turned back, in the slight cool of the May evening, to my tryst with the ferryman at Eriskay pier. The children scampered amongst the rocks, Eriskay children and Glasgow children, for the Catholic orphanages find homes for their charges in the Catholic Isles.

These had just arrived; soon they would be chattering in Gaelic.

Neil Campbell arrived, immensely pleased with the idea of an evening journey across to Barra to fetch some-one back from a cattle sale. The sea was undoubtedly the best place in the heat wave.

CHAPTER VIII

THE RIDGE ON THE EDGE OF THE WORLD

THE mountains of South Uist rise like a wall against the Minch, a wall of rock, breached here and there by the fiord mouths. On the west side of the island the Atlantic breaks on the long sandy beaches, behind which lies the machair; behind that again are the moors. But on the east side there is the great lift of the mountains, with crags and cliffs and deep glens. At the foot of these mountains the Minch is from 10 to 20 fathoms deep and shelves rapidly; but on the west coast of Uist you must go out nearly four miles to reach the ten fathom line, and up to eight miles for the 20 fathom line.

At the southern tip of South Uist, the eastern cliffs end in the great rock face of the Ru Melvick, rounded in cruel curves, inhospitable. Northward, the way opens between the rocky cliffs into the fiord of Loch Boisdale, the island's main harbour, a sea loch once guarded by Castle Calvay on the island at its mouth.

Boisdale fiord fingers up into the heart of the island, till only two miles separate its tidal head from the sands of the western machair. Loch Hallan, half-a-mile from the western beaches, drains into Loch Boisdale, so that Uist is here nearly cut in two.

Above Lochboisdale, to the northward, rises Beinn Ruigh Choinnich (902 ft.), the mountain of Kenneth's shieling; at its foot lies Cladh Choinnich, Kenneth's field, the site of an old chapel. A rugged mountain is Beinn Ruigh Choinnich, crags alternating with grassy slopes—the characteristic pattern of the ice-moulded island hills. The hard gneiss was rounded by the ice sheet against the direction in which the ice moved, left craggy upon the side sheltered from the moving glacier. Choinnich looks down upon Loch Boisdale, a maze of sea and land, whose tidal beaches seem weirdly out of place so far inland, and upon the complex of fresh water lochs on the level moor at the head of the tidal inlet. It is claimed, though calculations indicate that it is quite impossible, that the hills of the north of Ireland have been seen from the top of Beinn Ruigh Choinnich. They are 134 miles away. Mirage might bring them into view.

Next to Choinnich is the higher Triuirebheinn (1,168 ft.) and then Stulaval (1,227 ft.). North from Stulaval is another fiord, Loch Eynort, with its tidal arms reaching to within two miles of the opposite coast, and, like Loch Boisdale, receiving streams from the western lochs which lie in the sound of the Atlantic.

Beyond Loch Eynort rises the splendid mountain ridgeway of South Uist, the spine of Beinn Mhor (2,034 ft.), the castellated height of Feaveallach (1,723 ft.) and the overhanging rock of Hecla (1,820 ft.).

Again the ground falls, this time to the sea loch Skiport (Norse, ship firth), and here the island of South Uist is indeed cut in two, for Loch Skiport is linked

directly to the amazing Loch Bee. Loch Bee, a great
shallow expanse of water in the middle of the northern
section of South Uist, also drains into the Atlantic at
Liniquie. In the summer heat this great blue expanse of
water is an extraordinary sight, for the main road is
carried across the middle of it on a narrow built-up
causeway. The cattle crossing it on the way from the
sales form a shaggy caterpillar wriggling over the loch.

Dean Monro writes of Loch Bee as though the subsidence and erosion which have linked it to the west coast
had lately occurred (*c.* 1549):

Ther is ane maine loche callit Lochebi, three myle lang, and a
arme of the sea has worne the earth, that was at the ae end of this
loche, quhilk the sea has gotten enteries to this fresche water loche,
and in that narrow entries that the sea has gotten to the loche, the
countreymen has bigit upe ane thicke dyke of rough staines, and
penney stanes caste lange narrest, notwithstanding the flowing streams
of the sea enters throughe the said dyke of stanes in the said fresche
water loche, and so ther is continually getting stiking amange the
rough stains of the dyke foresaid, fluikes, podloches, skatts, and
herings.

The northern tip of South Uist, a level moor dotted
with lochs, lying between Loch Bee and the South Ford,
is thus in reality a separate island. It would not need
much further subsidence to cut the island across again
along the lines of Loch Eynort and Loch Boisdale.

Along these high hills of South Uist runs a great belt
of crushing and thrusting in the rocks. In the very remote past the ancient gneiss has been subjected to great
thrusting movements so strong that a great mass of rock
has over-ridden the uncrushed rocks to the westward.
Along the line of thrusting and movement the gneiss has
been so crushed, rolled out, comminuted and fused that

it has become a black and glassy flint-like 'flinty-crush' rock. The direction of movement may have been either from west to east or from east to west; the western uncrushed gneiss may have pressed east under the thrust planes, or the eastern rocks may have been sheared and forced westward over a firm rock massif.

North to south through the Isles this belt of flinty-crush, or shear and thrust, can be traced, through Gleann Mor in Sandray, curving through the Barra hills, along the east side of Eriskay, along the foot of the South Uist hills on their west flank, along the western face of the North Uist hills, through eastern Harris and then curving inland through Lewis to Ben Barvas, and out to the Minch at Tolsta. The thrust plane can be traced for all this distance, but in South Uist the pattern of the movements is clearest.

There along the western flank of the mountain line is the flinty-crush rock formed along the plane of movement and over 100 feet thick near Clett on Triuirebheinn. Above it the gneiss, often much shattered and sheared, forms the tops of the mountains. Finally, further east, lies a thrust plane along which the movement has not been quite so intense and the gneisses are ground down, not to black flinty crush, but to mylonite, a rock slightly less crushed. These mylonites are flaggy rocks, green in colour, and it is they that were quarried for roofing slates in Stuley Island and were used on Ormaclett Castle roof.

The thrust-plane itself is gently inclined, dipping at about 27 degrees to the east. Because of its low dip, its outcrop on the ground is affected by the changes in topography and its mapped line v's down the deep glens between Hecla and Beinn Mhor.

The crushed gneiss between the two main thrust planes has very well developed joint planes in it. They trend N.N.W. and have a marked influence on the South Uist hill scenery, as witness the crags of Beinn Mhor. The belt of mylonite weathers more readily than the other rocks and it seems to have determined the line of the South Uist east coast.

The gneiss of the east coast, too, weathers rather differently from that further south. In place of the geos there are cave-like hollows with less sheer walls, and the ground tends to steep slopes rather than high, precipitous cliffs.

Stulaval was my first South Uist top. The name itself, Norse, is of doubtful meaning. *Val*, of course, is the usual Norse word for a hill *fjall*, English fell.

I left Lochboisdale on a dull May morning, crossed the stream from Loch a'Bharp at Auratote, and followed a very faint path across the moors, past lochs black with peat stain. I made a diagonal across the flank of Triuirebheinn to gain the top of the ridge beside the rocky knob of Clett. Across the ridge I looked down upon a beautiful little corrie loch, Loch nan Arm. It lies in the hollow of the hills, Triuirebheinn on the one side, Stulaval on the other, separated from the big Loch Stulaval to the west by a rocky barrier, and with, to the east, a glimpse of the sea through the Bealach a'Chaolais ('Pass of the Kyle' or Sound) between South Uist and Stuley Island).

The little lochan is almost round, and its ripples glinted almost directly below me in a shimmering pattern. Round it rose the steep hillsides, rock showing here and there amongst the heather. Beside me, on the flank of Clett, was a deep gut of bare earth cut by a cloud-burst.

I climbed down to the lochan and walked round it,
through the tall heather, past bushes of wild rose and
stunted rowan. At the south-east corner is the Carragh-
broin, the Stone of Sorrow. Story goes that here was
fought a duel upon the loch shore, and that one of the
contestants, badly wounded, staggered back and collapsed
upon this rock.

Across the loch, under the crags and screes of the
Bealach a'Chaolais, I saw the rickle of stones marking the
site of an old earth-house. Coming up to them, I found
growing beside the ruined underground house the plants
that always prefer to grow near places of human habitation, nettles and raspberries, and the rowan planted to
keep off evil spirits. These earth-houses date from the
Celtic Iron Age and sometimes seem to have been underground places of refuge, though the more elaborate ones
may have been permanently inhabited. This particular
house is called Tigh nan Leacach, the House of Flagstones,
and is built out of the blocks fallen from the crag's face
above.

From the Tigh Leacach the side of Stulaval rises in a
long ridge which trends north-west to the summit, a mile
away. I climbed up the first sharp brae by a rock face
studded with little red garnets, and then walked up the
long grassy slope to a level haunch of the mountain at
800 feet. This haunch rose at its further end to the summit, a crest of rock marking the edge to the south-west
and leading up to the top. Upon the haunch were two
little lochs with bogbean growing on them, and deep peat
hags through which I threaded a way. Below me lay the
little Stuley Island with the green ridges of old lazy beds
marking the sites of old cultivations. On the mainland

of South Uist, too, at the seaward end of the Bealach a'Chaolais, there were more old greens and the rickle of stones of a ruined house. The wind came strongly from the south-west, and I, electing to go up the spine of rock, was pressed against it forcibly. But the cloud was breaking up and the sun came out, lighting up the landscape of moor and loch.

From the top of Stulaval, a grassy top with little outcrops of rock, I looked down over the moors to the pale green machair, the brown dots of black houses at Daliburgh, the flash of the beaches and the blue Atlantic. Across the sea were Eriskay and Barra, and beyond I saw the rise of Mingulay cliff. The South Uist moors were a maze of water, fresh and salt, the town of Lochboisdale almost an island amongst them.

To the northward, the side of Stulaval drops steeply to the sea loch Eynort, and there I found a sheltered hollow for lunch. Across Loch Eynort Beinn Mhor rose, a long ridge, grassy upon its lower slopes, grey scree spilling from its summit rocks. Beyond lay the tops of Hecla and to the east I looked towards the rocky coastline and then across to Skye. From Stulaval I could trace the limits of the ice sheets, for all the lower ground was rounded and moulded by them, but the tops of Beinn Mhor and Hecla rose ruggedly above the topmost limit of the ice.

Immediately below was the complicated and island-strewn fresh-water loch, Snigisclett, a detached portion of which is called Loch Drollavat, Troll's Loch. The colouring of the Hebridean lochs can provide curious contrasts. The sea fiords, Loch Eynort for instance, barely half-a-mile from Snigisclett, are, in the sun, a hard

H

and vivid blue, the clear water revealing the details of
the seaweed beds. But the fresh-water lochs, deeply
stained with peat from the moors, are a much deeper,
gentian blue, whilst the little corrie lochs like Loch nan
Arm tend to an inky blackness.

Some of the many islands of Snigisclett were very
green, and I suspect that there may have been duns or
houses on them in the past.

I left Stulaval and went down over a long heathy slope
and across a boggy flat, beyond which rises the low ridge
of Shuraval—Pig Mountain. The bog led down to the
Hornary River, which I followed to Mingary on the main
north-south road. The brown stream was edged with
dwarf willows, marsh marigolds and primroses. It flows
from Lochs Drollavat and Snigisclett, and at Mingary
enters a couple of lochs where the South Uist mill used
to be. These in turn drain into Loch Kildonan on the
machair. This loch is linked to Loch Ollay to the northward and it in turn is linked to the head of Loch
Eynort. Thus the water collected on the shore of Loch
Eynort makes a turn across the island before flowing back
into the eastern sea loch! Some of it, of course, probably
seeps through the machair sand to the Atlantic.

The name Loch Eynort is Norse but the meaning is
doubtful. It has been suggested that it means Evind's
firth, or, which is more likely, lonely firth—*einfjoror*.

It was on the Hornary river that I fell in with a keeper,
one MacDonald by name, a gun under his oxter and his
pocket full of primroses. He was looking for the nest of
the hen harrier which breeds there every year.

The hen harrier makes its nest in the long heather.
She constructs the nest as she lays the eggs. Soon we saw

the male bird, who has a good deal of white in his plumage, flying over the moor; then, with a whirr, the brown female got up off her nest and both of them circled watchfully as we went into the heather to look at the nest. It contained six white eggs. Nearby were the remains of last year's nest.

The keeper also showed me a crow's nest made on the ground amongst the heather and lined with sheep's wool; and later we found a pipit's nest with four small brown eggs. An owl was flying about, but we could not find its nest. Owls I had always connected with nests in hollow trees, but in treeless Uist the birds must make do with the ground or the cliffs.

So I came to Mingary, with the shell of the old corn mill by the loch, a slated building in contrast to the miller's own home which was thatched. Mingary was the birthplace of Flora MacDonald. The actual house is now ruined. She was a native of South Uist and her father was Ronald MacDonald of Milton near Mingary. He was a cadet of Clanranald and died when Flora was a year old. Her mother's second husband was Hugh MacDonald of Ormadale in Skye. Flora's brother succeeded to the Milton property, and she was on a visit to her Uist relations when she was persuaded to take Prince Charles out of the Long Island and across to Skye.

It was in the May heatwave that I climbed Beinn Mhor and Hecla, the ridge on the edge of the world. The sky was blue and clear, the sun scorched all day, and treeless Uist sweltered and baked beneath it.

I had first seen these tops from the deck of the *Loch Mor*, coming south from Loch Maddy; it is a high range, and very high indeed it seemed that evening with the

sea grey and choppy, and the mist rising and falling upon
the hilltops. The rocks of Hecla seemed, from the sea,
to form a conical spine, till the mist curled round them
and hid them. 'And what,' asked the man at the wheel,
'would you do if you were there and that came down
suddenly?'

I began the climb of Beinn Mhor from the turn down
to Stoneybridge on the main road, making a way up the
gentle rise of Beinn a'Charra (450 ft.). A little below
the top of the rise, but placed on the skyline to catch the
eye, is An Carra, a Megalithic monolith of unhewn gneiss,
some 17 feet high. I turned from it and went along the
ridge which leads toward Beinn Mhor, making my way
round the boggy hollow of Glac Auscar to the slope
of the big mountain itself. Immediately above was the
rocky knob which sticks out from the mountain flank
like a carbuncle and to this I was making my way. This
knob is called Spin and is at a height of 1,162 feet. Where
it joins the flank of Beinn Mhor are a few little pools and
a clear streamlet running from them, from which I drank
—the last supply of fresh water that I was to have until
I came down off Hecla in the evening.

I turned and looked back to the white and green of
the machair and the glint of the sea and the lochs; immediately below were the vivid greens of old shielings.
One of these is called Ari-nam-ban, Shieling of the
Women, because there once was a nunnery there, beside
the shore of Loch Eynort. A pleasant spot indeed.

The heather had died out at 1,000 feet, and from
Spin I made an easy way up the steep grassy slopes of
Beinn Mhor and then over the grey screes, lichen
grown, toward the high southern top. Above me the

summit rocks stood like a black wall against the blue sky.

From Eoligarry in Barra Beinn Mhor looks like a great table mountain, a level plateau, but when I came out upon the top (2,034 ft.), I found myself upon a narrow ridge. To the south-east it dips down to the sea in a broad and grassy shoulder, the Buail 'a 'Ghoill (*Buail*, from Norse *bòl*, a place for milking cattle). The ground narrows suddenly to the highest point, a small rocky platform, from which the crags fall sheer 850 feet to Glen Hellisdale, the higher faces actually overhanging. Thence the ridge runs north-west for half-a-mile, a narrow knife of rock with turrets of gneiss along it, widening again toward the further top at 1,994 feet.

I sat beside the cairn on the little rocky plat of the summit which leans out over Hellisdale and looked at a view which reached from the Scottish mainland to St. Kilda. The mainland hills were blue in the heat haze; Coll and Tiree were very far away. Rum was a serrate line of hills and the Cuillin of Skye took up the same theme in a spiny dragon's back. Northward lay Mac-Leod's Tables, green flats and basalt cliffs, and the whole of Skye spread out before me. Southward were Stulaval, the lochs of South Uist, and, beyond, Barra and the Bishop's Isles.

Northward was the drop to the bealach between Beinn Mhor and Feaveallach, and beyond that the rise to Hecla with its rocky top. Looking to the other side of Hecla, I saw the lone hill of Benbecula, the sugar loaf shapes of the Harris hills, the Shiant Isles and the Monachs.

Fifty miles across the shimmering sea to the westward rose St. Kilda and neighbouring Boreray, the stacks standing clearly off the coast though the cliffs were blue with haze. All day St. Kilda was in my view, faintly unreal, so that I turned again and again to look at it, to make sure that it had not vanished like a dream. It seemed that the ridge of Beinn Mhor and Hecla was upon the very edge of the world, and that Fordun (*c.* 1400) was right when he wrote of St. Kilda 'the Irte, which is agreed to be under the Circius and on the outskirts of the world, beyond which there is found no land in these bounds'.

Colours were very bright, the hard blue of the sea, and the deeper, softer blue of the inland lochs, the greens and browns and yellows of the moors, the white of the beaches.

I looked down into Glen Hellisdale, the deep valley between the slopes of Beinn Mhor and Feaveallach, the dark corrie lake of Hellisdale on its floor under the crags. Beyond the glen the twin green slopes of the Cas fo Deas and Cas fo Thuath (*Deas*, south; *Tuath*, north) lead down from Feaveallach to the sea, with the hollow of Glen Corodale between them (Corodale is Norse, *Kóri's* dale).

Of one of these glens, I am not certain which, Martin Martin wrote:

There is a valley between two mountains on the east side called Glenslyte, which affords good pasturage. The natives who farm it come thither with their cattle in the summer time, and are possessed with a firm belief that this valley is haunted by spirits, who by the inhabitants are called the great men; and that whatsoever man or woman enters the valley without making first an entire resignation of themselves to the conduct of the great men will infallibly grow mad. The words by which he or she gives up himself to these men's conduct are comprehended in three sentences, wherein the glen is twice named, to which they add that it is inhabited by these great men, and that such as enter depend on their protection. I told the natives that this was a piece of silly credulity as ever was imposed upon the most ignorant ages, and that their imaginary protectors deserved no such invocation. They answered that there had happened a late instance of a woman who went into that glen without resigning herself to the conduct of these men, and immediately after she became mad, which confirmed them in their unreasonable fancy.

When the South Uist people were herding their cattle amongst these hills they used to sing to them. One of the songs was a herding blessing (Beannachadh Buachaill-leac) in which Bridget (Bride), Columba and the Virgin are invoked to protect the animals from, among other things, the fairy darts (stone arrow heads) and the evil eye. This is the song, with the translation made by Alexander Carmichael for the *Crofters' Commission Report*:

> Cuireamsadh an spreidh so romhan,
> Mar a dh-orduich Righ an domhan
> Moire ga'n gleidheadh, ga'm feitheadh, ga'n coimhead,
> Air bheann, air ghleann, air chomhnart,
> Air bheann, air ghleann, air chomhnart.

> Eirich a Bhride mhin-gheal,
> Glacsa do chir agus d'fholt,
> O rinn thu daibh eolas gu'n aura
> Ga'n cumail o chall's o loc,
> Ga'n cumail a chall's o loc.

> O chreag, o chabhan, o allt,
> O chara cam, o mhille sluic,
> O shaighde nam ban seanga sith,
> O chridhe mhi-ruin, o shuil an uilc,
> O chridhe mhi-ruin, o shuil an uilc.

> A Mhoire Mhathair! cuallaichs an t-al gu leir!
> A Bhride nam basa-mine, dionsa mo spreidh!
> A Chalum chaoimh, a naoimh is fear buadh,
> Comraig-sa crodh an ail, bairig am buar,
> Comraig-sa crodh an ail, bairig am buar.

(I place this flock before me,
As 'twas ordered by the King of the World,
Mary Virgin to keep them, to wait them, to watch them,
On ben, on glen, on plain,
On ben, on glen, on plain.

Arise thee, Bridget, the gentle, the fair,
Take in thine hand thy comb and thy hair;
Since thou to them madest the charm,
To keep them from straying, to save them from harm,
To keep them from straying, to save them from harm.

From rocks, from snow wreaths, from streams,
From crooked ways, from destructive pits,
From the arrows of the slim fairy women,
From the heart of envy, from the eye of evil,
From the heart of envy, from the eye of evil.

Mary Mother, tend thou the offspring all,
Bridget of the white palms, shield thou my flocks,
Columba, beloved! thou saint of best virtues,
Encompass the breeding cattle, bestow thy protection
     on the herds,
Encompass the breeding cattle, bestow thy protection
     on the herds.)

I walked along the ridge of Beinn Mhor, the rocks
hot to touch, and from the further end went down to
the hollow of the Bealach Hellisdale, the pass between
Beinn Mhor and Feaveallach. The mountainside falls
steeply, grassy slopes alternating with rocky crags whose
lower sides are steep and sometimes overhanging. The
top of the bealach is a bare rocky bar at a little below the
thousand feet contour; immediately below it lies a little
rock pool of dark water.

From the pass a line of crags runs upward toward the

summit of the middle hill, Feaveallach. From the foot of these crags rise springs beside which were green cushions of moss and clumps of starry saxifrage, with primroses, celandines and roseroot on the rocks above. It was too hot and dry for the springs to yield more than a mere dampness on the ground beside them.

Feaveallach, with a drop of almost a thousand feet to the tops of the bealachs on either side, is a pleasant hill crowned with a rocky and castle-like mass of gneiss. To the west the rock is precipitous, but from the other side a grassy slope takes one up to the top of the crag. It is a very central place, with Beinn Mhor on the one hand and Hecla on the other, and the glens between them leading down to the sea. Northward one can look into the beautiful Glen Usinish, with the big dark corrie loch of Corodale in it. Corodale loch is partly held back by a moraine of one of the local Uist glaciers, formed in the waning phases of the Ice Age.

Straight out to sea I looked across to MacLeod's Tables, and close at hand was the curve of Usinish ('House Headland') Bay, near which are the remains of several more earth-houses. One of these is fairly complete; it is arranged in the wheel shape so common in the earth-houses of North Uist.

Beyond Usinish Bay a solitary rock with a crop of green grass on the top of it stands just offshore, a mere geo-like cleft separating it from the mainland. This cleft is called Nicolson's Leap (Leum MacNicol). The curious thing about the Leap is that the same story is told about it as about a similar place near North Tolsta in Lewis, Dun Othail. The same story also comes from France, where it is linked to a Chateau Roux.

Here follows the Uist version of the story. A certain MacNicol was, for some offence, sentenced to be mutilated, but managed to escape. At the same time he succeeded in carrying off the Chief's only son, and with the child in his arms sprang across the rift to this stack at Usinish.

MacNicol threatened to fling the child off the rock unless the Chief himself also consented to be libbed. After various attempts had been made, unsuccessfully, to deceive MacNicol, the Chief, to save his son, submitted to the operation. MacNicol then picked up the child and leaped with it into the sea, exclaiming, 'I shall have no heir, and he shall have no heir.'

The French version differs in that it is the top of a castle to which the child is taken. Whether the story reached Uist and Lewis from France, as it might have done, or whether they were developed independently, is a matter for speculation.

In the heat I left Feaveallach somewhat wearily, and went down its shoulder toward the Usinish bealach. A little way down, a couple of tarns lay blue in the sun, held in hollowed basins of gneiss. They were too inviting to pass and I halted to bathe in them.

Across the bealach ran the trace of an old track from Howmore to Usinish, its line clear on the firm ground at the top of the pass, lost in the peat hags on either side. The surface of the gneiss was weathered almost white and it flashed and dazzled in the afternoon sun. Hecla, its summit a crag overhanging, a long grassy ridge leading west from it, rose above me and I began the ascent of the steep scree-littered slope. The heat seemed to increase, and when I sat down to pause all the earth and heat seemed to radiate heat over me, so that it was cooler to get up and go on.

The top appeared close at hand, and yet it did not seem to get any nearer. Eventually, however, I did come out on the rock of Hecla (1,820 ft.), Hecla that the Norse named. It means 'hooded shroud', probably because, as when I first saw it, its peak withdraws into a hood of mist at frequent intervals. Beinn Mhor across the way is, of course, good Gaelic, the big mountain, one of the few principal Long Island hills with a Gaelic name.

I went round to the north side of Hecla, where there was an overhanging ledge with a cool pool of shadow underneath. Below me the ground fell away to the moors and lochs of the north of South Uist, the maze of Benbecula, and beyond them the hills of North Uist, the fords between, and Harris beyond, with smoke rising from a peat cutter's fire.

This country of Corodale and the high mountains of South Uist saw a good deal of Prince Charles when he was skulking in the Long Island. He spent twenty-two days in a forester's cottage at Corodale, to which he came on 14th May 1746. This must have been one of the pleasantest times of his fugitive days. While he was there he was visited by both MacDonald of Boisdale (who had refused to help him when they had met in Eriskay) and Hugh MacDonald of Baleshare in North Uist. MacDonald of Baleshare wrote an account of the meeting.

When Baleshare heard that the Prince was in the Long Island, he crossed the strands to South Uist and went to see Boisdale, and the two decided to visit the Prince. To avoid suspicion, they each went a different way.

The Prince, who was wearing the kilt, welcomed

them warmly and insisted that they stop the night with
him. Boisdale then insisted on changing his shirt and
being shaved before they began the serious business of
drinking. 'Then wee began with our boul frank and free;
as we were turning merry, wee were turning more free.'
Boisdale, the only Protestant of the party, reached the
stage of telling Charles that the two chief objections
against him were Popery and arbitrary government.

'Wee continued this drinking for 3 days and 3 nights.
He still had the better of us, and even of Boystill himself,
notwithstanding his being as able a boulman, I dare say,
as any in Scotland.'

This drinking does not seem to have affected the
Prince's skill as a marksman, for Hugh MacDonald's
account relates that:

Lachline M'Donald of Dremstill, who supplyed him and the few
with him at Glencoridile with victulls tells me he was the man that
attended him still while in the hills a-hunting. He kept plenty of all
sorts of fouls in this hutt he stayd in and deer venison plentifully. But
one day as they happend to go a-hunting the Prince with his feusee in
his hand stood on a hillside and whistled so exact that you coud not
distinguish it from a plover. Some gather'd about him, of which he
shot two on wing and two on ground. Lachline Dremstill said the
art behoove to be witchcraft, for if it was not so the plovers woud
conveen to his whistling as to his highness's. Dremstill takes the
fewsee and falls a whistling, but tho' he stood there yet no plovers
cam to his relief. The Prince a second time takes the feuzee, whistles
and gathers a croud of the plovers about, and shot a good many. He
said he never seed any to paralele with him at the gun, and that he'd
never risque being starv'd while he was master of the feuzee and
plenty of ammunition. Dremstill tells me as they were coming away
from Glencoridile, and the parties by this time landed in South Uist,
as his highness was crossing a burn he miss'd his step and fell on his
ribs on a pointed ston, which hurt him severly. He gave a heavy
groan and made no more bemoan. He was all this time very ill of a

bloody flux and sever fits of grinding, yet still was firm in courage, and insisted he'd never be taken while among his Highland freinds.

The Prince was back in the Corodale district again toward the end of his time in the Isles, hiding in a cave whilst the final arrangements to get him away were being made with Flora MacDonald.

I went down from the top of Hecla to the moor below and the long level tramp back over the bogs to the main road at Snishival. It was a long four miles; the streams the map shows on the flank of Hecla were nearly dried up, so that I did not hear that most blessed sound, the splash of water, till I reached the large Abhainn Roag itself (*Abhainn*, a stream). It is a fine brown stream, rising in the bealachs on either side of Feaveallach, and flowing to the loch complex on the machair at Howbeg and Snishival. Dwarf willows and rowans grow along its banks, and the cuckoo was calling insistently.

Where the stream makes a sharp bend as it nears the road bridge there is a green meadow-like flat with an entrenchment across it. This dyke was made by some MacDonalds who were waiting their time to deal with an invading party of MacLeods. The MacLeods, who were from Skye, landed at Loch Skiport and began to make their way across the country. The MacDonalds sprang upon them from their prepared position and totally defeated them.

So I came back to the road and drove back to Lochboisdale. In the evening sunshine the South Uist hills were very clear and velvety green, their screes hidden by the distance, their summits deceptively close. In the mouth of Boisdale loch, apparently very near, was framed the massive hilly shape of Rum.

CHAPTER IX

THE HILL OF THE FORDS

BENBECULA, Beinn a'bh-faodhla, the mountain of the fords, is the most curious of all the divisions of the Long Island. Linked by its strands to the two Uists at low water, it becomes a separate island at high tide, an island low and little, an island of machair and bogland whose highest hill is a mere 409 feet above the sea.

North to south the island is only some six miles long; east to west, at most just over eight miles broad. To the west side there is a fine machair and a string of beautiful sandy beaches; to the east, a maze of sea lochs and little islands. Between the two shores lies a level moor, for the most part well under 100 feet above the sea, and all threaded and interwoven with lochs. Towards the middle there is the solitary hill, a little conical mole-heap called Rueval (409 ft.).

To the north and south stretch the fords, the strands. The South Ford, across to South Uist, is a short crossing over very white sand, firm and dry at low water. The North Ford, across to North Uist, is of greyer sand, and never completely dry, so that if you would avoid a wetting you must cross on horseback or in the pony trap, and it is also considerably longer. Here are drifting quicksands, the safe route changing with each winter's storms, so that the old guide cairns would take you hopelessly into the quicks. Because it is longer and more dangerous, there have been fewer fatal accidents than on the South Ford, with which people are more apt to take liberties.

Now, the South Ford is no longer in use, for the necessity for quick transport between the important R.A.F. aerodrome at Balivanish in Benbecula and the main port at Lochboisdale in South Uist made the building of a bridge essential. This bridge is nearly half a mile long, a straight line of blue-black tarmac between white concrete parapets, raised up on concrete piers above the tide.

The North Ford, too, could be bridged in similar manner, though the bridge would have to be very much longer. Part of the way could, however, be a causeway. Undoubtedly, in time, the project for the North Ford bridge will materialise, and the pony and trap at low tide, and the motor boat at the flood, will cease to ply between Carinish in North Uist and Gramisdale in Benbecula. North Uist has some doubts about the matter, for would not their port of Loch Maddy suffer if a good road ran all the way, the length of the Uists? And again, there is the matter of the Sunday. For a road bridge might bring the South Uist people holiday-making into North Uist on the Sunday and that would not do at all. For to suppose that the people of the Long Island are all of the same mind would be a great mistake. The spiritual climate of the islands differs so much that, going ashore blindfold, you would know at once which island you were on. Benbecula is placed on the very fulcrum of the see-saw, on the line where two opposed religions meet.

Southward the people are all Catholics; northward they are all Protestants. In little Benbecula there are people of both beliefs, but across the North Ford is the country of the heretics. And there are a few folk across the water who do not want to be made a Siamese twin with the light-hearted Catholics of the south.

At a guess, I should suppose that about a third of Benbecula is loch-covered. Most of the lochs are very shallow, with boulders sticking up through the peaty water. They have various islets and there are old duns upon some of them. Thus the southern Loch Olavat has no fewer than three duns on islands: Dun Mhic Uisdein (the fort of the son of Uisdein), Dun Ruadh (the red fort) and Dun Aonais (Angus' fort). There is a second Loch Olavat in the north of the island, two miles away. Olavat is probably Olaf's Loch (Norse *vatn*, water, is equivalent to Gaelic *loch*, English *lake*). If so, Loch Olavat is a mere tautology. Another interesting fort is Dun Buidhe (the yellow fort) on Loch Dun Mhurchaidh in the north of the island. Here it is said the captain of Clanranald lived at one time, and leading out to the island fort is a substantial causeway, 200 yards long.

To look down upon Benbecula from the hills of either of the Uists, or from Rueval itself, is almost to echo MacCulloch: 'much amusing display of a sort of ichnographic scenery, arising from the labyrinthine disposition of the land and water, may be seen by ascending the hills, but there is scarcely anywhere a subject for the pencil'.

If, again, upon a cool autumn evening, when the many lochs of the island begin to give off a thickish mist, you look across the ford to Benbecula, Rueval alone shows above the smooth white blanket of mist. And, driving across the island, it is so flat and low that you look ahead, northward, to the North Uist hills and the mountains of Harris rather than at the moor beside you.

Balivanish, where the big aerodrome is and whose buildings have become the social centre for both Benbecula and South Uist, is the site of an old monastery. The name means Monk's Town, and here was Teampull Chaluim Chille, St. Columba's church. It seems to have belonged to the monks of Iona and to have been founded about 1390 by Amie, the wife of John, Lord of the Isles.

South from the airport is Nunton, with a fairly intact little ruined chapel in the burying ground. The nunnery buildings themselves were demolished to build Clanranald a new house. The nunnery also seems to have belonged to Iona. Martin Martin relates how the people of Nunton a little time before his visit there (c. 1695) had unearthed a stone vault at the east side of the town. This vault was full of small bones which some people thought were those of birds, others of pigmies.

The proprietor of the town, enquiring Sir Norman Macleod's opinion concerning them, he told him that the matter was plain, as he supposed, and that they must be the bones of infants born by the nuns there. This was very disagreeable to the Roman Catholic inhabitants, who laughed it over. But in the meantime the natives out of zeal took care to shut up the vault so that no access can be had to it since; so that it would seem they believe what Sir Norman said, or else feared that it might gain credit by such as afterwards had occasion to see them.

Between Nunton and the end of the South Ford road bridge at Creagorry is Borve Castle, a small but solid ruin. In height it still rises 30 feet, and the walls are from 5 to 9 feet thick. It is only 60 feet by 36½ feet in

I

size. Ranald of Benbecula is mentioned in 1625 as of
'Castellborf', and the castle was the chief stronghold of
the chiefs of Benbecula. Down on the sands, between
the sea and the castle, was a chapel, Teampull Bhuirgh,
Borve church, but it is now almost overwhelmed by the
blown sand.

It seems that there must have been some sort of a
castle at Borve from very early times, for the name *Borve*
is Norse and means simply fort or castle (Norse, *borg*).

Benbecula is closely linked with the story of Prince
Charles in the Long Island, for there he landed a fugitive,
and thence he sailed for Skye with Flora MacDonald.

Prince Charles was only able to get to the Long Island
safely because the Government search parties were convinced he had made for St. Kilda and General Campbell
had hurried off there to look for him. Meanwhile, on
26th April 1746, Prince Charles left Borrodale on Loch
nan Uamh in a small eight-oared boat. With him were
Donald MacLeod, a Skyeman who was Charles' guide and
helper for most of his Long Island stay, O'Sullivan, O'Neil,
Allan MacDonald, Edward Burke and seven boatmen.

Donald MacLeod said that they should not go because
stormy weather was brewing, but the Prince insisted.
Once on their way, the storm began, and the Prince
begged to be taken back to the mainland, saying he would
rather face the enemy guns than that sea. But MacLeod
was now the obstinate one, for they had little chance of
a safe landing in such weather, and in black darkness,
with neither compass nor lantern, they succeeded in
making the headland of Rossinish on the east coast of
Benbecula. The crossing took them about eight hours.
The storm continued for some time after their arrival.

At Rossinish they spent two days in a deserted hut, and on the 29th again set out in their boat for Scalpay in East Loch Tarbert, Harris. There they stayed with one Donald Campbell, who was the only tenant of the island of Scalpay and a friend of Donald MacLeod. On the first of May Donald MacLeod went to Stornoway to try and get a ship for Charles. This he nearly succeeded in doing, sending word to Charles that all was well and that he could come on to Stornoway, which Charles did, arriving there on 5th May. Meantime, suspicion had arisen in Stornoway, and Donald became too eager in his bargaining, eventually trying to buy the ship he wanted at any price. In fact, the Presbyterian preacher in South Uist had learned that the Prince was in the Long Island and sent word to Stornoway, and Stornoway now had it in its head that the Prince was close at hand with 500 men.

'Well then,' said Donald to the men who were in command of Stornoway's hastily mustered citizens, 'since you know already that the Prince is upon your island, I acknowledge the truth of it; but then he has only but two companions with him, and when I am there, I make the third. And yet let me tell further, gentlemen, if Seaforth himself were here, by God he durst not put a hand to the Prince's breast.'

Indeed, the Lewismen would not harm Charles, but they flatly refused any sort of help. So Charles went to Lady Killdun at Arnish by Stornoway, leaving again on 6th May for Scalpay. Seeing some ships which they thought were men-o'-war, they put into Loch Iubhard and spent some days on a small island there, eventually getting back to Scalpay on the 10th. As Donald, who was likely to get into trouble for entertaining the Prince,

was now also in hiding, the party had to go on. Captain
Ferguson's ship saw them, but they escaped by rowing
into the shallow water where the big boat could not
follow. Next day they were still coasting south and,
having eaten all their bread, made drammach with salt
water (raw oatmeal moistened with water). The Prince
ate heartily of the mixture, Donald MacLeod watching
him the while and wondering how he could possibly
manage so much of the stuff.

That day they landed again on Benbecula, again on
the east coast, at Loch Uskavagh, where they stayed
three nights in a grass-keeper's bothy. The door of this
hut was so low that they dug down under it and laid
grass and heather so that the Prince could crawl inside
more easily.

On the 14th they went on to the forester's hut in
Corodale. There again the Prince had a narrow escape.
A lad came to the door while Edward Burke was cooking
some venison collops and snatched one out of the pan.
Burke struck him, but the Prince remonstrated with him,
fed and clothed the boy, praying that God would help
the poor and needy. The boy went straight back and
announced the Prince's whereabouts, but was merely
laughed at for a fool.

As the search for the Prince gained strength, Charles
had to leave Corodale. He went to the island of Wiay
off the south-east coast of Benbecula, where he stayed
four nights, then went for a further three nights to Lady
Clanranald's at Rossinish, Benbecula. The soldiers were
now patrolling the area, so the Prince went back to
Corodale by boat, camping at Usinish for the night. On
the following day, the 14th June, they sailed to Kyle

Stuley and reached Boisdale on the 15th, taking shelter at Castle Calvay. It was then that they learned that Boisdale himself was under arrest. This was a great blow, for Boisdale knew all the hides in the Long Island. It was said that the Prince need never have left the Long Island so long as Boisdale was free to suggest fresh hiding places.

It was then imperative to get Charles away, for the search was so intensive that, not knowing the country intimately, the party had little hope of remaining hidden, and it was then that Flora MacDonald came to the rescue. The plan for the Prince's escape seems to have been thought of by Captain Hugh MacDonald of Armadale, who was in command of a company of militia stationed in Benbecula, 'an enemy in appearance yet a sure friend in heart'.

Neil MacEachain now appears on the scene in a prominent part. Neil was born at Hoebeg, the Mac-Eachains being a South Uist sept of MacDonalds. He guided the Prince and O'Neil to a hut near Ormaclett where the Prince and Flora had their first meeting. Flora agreed to the plan and Charles was guided by MacEachain to a cave near Corodale, where he hid while Flora went to Benbecula to make the final arrangements.

Flora undertook the task very much against her will. 'What will people say of me?' was her complaint. O'Neil talked her round, telling her she would earn immortal fame. He further offered to marry her, but she refused. Indeed, she would on no account let him come with them to Skye. When O'Neil and Flora met again as prisoners, she gave him a slap on the cheek 'with the loof of her hand', exclaiming, 'To that black face, I owe all my misfortune.'

The fords were now guarded, so that on 23rd June Neil MacEachain took the Prince northward from Corodale by boat, back to the Island of Wiay. Next day they went on to Rossinish and stopped in the house of Clanranald's chief tenant. During the next day it poured with rain, but, as the soldiers were searching the houses, the Prince and O'Neil had to go out and hide under a rock all day. This cave was on the east face of Rueval.

Meantime, Flora MacDonald was with Lady Clanranald at Nunton, putting the finishing touches to the Prince's disguise as Betty Burke. It was Lady Clanranald who supplied the clothes. She, her daughter Peggy, Flora and Flora's brother Milton, all came to Rossinish on 27th June. While they were having their supper, news came that forces led by General Campbell, Captain Scott and Captain Ferguson were closing in on them. They moved southward, across Loch Uskavagh. Next morning a message came for Lady Clanranald to attend General Campbell at Nunton, and she had to leave the party.

The same evening, 28th June, the Prince, disguised as Betty Burke, with Flora MacDonald, Neil MacEachain and a crew of Long Island men, sailed for Skye. Incidentally, the Uist boatmen returned at once to South Uist, were questioned, and under threats told all they knew, so that all the details of Charles' disguise, etc., were almost at once known to the authorities.

The Long Island tradition is that, as the wind was against them, Flora's boat first sailed northward and they made a landing in North Uist at Aird Maddy. They rested in the house of a crofter called Eobhan MacPherson. A MacDonald who had fought at Culloden recognised the Prince there but did not tell MacPherson who he was

till the party were well away again. When the MacPher-
sons knew whom they had entertained, the three young
daughters fell to fighting for possession of the stool on
which he had sat, the youngest losing two of her teeth in
the struggle. As she had suffered so much for the cause,
she was eventually awarded the stool.

The Long Island people used to refer to Prince Charles
as Am Buachaille Buidhe, the yellow-haired shepherd.
By using this name they could talk about him without
arousing any suspicion in the minds of outsiders.

Neil MacEachain went to France with the Prince,
where he joined Ogilvy's regiment. He died there in
1788. His son was Marshal MacDonald, created Duke
of Tarentum by Napoleon. The Marshal went back to
South Uist to visit his father's old home in 1825. When
he came to the river at Howbeg, he stopped and raised
his arm, exclaiming, 'That is the River of Hough, I know
it from my father's description. Many a salmon my father
killed there.' When he left, he took earth from the
floor of the house where his father was born and asked
that it should be put in his coffin when he died. The
Marshal also took potatoes from his grandfather's garden,
and went over to Corodale to take a few stones from the
Prince's hiding places there.

Dr. Johnson, remarking on the fact that in his Hebridean tour he was not able to visit any of the Catholic
islands, wrote: 'Popery is favourable to ceremony; and
among ignorant nations, ceremony is the only preserva-
tive of tradition. Since protestantism was extended to
the savage parts of Scotland, it has perhaps been one of
the chief labours of the ministers to abolish stated obser-
vances, because they continued the remembrance of the

former religion. We therefore who came to hear old traditions, and see antiquated manners, should probably have found them amongst the Papists.'

The same still holds good to-day; it is in the southern Catholic Isles that the folklorists have reaped their richest harvest. The early Christian missionaries tended to try to make over rather than violently alter the religious ideas of the Celts. The pagan holy well was blessed, the temple site became that of the church. The old ideas still lingered; as time went on, ancient memories of pagan gods and goddesses were sometimes confused with those of Christian saints. The notable example is St. Bride, who in Hebridean folklore is confused with Dana, the Mother goddess who assists man in all his doings.

The stories of the Celtic saints show them accepting the challenge of the old gods as such. There is the one about St. Columba and the Druid, Broichan, at Inverness. Broichan threatened to raise such a storm on Loch Ness that Columba would be unable to leave on the day planned. Columba accepted the challenge quite seriously and when the storm did, in fact, materialise, called upon the Christian God as a power stronger than the Druid's and set sail in the teeth of the wind. Very soon the wind veered round in his favour and took him safely down Loch Ness. The tale has an air of a competition in magic; Columba was far too level-headed to have had much belief in the Druid's powers, but to accept the challenge and get the better of Broichan was an astute psychological move.

However, the Islands have preserved a curious mixture of traditions in which pre-Celtic church and Norse belief and magic have frequently acquired a Christian twist and veneer. At the Reformation the Protestants struck hard at this body of tradition, perhaps mainly for the reason Dr. Johnson mentions. Although these old customs delight the folklore collectors, if the people who carry them out do in fact believe them they may be a very evil thing indeed. If in seventeenth century Scotland men could seriously sacrifice a bull to St. Maelrubha so that the sick wife of one of them might recover, the Presbyteries were right to strike hard.

Unfortunately, the Protestant churches did not bring as much enlightenment as they might have been expected to do. If there was idolatry of the saints, they tended to replace it with idolatry of the Bible, and to clamp a narrow Puritanism on the normally gay and cheerful Celt.

So in the Outer Isles Benbecula divides the Protestants from the Catholics, the unbroken tradition from the broken one. But old traditions are dying everywhere to-day. The steamer and the aeroplane, the motor-car and the radio set, the daily paper and the tractor, these things in a few years have done more to kill the old beliefs than all the centuries of Protestant preaching.

After the Reformation, the Long Island was left very much to itself so far as religion went. It was then that Catholicism spread in the Southern Isles, for a few priests managed to get to the Isles, and, in spite of much hardship and danger, reconvert the people. In 1753, a Captain Barlow of the Buffs, stationed in the Long Island, could write of Benbecula:

The Inhabitants are all bigotted Papists, and frequently make their Boasts to the Soldiers when quartered there, of what execution they did against the King's Troops at the Battle of Prestonpans. There is a Presbyterian Missionary resides in this Island but he has a miserable time of it. He set some Men to work with an Intention to build himself a House, but he has never been able to compleat it, for what was built in the Day, was almost demolished in the Night by People unknown, and the poor man durst not complain for fear a worse Treatment should ensue.

One very curious ritual for looking into the future was the Frith, which survived in the Isles until fairly recent times. It does not appear to have ever been used on the Scottish mainland. Uist calls it 'Frith a rinn Moire dha Mac', the Frith that Mary made for her Son—which enabled her to find her Son among the doctors in the temple. In other words, a Christian interpretation has been put on a pagan custom, for the Frith was a Norse importation. In Norse the word is *Frett*, and means 'to enquire of the gods about the future'. To carry out the Frith one rose before sunrise on the first Monday of the quarter and, bare-headed and bare-footed, eyes closed, went to the door of the house. A hand was put on either jamb, and the gods were invoked to reveal the future. The enquirer then opened his eyes and looked straight ahead. Whatever he saw was taken as an omen of the future. A raven is a bad sign, as is a woman with red hair, but a man approaching or a bird on the wing is a good sign. For the Mackintosh clan a cat is a good sign, as is a pig for the Campbells (the boar in the Campbell crest), and so on. In Benbecula the following rune was repeated when making the Frith:

> Mise dol a mach orra shlighe-sa, Dhé,
> Dia romham, Dia am dheaghaidh,
> Dia am luirg;
> An t-eòlas rinn Muire dha'Mac
> Shéid Brighid thromh bas (glaic)
> Fios firinne, gun fhios bréige:

> Mar a fhuair ise gum faic mise
> Samhladh air an rud a tha mi fhéin ag iarraidh.

(I go out in thy path, O God; God be before me, God be behind me,
God be in my track; the knowledge which Mary made for her son,
Bridget breathed through her palms, Knowledge of truth, without
knowledge of falsehood; as she obtained her (quest) so may I too see
the semblance of that which I myself am in search of.)

In the old days in the Isles, everything one did, from
getting up in the morning to going to bed at night, seems
to have been accompanied by the appropriate rhyme or
prayer. For instance, at night, when the fire was smored,
this prayer was said over it:

> Tha mi smaladh an teine,
> Mar a smalas Mac Moire;
> Gu mu slan dha'n taigh's dha'n teine,
> Gu mu slan dha'n chaideac uile.
> Co siod air a lar? Peadair agus Pal,
> Co air a bhi'eas an fhaire noc?
> 'Air Moire mhin-geal 's air a Mac.
> Beul De a thuradh, aingeal De a labhradh.
> Aingeal an dorus gach taighe,
> Ga'r comhnadh's ga'r gleidheadh,
> Gu'n tig la geal a maireach.

> (I smoor the fire,
> As it is smoored by the Son of Mary.
> Blest be the house, blest be the fire,
> And blessed be the people all.
> Who are those on the floor? Peter and Paul.
> Upon whom devolves the watching this night?
> Upon fair gentle Mary and her Son.
> The mouth of God said, the angel of God tells.
> An angel in the door of every house,
> To shield and to protect us all,
> Till bright daylight comes in the morning.)

You cannot smore a modern stove or fireplace. The

operation refers to the peat fire made on the earth floor
of a black house, which you can draw together and cover
with ashes so that it smoulders all night, ready to burn
up in the morning. Fire, of course, is regarded as holy
by most peoples. Especially holy is the fire made 'naturally', by friction (need fire), and the Hebrideans probably prayed over their fires long before the first
Christian missionaries arrived.

There is a curious little legend of how the Outer Isles
acquired their collection of charms. These charms are
called Eolais or Eolas, knowledge. St. Columba had two
tenants, one of whom was single, the other married with
a family. The single man complained to the saint that
he had to pay the same rent as the family man, who was
obviously able to make more as he had more people to
work for him.

Columba told the man to steal a shilling's worth of
something and restore it to its owner at the end of the
year. So the man stole Columba's own little book of
eolais (charms) and then went off with it to the Long
Island. There he gave permission to anyone to read it
for a fixed charge. Thus the Outer Isles learned the spells
of Columba and the man made his fortune. When he
returned the book to the saint, the latter burned it,
fearing he would earn a reputation for knowledge and
power which he did not deserve.

CHAPTER X

THE THREE HILLS

IF you sail southward from Loch Maddy in North Uist, three hills will dominate your going. First, two conical hills rise close together, the North Lee (823 ft.) and the South Lee (920 ft.), with a deep V-shaped cut between them through which the last light of the sunset gleams golden. South from the Lees is the narrow opening of Loch Eport, a fiord which seems to lead across North Uist to the Atlantic. And beyond Loch Eport rises Eaval (1,138 ft.), a splendid mountain shaped like a pyramid and the highest top in North Uist.

These three hills continue the line of the South Uist mountains, broken by the level moor of Benbecula. Though lower and separated, they are yet a worthy continuation of the great southern ridge. And to understand the build of North Uist it is to the tops of the mountains that one must go, there to look down upon the most complicated pattern of lochs in all Britain.

It was on a rather cold October morning that I set out for the two Lees. The sun was bright, but there was a skim of ice on some of the lochs and the bogmoss was crisped with frost. Across the Sound of Harris the mountains of that country rose white against a blue sky;

the Uist hills themselves were pricked out with snow.

To save three miles of walking round one of the many arms of the sea that made up Loch Maddy, I went down to the pier and got a rowing boat to take me across the narrow stretch of water, beyond which the moor stretched, more or less clear of lochs, to the foot of the North Lee.

A sort of a path took me part of the way, then I went cross-country, past the green mound of an old shieling, towards the rocks at the foot of the hill. A hoarse lowing noise, like that of an irate cow, echoed twice across the moor; then came a wheezing cough. I looked toward little Loch na Hostrach. Surely those animals were not cows? Surely one of them had antlers?

In fact, the whole moor seemed to be alive with deer, the stags with harems of hinds. The click of antlers came from a hollow on North Lee itself; the roaring sounded from every hollow among the crags. I avoided one herd only to walk into another. The deer of the forests of Harris and Lewis are smaller than the red deer of the mainland, but these North Uist animals were very fine beasts, high in the shoulder with great shaggy coats and a royal spread of antlers.

The low autumn sun was coming up over North Lee, and as I went up among the rocky crops that build the mountain it was almost blinding. As I came to the top, a top of ice-smoothed gneiss, I came face to face with a belling stag who was stationed a little below the summit on the other side. We glared at one another momentarily and then I tried to make believe I had a gun, so that the creature turned and slowly trotted off. The rutting stag is usually in a somewhat aggressive frame of mind.

In the haze across the Minch I could see Skye, snow whitened, but the mainland beyond it was invisible. Northward were the white hills of Harris, and southward the slightly less snowy ridge of Beinn Mhor and Hecla in South Uist. Below me lay a pattern of golden-yellow moor and vivid blue water, North Uist itself, the shadow of North Lee a black triangle on the ground at its foot.

To the north of the hills was the opening of Loch Maddy, with its bays fingering deep and complex into the land. To the south the dark shadow of South Lee lay black on the moor, and beyond it was the fiord of Loch Eport cutting across the island almost to the Atlantic coast. To the west were the central hills of North Uist, rounded moorland tops, and between them and the two Lees lay a jigsaw pattern of lochs, bays and headlands, of islands with duns on them. The loch most prominent was Scadavay, the most involved fresh water loch in Britain.

All this network was vividly coloured, the moor golden and the water sparklingly blue, the tangle yellow-brown on the rocks at Loch Maddy, the shadows of the two hills black upon the land below them; a splash of red was the funnel of the *Ulster Star* at the pier. From all around came the roaring of the deer.

To look down upon the network of water, the brown hills of the Uist interior, the rocky knobs of Crogary More and Beg, and Maari linked by a ridge, the more rounded shapes of Marrogh and Uineval, Loch Maddy town strung out on an arm of dry land, is to see the map come to life and put meaning into the figures.

For instance, the total area of North Uist parish, including some islands off the coast, is 103,274 acres. Of this area, 8,000 acres are covered by fresh water lochs and 20,000 by foreshore and tidal waters. The Ordnance Survey map shows 125 different fresh water lochs on the main island itself. The sea loch Maddy, in which is the island's harbour, has a shore line at high water of 43 miles and penetrates through a maze of islands deep into the land. Many inland lochs are brackish, being reached by the highest tides. Most of them are very near sea level; the highest loch surveyed by the Bathymetrical Survey was only 35 feet above sea level, and Loch Scadavay is a mere 16 feet. A very little further subsidence would not only link up the existing lochs but flood the land between them.

Beyond the South Lee I could see Eport, which to me is the oddest loch of the whole collection. It is a sea loch, and the mouth opening into the Minch is a mere cleft in the cliffs, at its narrowest point only 60 yards across. In this narrow mouth the water is from 7 to 15 fathoms deep, in the main loch up to 10 fathoms. The narrow entry is about 1,200 yards long, then the fiord opens out to about a mile in width. Further on, it narrows again, sending off branching fingers at its further end, nearly seven miles from its mouth. The head of the loch is only about a quarter of a mile from the bays on the west side of the island. Throughout its length the main line of the fiord is perfectly straight, trending east to west.

These two sea lochs, the narrow mouthed Loch Eport and the wide mouthed Loch Maddy, are a result of recent subsidence of the land and of the sea breaking into a fresh water loch. Loch Uskavagh in Benbecula has been similarly formed.

This then is the shape of North Uist, complicated

sea lochs and fresh water lochs to the east and three high
hills. Beyond, to the west, lies a group of lower hills
in country which is thickly covered with peat. And
sweeping around the island, from the north at Port nan
Long to the south at Carinish, there is a broad fringe of
good machair land with the sandy beaches that are found
on the west side of all the islands. Upon this western
edge live most of the people, for the peaty interior is of
little use. It is well to remember that the peat is a late
growth here, after the time of the people who built the
stone cairns and circles, and that once the whole island
was inhabited. The peat is now some 15 feet thick and
of very high quality.

I left the summit of the North Lee and went down
the steep side toward the South Lee. Between lies a
deep and narrow glen, on either side of which the hills
rise some 600 feet. Crags and stretches of turf and
heather, with stray flowers still on it, led down to the
dark little loch on the floor of the cleft. Then, by the
same kind of country, I climbed up again. The water
is black with peat, and the sun kept away by the steep
glen sides. This small loch is dammed at one end to
form a reservoir for Loch Maddy.

The South Lee is the higher of the two, with a broad
undulating top of bare rock and rough grass. There I sat
down to look at the lochs again, to be suddenly roared
at by a stag who came clattering up over the rocks. He
was very reluctant to trot away. Under the shelter of the
rocks were little patches of granular refrozen snow and
the wind was keen.

Across Loch Eport I could now look to the lovely
symmetry of Eaval, which rose from a glittering ring of

K

lochs. The Norse name is probably from *Ey fjall*, Island hill, for it is a hill that is almost an island. To the north and west the fresh water Loch Obisary laps round it, the deepest loch in North Uist (151 ft.). To the south there is the sea coast bordering on the sound between Uist and Ronay Isle in the North Ford gap, and to the east two small lochs, Loch a'Gheadais, with a dun on it reached by a twisting causeway, and Loch Surtavat. To the south-west on another small loch, Loch Dùn an t-Siamain, is another dun, fairly well preserved and linked by a causeway to the shore. The level of this particular causeway indicates that the water level is lower than when the fort was built.

Taking a line around Eaval on the 100 feet contour line, or slightly below it, the base of the mountain measures 6 miles round. Of this, about 4½ miles abuts on either fresh or salt water. In fact the ascent of Eaval seems to entail either a very great deal of bog-hopping and walking around lochs or else a boat.

In the low sun all this water sparkled silver as I looked against the light, while to the west it was all deep blue. A small lobster boat traced its way along the shore of Loch Eport. Loch Hunder (Hound Loch) below the South Lee attracted me with its dun and causeways linking the dun to the shore and then to another island, where cattle could be housed. I turned down the face of the hill towards it.

There is another dun in this country—upon the flank of the South Lee towards Loch Eport and near an old shieling called the Buaile Caragarry. It is placed on a rocky ridge and inside the fort is a primitive beehive hut built of unhewn slabs of gneiss.

As I went down the steep grassy slope towards the loch, I turned to look back towards the rocks of the summit in time to see a large stag standing upon them. Outlined against the bright sky, he stretched his neck, heavy with a grey mane, and roared with open mouth. Eight hinds now came in sight, upon the hillside beside me, and the big stag turned down the slope to join them. I had the party outlined against the glint of the Eaval lochs, the hinds fearless, watching me with feminine curiosity, the stag shifting restlessly, a little suspicious.

And as I went back towards Loch Maddy after looking at the duns of Loch Hunder, I met several further groups of deer. All through the frosty starry night Loch Maddy town could hear them roaring. Similarly, the croak of the corncrake allows it no rest in summer. Later, as the feed got scarcer, the deer would be down on the roads; but that autumn day they were magnificent upon the hills, their branching antlers against the sky and their belling echoing from the snow-flecked crags.

CHAPTER XI

THE COUNTRY OF THE CASTLES

THERE is not much shipping in Loch Maddy now, though Martin Martin was told that there had been 400 sail loaded there with herrings. It is a somewhat tricky harbour with its multitude of islands, and its little pier built on a rocky promontory deep in the heart of the sea loch. Always as you pass the lighthouse on the Weaver's Point you will feel the lift of the waves under the keel, and as like as not there will be white crests around the Maddy rocks even if the water within the sea loch is calm and still.

They will tell you that Loch Maddy is the Loch of the Dogs, and that the dogs are the two basalt rocks at the mouth of the bay: Maddy Beg (Little Maddy) to the north and Maddy Mhor (Big Maddy) to the south. Some way down the coast and out of the sea loch stands Maddy Gruamach (Sour-faced Maddy). So in North Uist you will meet three words for a dog; the Norse *hundr*, hound, in the place-name Loch Hunder, the Gaelic *cù* of the ordinary speech, and the Gaelic *madadh*, in English spelling Maddy. Madadh also covers fox—*madadh ruadh* (red dog) and wolf—*madadh allaidh* (wild dog). But since *madadh* also does duty for the common mussel, perhaps

Martin Martin was right when he said that the name referred to the numerous mussels on the three rocks.

Strung out along the inlets of the sea loch is the town of Lochmaddy, North Uist's principal centre, with a hotel and a police station, among other amenities. Up the promontory runs a good tarred road to branch in two a mile inland and encircle the whole island. This is the main road, and bordering it are the different townships where the people live. Within the girdle of the road are many of the lochs and the sterile moors, crossed only, north to south, by a rough track made originally as a relief measure in the potato famine.

Perhaps first you will go southward to Carinish on the North Ford and Trinity Church, crossing Loch Scadavay on a built-up causeway. There is a peculiar fascination about this part of the road. The wind sings through the telegraph poles, which huddle in the distance as the road dips and rises. In the October sun the moor grass is yellow and red, the dead brackens russet and the lochs a gentian blue. Here the road crosses a loch by a little bridge, here a long seaweed-fringed finger of the sea comes close, grey water slipping off pale muddy sand. At the end, at Carinish, is a turning place for cars, and the wheel tracks of the pony trap lead away over the grey sand of the North Ford, the windy desolate gap between the isles.

In winter the road may be iced so that a car cannot climb the undulations; or the snow may bury road and loch alike—at least one man has been drowned by straying off the road into a loch.

Upon a ridge there is the great cairn of Barpa Langass, a dark heap against the skyline as you look northward

from Carinish. And as you come toward Carinish, upon
the salty grass beside the sea you will see a brown ruin,
the great church of North Uist, Teampull na Trionaid.

The church of the Trinity is built in rather small and
largely unhewn blocks of local gneiss, all blotched with
golden crotal (lichen). The mouldings of the windows
are gone, and as you clamber in from the nettle-grown
graveyard you see that the whole of the floor of the
church is deep in rubble. What is underneath it? It is
said that there was once a three-headed giant carved in
stone on the building—presumably a representation of the
Trinity—and that inside there were carvings like those
of Rodil in Harris. At the beginning of the nineteenth
century a man called Macpherson remembered seeing
carvings of animals, armed men, angels and so forth in the
church. Perhaps some of them are still buried there.

The church itself is some 61½ feet by 21 feet in size,
with walls nearly 4 feet thick and rising to a height of
from 17 to 20 feet. Off this main building there is a
vaulted passageway which leads into a smaller building,
some 23 feet long, called Teampull Clann a'Phiocair
(MacVicar's Church). This second building is not a
church but a house, and is a later addition to the church.
Perhaps the priest lived there. There is a MacVicar
commemorated on a recent headstone in the graveyard
by the church.

The date of the present building is somewhat in doubt.
The lancet windows are a sixteenth century style but the
plan is fourteenth century.

'In 1389 Godfrey of Íle, Lord of Wyst confirmed to
the monks of Inchaffray the chapel of the Holy Trinity
(at Karynch) in Wyst, as granted to them by Cristina the

daughter of Alan the true heiress and Reginald called M'Rodry the true lord and patron' (*Origines Parochiales Scotiae*).

Cristina lived about 1309. Tradition believes that Amie M'Ruari was the founder of the church about 1390, but it seems more likely that she repaired rather than built it. It is probably a very ancient church site. Amie M'Ruari married John, Lord of the Isles. Godfrey was her son.

Up on the low salty machair beside Teampull na Trionaid and the North Ford was fought the battle of Carinish, an affair of swords and bows and arrows, in 1601. Feith na Fala, the field of blood, is the name by which the battle field is still known.

The cause of the battle of Carinish was the feud between the MacDonalds of Sleat and North Uist and the MacLeods of Dunvegan and Harris. The affair boiled up to fighting point when Donald Gorm Mor MacDonald divorced his wife, one Mary MacLeod, and rudely sent her home. Her brother was a Sir Ruaridh Mor MacLeod and he at once sent his kinsman Donald Glas MacLeod to lay waste North Uist. Donald Glas took with him from forty to sixty men and, having arrived in North Uist, they made their way to Teampull na Trionaid 'to tak a prey of goods out of the precinct of the church of Kiltrynad wher the people had put all ther goods and cattal, as in a sanctuarie'.

Now Donald Gorm Mor MacDonald had a near relation called Domhnull Mac Iain 'ic Sheumais (Donald son of John, son of James), and this gentleman with a party of sixteen men attacked the MacLeods at Carinish. The MacLeods were cut to pieces, only two reaching their

boats at Loch Eport. Donald Glas managed to escape to
the tidal island of Baleshare off the North Uist coast at
Carinish, but was overtaken, hit over the head and killed.
It is said that his body was buried at Teampull na Trionaid,
and in 1840 a skull with a gash in it was lying about in
the church there. The other MacLeods were buried
where they fell, at Cnoc Mhic Dho'uill Ghlais (the
hillock of Donald Glas) beside the shore.

Donald Mac Iain was an Eriskay man, but he moved to
Carinish about 1650 to live there permanently. It was
Donald Mac Iain's great-great-grandson, Angus MacDon-
ald, who was the tacksman of Eriskay with whom Prince
Charles spent his first night on Scottish soil.

Alternatively you may go north from Loch Maddy,
the road snaking by the complex Loch Blashaval, a division of Loch Maddy itself, and the hill Blashaval (361 ft.)
rising upon the other hand in heathery slopes. Perhaps
you will see a heron fishing on the seashore or, more
probably, the companies of whooper swans swimming
upon the lochs. These swans are a winter or autumn
sight, graceful whether riding the air or the water, their
harsh voices filling the air. Martin says that when the
people of North Uist took a swan for food they made a
negative vow: they swore not to do something which was
itself impossible. In the old stories bewitched people
might be changed into swans.

Beyond Blashaval is Loch an Duin, the loch of the
duns, practically fresh water at one end, but salt and
entered by Loch Maddy at the other. There were four
island duns upon the loch, and of them a broch, Dun
Torcuill, has walls still rising about 10 feet. It is the best
preserved broch in North Uist.

Most of the duns of North Uist have served as quarries for new buildings, dykes, houses, roads. Dun Skellor built several farm steadings, Dun an Sticer, Newton Ferry, made dykes, Dun Tomi a house in Vallay Island. But North Uist is a country of duns, of castles. The sites number nearly 100, on islands, in lochs and on rocky heights.

Beyond Loch an Duin a road branches to the north, to Port nan Long, commonly called Newton Ferry. The way lies between the machair land, with a graveyard dedicated to St. Columba, and two moory hills, Beinn Mhor, 625 feet (the Big Hill) and Beinn Breac, 450 feet (the Speckled Hill)—a pattern of brown moorland and steel-grey rock. Under these hills, on an island in a loch, is Dun an Sticer, which is another old broch, and several other fort sites are to be found by the road between the turn off the main highway and the ferry.

Port nan Long, the ship harbour, looks across to the island of Berneray, a pleasant machair-covered island; as it is devoid of peats, the inhabitants have to go and fetch them from overseas. Martin says that at one time the peat on the small island of Lingay between Boreray and Berneray was held sacred and though it would have served the people of these islands they durst not cut it.

From Port nan Long the ferry-boat runs across to Berneray. But the main supplies are transhipped to a small boat at Loch Maddy pier, and then make the rough journey round the Weaver's Point and the skerries and rocks of Hoebeg. Once, many years ago now, the boat set off as usual but never arrived at Berneray. No trace was ever found of the boat or her crew.

Tradition has it that a ship of the Spanish Armada was

wrecked at Port nan Long, and that at very low tides the wreck may yet be seen.

The main island road runs on westward, past Dun Aonais on its loch and Loch nan Geireann with its prehistoric kilns. Northward, the sea has broken deep into the machair land, so that two long spits reach out—the Port nan Long machair and the Machair Leathann—and between them is an Oransay, an ebb island. There is a broad bay at high water, sand at low tide. West of the Machair Leathann is another great strand, Vallay Strand, and at the end of it the Island of Vallay, a dune country covered with bright green machair turf, with a track across the sands leading over to it. And beyond that are the north-west point of North Uist and the great rocky cliffs of Griminish.

On Loch nan Geireann is Eilean an Tighe, where have been found a series of Neolithic kilns. They are of a horizontal type and resemble some found at Farnham in Surrey belonging to the Roman period. The firing ovens were at the back of a large hearth, the flames being led back over them, stone baffles keeping them from coming in contact with the actual pottery. This discovery of pre-Iron Age pottery kilns is the first in Western Europe and is quite a new one. There is a series of kilns and a series of pottery shards from them, ranging from simple undecorated pots to more elaborate types and decorations. One decoration was made by pressing a cockle shell edge, into the soft clay. A similar decoration has been found on pottery in Southern Catalonia.

Eilean an Tighe made a very high grade ware and made it in bulk, obviously selling it to all the neighbourhood. The pottery is very similar to that found in

Orkney, and it was thought that Uist might have sent it that far, but a geological examination of the crushed rock used to make the grog (crushed rock or old pottery mixed with the clay) showed that in each place strictly local rocks were crushed for this purpose. Orkney therefore did not receive ware from Uist.

But the find gives a new light on life in the Stone Age Hebrides. The Islands were well populated, almost free from peat, the people civilised enough to build great tombs and circles of stone and to manufacture high grade pottery. And North Uist itself extended further north, south and west than it does to-day, and had woods, for the tomb on Clettraval yielded birch wood charcoal together with Eilean an Tighe pottery. This production of Hebridean pottery did, in fact, become much less expert as time went on. The people used to make their own pots right up to the middle of the nineteenth century, and they made them then in a very primitive fashion without a proper kiln for firing.

The Machair Leathann, which reaches out northward from the village of Grenetote, is one of the finest machair and beach strips in the Isles. It is about three miles from Grenetote to the Ard a'Mhòrain at the end of the half-mile wide strip of turf, and on either side is a fine beach.

Where the land broadens toward Grenetote is Sollas, the present emergency landing strip. Originally the planes used to land on the eastern sand, the Traigh Ear. I drove over its firm ripple-printed surface as far as the spit called Corran Ard a'Mhòrain (*corran*, a sickle, the shape of the spit), where the sand softens. The autumn sun glinted on the wet and rather grey sand, stray strands of brown tangle were littered about, the machair grass

on the dunes was golden in the morning light, the sea
very calm. Oyster catchers, gille-Bhride (Bride's ser-
vants), fluted 'Bi glic, bi glic' ('Be wise, be wise'), as the
Gaelic mimic has it.

Ahead was the Ard a'Mhòrain, a low hillock (130 ft.)
of sand buttressed by rock, the rocks themselves cropping
out upon the end of the headland. Banks of variegated
shingle mingled with the sand as I came up to the rocks,
and, going round them to the very tip, I came to the old
burying ground of the Ard a'Mhòrain.

It faces out to sea, to the islands of the Sound of Harris,
Boreray, Berneray and Pabbay, and looks beyond to the
Harris mountains themselves. Here are buried, in a little
enclosure, the MacLeans of island Boreray. Most of the
graves are marked by unhewn stones, but some record
burials up to the 1920's, and I tugged the grass aside to
read 'Erected by John McLeod, Owner of the Sloop
Maria Loch Mady, March 14th, 1812'.

Two hundred yards west of this burial ground, on a
flat face of dark gneiss facing the sea and forming part of
the first outcrop of rock that you come to on the way
from the Corran spit, is cut a cross. It is a simple Latin
cross, 14 inches high and 7 inches across, and, in the
particular light in which I looked for it, difficult to find.
In fact, I only discovered the thing by stroking all the
likely faces with the tips of my fingers. Crosses of this
sort cut upon rocks and stones are found throughout the
Isles and are fairly old. This particular cross is below the
highest tide level.

Nearby there is said to be a well called the Well of
the Priest or the Well of the Cups, but I did not satis-
factorily identify it, though there certainly were several

small springs close to the cross. The cups refer to a cup-marked stone. As one of the rocks on the beach weathers naturally into cups, I doubt whether the cups really are hand carved.

I walked back to Grenetote over the top of the Ard a'Mhòrain, with a splendid view out to sea to the lonely Haskeir Islands, and along the eastern Traigh Iar. Here are white beaches and a few rocky skerries, the Atlantic roaring in on them, in sharp contrast to the calm upon the eastern side of the Machair Leathann.

Upon this machair there are several kitchen midden sites and some underground houses, and I myself sought out the ruin of Udal. Udal village was placed upon the grass against the western beaches, the roar of the sea about its little fields, whose walls you may still trace. Where the wind had scooped out a dune, I saw the walls of old houses, layers reddened with fire, and the kitchen midden refuse—the shells and bones which were flung out by the inhabitants. I found many fragments of coarse pottery among the winkle, cockle and limpet shells, and bones of sheep, ox and whale. I also found a piece of iron slag, for the Udal folk did their own smelting, and there were many white quartz pebbles, some split across, which one could use as a strike-a-light. The results of systematic search at Udal have yielded a good deal of rough pottery, human bones, hammer stones, pins made of bone and soapstone vessels. Slag has been found and a whorl of sandstone such as was used to weight the spindle in spinning. Some rivets of Viking type also turned up.

But Udal is not a mere prehistoric kitchen midden site; we have the story of its ruin, though to understand the feud that ended Udal, one must understand the complicated affairs of Amie M'Ruari.

David II of Scotland confirmed by charter Ranald M'Ruari's hold of Uist and Barra. But in 1346 Ranald was treacherously slain by his superior, the Earl of Ross, and his lands passed to Amie M'Ruari, the woman who repaired Trinity Church at Carinish.

John, Lord of the Isles, married Amie and thus obtained her lands. By her, John had three sons and a daughter: John, who died before his father; Ranald, who was the founder of Clan Ranald; Godfrey; and Mary who married MacLean of Duart. Having got hold of Amie's lands, the Lord of the Isles divorced her and married a daughter of Robert II, by whom he also had three sons. These sons were Donald, who succeeded as Lord of the Isles; John Mor, the Tanister, from whom sprang the MacDonalds of Dunyveg in Islay and the MacDonalds of the Glens in Antrim; and Alastair Carrach, who was the originator of the MacDonalds of Keppoch.

Now Godfrey, Amie's son, held the North Uist lands from about 1389, and his descendants, the Siol Gorrie (seed of Godfrey), lived at Udal.

In North Uist there was another sept of MacDonalds, the Siol Murdoch, descended from Murdoch, a bastard son of Angus Mor of Islay (died c. 1293), and between these two septs there was a deadly feud. Siol Murdoch were the stronger, but Siol Gorrie the more cunning.

The Siol Gorrie decided to exterminate the Siol Murdoch, and accordingly went over to the Loch Hosta district where the sons of Murdoch lived. There they cut the banks of a lake and drowned a large number of their enemies. The flood water is said to have formed the present Loch Hosta on the west coast.

But not all the Siol Murdoch were drowned, and the survivors set off for Udal. Siol Gorrie, taken by surprise, were all killed but one, and the village was burned. The survivor reached Boisdale and his descendants lived there for many generations. But Udal was dead, and the sand blew in over the blackened walls.

In complete contrast to the sands of Udal are the rocks and heathy moors of Griminish Point, a little over five miles to the westward. There against high cliffs the Atlantic pounds, and out to sea one can see the natural arches eroded in the Haskeir Islands and the spray leaping on the cliffs. The Griminish (Grimr's ness) cliffs themselves are all seamed with geos and arches cut out of bands of dark hornblende gneiss. One system travels right across the headland and the roof of it has fallen in so that there is a great round hole in the grass. Looking down, one can see the sea lapping into it under a rock arch, and flecks of spume come floating up out of the hole. Sloc Roe (*sloc-a-rodha*, the Pigeon's Cave) is the name of this blow hole; another one is some miles to the southward at Tighary Point and is called Sloc-a-choire, hole of the cauldron. Sloc-a-choire is said to spout 200 feet into the air when a storm is running, but while I was on the cliffs it never seemed to be doing anything at all. The rock arch between the sloc and the sea will, according to legend, give way one day under the weight of a newly wed couple.

If you go southward along the cliffs from Griminish you come first upon a quiet little bay called Scolpaig Bay, an arc of white sand, some multi-coloured shingle, a

small piece of dune at the back of it, and a rock bar out
to sea breaking the force of the waves. Cross a few yards
of headland from this quiet corner, and you are at Port
na Copa, with a high sea breaking on black rocks and
the land behind sodden with foam and spray.

Port na Copa, the harbour of foam, seems to gather
unto itself all the froth and foam produced by the
beating and churning of the Atlantic round its rocks, and
this foam drives inland, sometimes piling up 15 feet deep
on the beach and 5 feet deep on the field at the back of
the bay. But about most of the rocky inlets and geos of
this coast you will come upon pelts of froth thrown up
on the rocks.

Upon the rocks beside this beach have been found
the traces of an old quarry for millstones—the small hand
querns which every household once used. Some unfin-
ished querns were lying there and there was the trace of
one on a rock ready to cut out. Another such quarry was
found out to sea on the Haskeir Islands. Millstones, of
course, have to be of a suitable sort of rock, and some
of the old quarries sent their products very long distances.
One popular stone was the Lochaber variety, a mica
schist with garnets. The soft mica wore away and left
the hard garnets sticking out like the teeth of a rasp.
Lochaber querns went all over the Highlands: a quarry
for them is known at Bruniachan, Glen Roy, near Spean
Bridge. Another much favoured rock was the gritty sandstone of Soay, off Skye. Every house had its quern 'and
the two stones doth lye on the house floore, and that
place is made cleane'.

Behind Port na Copa is a partly drained loch with an
island; an octagonal 'folly' is built on it. The tower is

on the site of an old dun. A Donald Herroch once lived
in the dun, till he was killed at the local sports by some
of his enemies. The method was ingenious. As Donald
made the high jump, one Paul slung a leather noose round
his neck so that he strangled. This Paul fled for sanctuary
to Cill Mhoire but was overtaken and slain.

Cill Mhoire is some three miles south from Donald
Herroch's island and Scolpaig farm, and between the two
places is another ancient church site, Kilphedder (Peter's
church), of which no trace remains. On the ground above
the old site, however, is a little pillar with an ancient
cross set up on it which came from Kilphedder graveyard. It was erected between 1830 and 1840 on this site
by Dr. Alexander MacLeod, one of the few factors who
have won the hearts of the tenants. An Dotair Ban, the
fair-haired doctor, had many schemes for the benefit of
Uist, including drainage plans, reclaiming the dunes by
planting bent grass and cultivating seaweed by setting up
stones for it to grow on.

There is no trace of the old church of Cill Mhoire
(St. Mary's church) on the rise of ground by the sea at
Houghary. The graveyard is divided into two parts, with
the recent burials on the slope towards the sea and the
old ones on the crest of the hill above. Here you will see
the burying ground of the MacDonalds of Balranald, des-

cended from Donald Herroch of the Scolpaig dun, who was buried here in 1460. Here, too, you will find a fine old saddle quern serving as a headstone; a broken slab with an interlaced Celtic design on it; a socket stone for a cross; a flat slab with a cross rather like that of Ard a'Mhòrain cut on it, and several other old crosses. One of these is perhaps the Water Cross, of which Martin heard; this the inhabitants set up when they wanted rain and laid down when enough had fallen.

Standing amongst the stones of Cill Mhoire, you will look to the Haskeir Islands, to the Monach lighthouse on the Monach Islands (also called Heiskers) and, far out, to St. Kilda and Boreray. Nearer at hand is a large complex of dunes called Beinn a'Bhaile (hill of the township), the lowest 'Ben' in all Scotland. It is 72 feet high.

I walked over the machair land towards this miniature mountain, through herds of Highland cattle and sturdy little ponies and past the fields where the potatoes were being harvested. A pony plough was turning up the lines and the people were then howking out the potatoes from the soft sandy soil with their little hooks and carrying them in baskets to the pits. These are small graves dug in the ground and covered with the dune sand. I watched a man making one, putting in a mixture of varieties, Kerr's pinks, a white sort, and a vividly red tuber. I asked what these last two were. The red one, he told me, had been in the ground for years (meaning that they saved their own seed) and, as for the white, 'Och, there was a wreck out there.'

You climb the dunes of Beinn a'Bhaile past an odd crop of rock, go through marram grass knee high, and come out on a crest of sand. The dune itself is level enough on the top for one or two small fields to be worked, and just below me I looked down on a party of potato diggers.

But the view is of mountain rather than lowland quality. Behind lie the brown hills of central North Uist; out to sea are the Haskeirs, St. Kilda, Boreray and the Monach Islands. Southward, I looked to the hill of Rueval in Benbecula, to the mountain ridge of South Uist, and, far away, to the arch of Heaval in Barra. And through the North Ford gap, eastward, the jagged line of the Cuillins of Skye was in sight.

From Houghary road end the main North Uist road runs southward to Carinish, past the grim square block of the West Ford Inn, where the strands lead out to Kirkibost and Baleshare. These two islands are machair strips isolated by the erosion of the sea, and it is said that the Monachs, seven miles out to sea, were formed in like fashion and that once there was a tidal strand leading out to them also. Tradition remembers the names of the people who made the last crossing of this strand before it deepened to a permanent channel. The island where the lighthouse stands is Heisker nam Manach (Heisker of the Monks) because there was once a colony of monks there, and the other of the two islands is called Heisker nan Cailleach (Heisker of the Old Women), commemorating a nunnery.

In the early part of the Iron Age many of the inhabitants of North Uist seem to have lived underground. Some were cave-dwellers. You will find shells and bones and bits of pottery in the caves of Druim na h'Uamh (ridge of the cave) on Eaval and Uamh a'Bhalbhain (the dumb man's cave) on the North Lee. Altogether North

Uist has eight inland caves; but more important are the artificial caves, the earth houses.

These earth houses are curious structures, built underground in drystone. Some may have been temporary hides, but in North Uist many were permanent residences. Often there is a big circular underground room divided into compartments by walls radiating like the spokes of a wheel. One earth house of this type excavated on the Machair Leathann had fourteen such chambers opening off from a central space with a hearth in it.

Earth houses have been found in all the main islands of the Long Island but they are most numerous in North Uist, where there are about fifteen known sites.

Valley Island has a good number, for the sandy soil lends itself to their construction. The site would be dug out, the house built and roofed and the sand piled back. The Valley underground houses show the wheel structure with, in some cases, a boat harbour by the neighbouring shore, and there is a well made system of drains also leading shoreward. Finds include a fragment of Samian ware and a coin of Constantius II (fourth century). With them were the usual household products, pottery, hammer stones, strike-a-lights, iron knives, weaving combs and spinning whorls, the inevitable quern and, rather interesting, a whalebone knife handle with an Ogham inscription. Bac Mhic Connain in Valley had inside its wheel house not only ordinary hearths but a small furnace for iron smelting. With the furnace were found moulds of clay and stone, and crucibles in which the molten metal could be melted and shaped.

We get a picture of a people making iron tools and bone tools for themselves, weaving their own beasts' wool, making pottery to cook their food in, and grinding the corn they had grown on the machair outside for their baking. They also gambled, for a bone die was found at Foshigarry. The numbers 3, 5, 4 and 6 were indicated on four sides, by dots enclosed in double rings.

I visited Foshigarry earth house site. It is about a mile and a quarter due east from the tip of Griminish Point, beside a sandy bay west of Callernish Point. Foshigarry was the name of a group of shieling houses which were placed upon the top of the earth houses and by which you can locate the site. Nothing is now to be seen of the actual earth house. The house was, in fact, not a single house but an underground village. It had a drainage system leading to the shore, and there, too, was a boat harbour. The coast is very rocky from Griminish to Callernish, and the underground village was placed at the one point where a boat could avoid the skerries and come in to the short stretch of clear sand.

Foshigarry pottery fragments had no fewer than thirteen different kinds of pattern ornamenting them. A number of pieces of pumice stone were found. These could not be got locally, and would be washed in by the tide and gathered off the beach by the people. They used them for smoothing the various tools they made out of bone. They worked quite a bit in whalebone, the creatures presumably being either hunted or stranded in the vicinity. I found a whale's vertebra tossed up by the tide close to Foshigarry when I was going round the cliffs.

There is another and different type of earth house in Uist, built not in the soft sand but in the scree fallen from a crag. Of this type is the house in South Uist at

Loch nan Arm under Stulaval. Another of this kind is a house in North Uist in the Loch Portain country. It was to visit this Loch Portain house and a couple of interesting duns near it that I embarked with the mails on the *White Heather* one drizzly morning.

Loch Portain is an inlet of Loch Maddy, and the district of Loch Portain and Hoebeg forms the northern shore of that sea loch. The district is linked with the outside world by motor boat and is virtually an island, Loch Maddy nearly cutting it off from the rest of Uist in the Loch an Duin district. A road, however, is now under construction, which will loop around Loch Maddy to join the main island road.

Loch Portain is the boggiest part of North Uist. It is a large bog, diversified with lochs and rocks and a few damp hills, with here and there an old shieling mound vivid green against the brown moor. That particular day it did nothing much but rain or drizzle and the mist drifted in quivering sheets about me. The peat was soft and slippery like butter; the bog moss gave beneath my feet and brown water oozed up.

But though the district was bleak the people of Loch Portain did not match it or their climate. The man who met me at the little jetty and seized me by the hand to help me out of the mail boat had the old and royal Hebridean manner. With a few ordinary sentences he made me feel that I was the one person Loch Portain was pleased to be receiving. When I came back, dripping rain, he gave me tea in his house before the sail back, and introduced his cat, which shook paws with me.

Tigh Talamhant (earth house) is the name of the Loch Portain underground dwelling situated on the shore of Loch Hacklett. To reach it you must go around the head of Loch Portain itself and climb straight up the brae to the south. A little way over this brae is Loch Hacklett, with a small stream running down from it into Loch Portain.

It is a pleasant, open loch, cradled in a hollow of the moors, and to the west side are a few low crags. At one point these come down to the water's edge, so as to enclose a small triangular plot of ground between the crag foot and the water, and upon this plot is Tigh Talamhant.

You may approach it by water, but you cannot approach it by keeping to the shore of the loch, because the edge of the crag bars the way on either side. At the back of the plot, however, where the crags run back, the rock gives place to a short and steep heathery slope, down which it is quite easy to slither. On the small plot you will see some big fallen boulders, grown over with fern and grass and heather. Under one block a tunnel leads down underground, and towards the other crag you will see a stretch of faced drystone walling through the cover of herbage. Below this, on a level with the loch water, is an entry into a narrow and low passage built in drystone. There is a strong draught along this passage, which seems to extend for some distance parallel to the loch shore. It is, however, somewhat narrow to crawl inside to explore, and has probably closed in with settling down in the course of time.

I got the impression that the whole little piece of ground must have been mazed with tunnels like a rabbit warren. Whether anyone lived there permanently, or whether it was a sequestered spot to hide one's goods in time of trouble, I do not know. Pathetically, the tree so dear to the Scottish homestead, the mountain ash, grows on the loch side by the mouth of the passage; its red berries were glistening in the rain.

These earth houses were used over a considerable period. Though they were built in the Celtic Iron Age, and though the Vikings seem to have kept out of them, they came into use again later on. Dean Monro wrote of North Uist (1549), 'Ther is sundrie covis and holes in the earth, coverit with heddir above, quhilk fosters maney rebellis in the countrey of the north heid of Ywst'.

CHAPTER XII

PORTRAIT OF THE MACHAIR

Machair and Traigh, these two words are the key to the beauty of the Outer Isles. It is the memory of the machair and the traigh that will be pulling you back across the Minch to the Islands, not that of the mountains or the rocks or the intricate lochs of the moors.

The machair is the sandy plain of the dunes; traigh is the Gaelic word for the white beach beyond it. The machair land is the wealth of the islands, dotted with villages and striped with the pale sandy fields, its short hard grass grazed by big herds of Highland cattle and ponies. The machair leads down to the traigh, where is the long curve of the white beach with the glint of the sun on the golden-green marram grass of the dunes and the Atlantic swell riding in, the wind lifting the spray off the wave crests.

The Hebrides can be bleak. The Minch crossing is too often an affair of grey water tossing between grey islands, stern rocks and landing at dusk at a windswept pier, while above the hills rise into mist wreaths and seem gigantic. The eastern side of the Long Island is a cheerless country, but the west side of the Long Island is entirely different. One recalls the low sun of the dawn building a shining path across the ripple-printed sands, the surf foaming on the skerries and the beach long and dazzling, with dark tangle strewn about on it.

And every traigh and machair has its own particular flavour. The Traigh Mhor of Barra, the cockle strand, has silver-grey sand which the tide leaves rock hard. Equally hard is the Traigh Ear of Sollas in North Uist— your feet ache with walking over it. Yet across the machair spit, facing the Atlantic, is whiter, softer sand, open to the full surge of the sea. In South Uist the beaches curve along the twenty miles of western coast; in Benbecula and North Uist they ring the western shores. Between these islands lie the wet strands of the Fords.

The spring comes late to the machair: it is May before it is yellow with primroses and the hollows are full of their scent while the wind keens over the dune tops. Later, the machair has a brilliant carpet of daisies, blindingly white like a shell sand, while on the lochs there are water-lilies.

The machair has its own sounds, distantly the roar of the sea, but close at hand the skylarks singing in the hard blue of the sky, the wail of lapwing and whaup and oyster catcher. Down on the beach, the turnstones run in droves at the tide marks. And scattered along the machair are the little townships with their friendly people and their sandy trackways.

It is not easy to portray this Hebridean machair to the southron who has never felt the salt-edged breeze, and the sand hard and unyielding under his feet, his ears singing with the deep throated roar of the surf. In the summer sun the sea is quiet and gentle; in the winter gale the waves come shouting and crying. One recalls the Uist place-name Lamrig E-eg-ir, Aegir's landing place. Aegir was the Norse god of the sea and the waves were his children; in the thunder and spray of an island storm the Norsemen's mythology seems less fanciful.

And then there is the wind. It flattens the wiry marram to the ground till the leaves draw circles on the soft dune sand. One may lie in the deep dune hollows, snug amongst the old faded shells and splintery bones, and look out to the wind-tossed sea, the long waves coming steadily in, five, six, seven of them, one behind the other, foaming steps leading westward to the blue line of the horizon.

Down on the sands a shower has passed, pitting the beach with pocks, each with its splashmark to the lee-ward side of the wind-driven rain. These are small showers, and this one has only crossed one end of the traigh, leaving a track of pitted sand whilst the rest of the beach is smooth and unmarked. Out to sea another shower is coming in, long shaking threads swinging from the dark clouds, veiling the hills as it crosses them, the half arc of a rainbow leaping from the sea at the back of the storm.

At the end of the traigh, between this beach and the next, a rocky bluff makes a little headland, the bare rock only showing here and there through the mantle of machair sand and turf. Below, the clean rock faces the sea, smooth and with a deep, vertical-walled geo cutting into it. The sea comes arching over the rock, tossing spray high as it breaks, the water swirling in creamy eddies, white and lustrous like icing sugar. Between the rocks, where the eddies meet, the foam lives longer to form a yellow-white pelt upon the water, a fleece floating on the uneasy sea.

Down on the beach the tide has torn up the long stalked tangle and rolled it neatly into bundles two feet high. It would be a poor soul who did not go down and give a glance to the strand-line.

For there are always odd things coming out of the Atlantic, wreckage and bleached spars, tropical things out of the Gulf Stream, cargoes of lost ships. Once you might have found the St. Kilda people's mails, sent out in an inflated sheep skin or a rough wooden boat in the hope that they would drift ashore and be found. One walks the traigh, piratical, desiring the sea gods, and the Virgin's treasury, to give of their plenty.

The machair and the traigh; these words recall the western beauty of the Outer Isles, lonely beaches and chimneys smoking in the township behind, tangle wet and glistening, and always the voice of the sea, strong and deep and unceasing.

CHAPTER XIII

LEWIS OF THE MOORS

Lewis is different. It is different both from the mainland that rises out of the sea across the Minch and
from the islands to the southward. It has a quality
of its own, a quality of spaciousness that comes of wide
open moors without high hills. These broad moorlands,
dappled with shadows, strewn with lochs full of water-
lilies and with dark peat cuttings, and with the distant
blue line of the Harris and Uig mountains, have the
bleak, keen beauty of the English downs. And the Lewis
people are different from other Hebrideans, in speech,
in manner, in habits.

You sense the difference as the *Loch Seaforth* comes
into Stornoway Bay. After all, most of the people in the
Outer Isles live in Lewis and Harris (30,000 out of
40,000), and after all, Lewis-with-Harris is the biggest of
the small islands off the British coasts. All this is reflected in the bigger steamer, the crowd off the train at
Kyleakin, and then, as you near the shore, the harbour
works and town of Stornoway.

The bay was christened by the Norsemen Steering
Bay, and probably their ships were often anchored there,
where the wide neck of land on which Stornoway town
stands, juts out into the bay.

The cable of the crane tightens and they swing your car on to the pier beside the site of the old Castle of the MacLeods. Around behind the office where you sign forms for the car's loading is a plaque upon the wall, in Gaelic and English, announcing the fact that here was the site of the old Castle.

It stood out in the bay, a little off the spit on which the village was first built, and perhaps it looked very much like Kiessimul in Barra. Tradition relates that it was built by the Nicholsons of Lewis, a clan claiming descent from the Norsemen. But afterwards it was the stronghold of the MacLeods of Lewis, the Siol Torquil, until they were driven out. It was demolished during Cromwell's time, and the remains were destroyed in new harbour works in 1882.

Stornoway is a curious little town, the older part all upon the spit dividing the outer and deeper from the inner and shallower harbour, and the new houses sprawling inland. Lewis Castle stands aloof across the bay with tree-clad slopes round it, a big pretentious building of last century; closer at hand the smoke rises from the kippering plants and the boats of the fishing fleet are packed neatly in the inner harbour. Every morning of the season they are there, shovelling herring into baskets and swinging them over to waiting lorries piled with empty boxes and barrels. The fish glitter in the sunlight, the little boats are brightly named so that you go from one to the other to see what will be next, and everyone is speaking Gaelic. Some of the boats, with names like *Tern*, will have the creature painted upon their wheelhouse; some will halt you with the name of their home town. Applecross caught my eye and set me wondering how many come from that small village. People will be going away with a dozen herrings threaded on a string for their own eating.

English multiple stores show their signs under the street names, written up in Gaelic and English so that anyone can learn that Mol a'Tuath is North Beach and Mol a'Deas South Beach. Buses galore come in from the country districts daily and rumble back again when the boat has arrived. By evening the bars always seem to be doing a brisk trade and people are finding the pavements suddenly uncertain. The Sabbath is an exception, for a Stornoway Sabbath is a matter of a long face and a black suit, even if you could not find your way home on the Saturday night.

I had half made up my mind that Stornoway might be resolved into two parts, one of which was kippers and the other the Nicolson Institute—that great school of the Isles that has sent its pupils right around the world—when the town's pipe band appeared. Against a background of herring boats chugging out to sea, of cairns of herring boxes and of the country buses working round the one-way streets, they marched and countermarched, resplendent in tartan, with the Caberfeidh crest, the stag's head, on their bonnets. It is a weekly event, taking place outside each hotel in turn through the season, and Stornoway folk gather in little straggly groups on the pavement to listen. Perhaps Stornoway is like that, a little drab and fishy at first acquaintance, but suddenly making the magnificent gesture. It bears a little of the same relation to the rest of Lewis that Portree bears to Skye—it is something of its own and in no way like the rest of the country. To see Lewis, you must leave Stornoway.

The main roads radiate out from Stornoway like the spokes of a wheel, southward to Harris, eastward to Point and Tiumpan Head, northward to the Butt of Lewis and Tolsta, westward to Callernish and Uig.

Eastward is the Eye peninsula, the 'Point' district, ending in the lighthouse and rugged cliffs of Tiumpan Head. The road goes past Stornoway airport and along a narrow neck of land, which, but for the artificial embankment, would have already yielded to the sea and made the peninsula a real island.

The land widens suddenly at the further end of the neck of land. There are red gritty beaches upon either hand, and a track leads off northward to the very edge of the encroaching sea, to the roofless church of St. Columba.

St. Columba's, Eye, is one of the great churches of the Outer Isles, and is supposed to have been founded by St. Catan in the sixth or seventh century. The present building, a roofless shell in warm red local sandstone, dates from the fourteenth century with fifteenth or sixteenth century additions. There was a priory there, and like Teampull na Trianaid in North Uist it was attached to Inchaffray. It is often referred to as the priory of Skairinche, probably skerry of the island ('*sker*' and '*innis*').

The present building is divided into two parts, a smaller rectangular portion 23 feet by 16 feet leading into a larger building 62 feet by 17 feet, like chancel and nave. There is a fine barrel arch over the door through the dividing wall; the windows of the building are narrow and splayed internally.

Undoubtedly the time to visit Hebridean churches is

in winter or early spring. In summer they are deeply
buried in a riot of nettles and cow-parsley, and amongst
this stinging jungle I picked a way to look at the carved
tombs. Erected on the kirk wall is a wonderfully carved
life-size representation of a MacLeod of Lewis, done in
dark hornblende schist. It is supposed to be Roderic II,
who lived in the latter part of the fifteenth century. He
was the father of Torquil IV and of Margaret MacFingone,
who was the mother of John, last Abbot of Iona. Roderic
wears a mail tippet, a quilted coat and a bascinet. The
details have weathered on the face of the carving but still
show in their original form on the sides, where, for
instance, one can make out the four strands of the sword
belt. On the mainland the tippet and bascinet went out
of fashion by the middle of the fifteenth century, but the
Outer Isles were far enough away to show a considerable
time lag in relation to mainland trends. In fact, the
Highlands still wore the quilted coat in the seventeenth
century.

Another stone, with a foliage and interlace pattern,
has also been fixed to the wall. When less worn, the
lettering round the margin was read as 'Hic Jacet Mar-
gareta Filia Roderici Meic Leoyd de Leodhuis vidua
Lachlanni Meic Fingeone Obiit MᵒVᵒIII'. In other words,
it is the tombstone of the daughter of chief Roderic on
the opposite wall.

I saw another fine carving, of much later date, with
a skull and cross-bone design, and one of the same style
as Margaret's with a sword. There is said to be a cup-
marked stone somewhere upon the church floor but the
nettles forestalled me. Here are said to be buried nine-
teen of the Chiefs of MacLeod of Lewis, one of the

M

principal clans supporting the Lord of the Isles. Who
were these MacLeods?

They claimed descent from one Olave the Black, a
King of Man and the Hebrides, who had a son called
Leod, and were therefore of Norse extraction. In the
thirteenth century the clan divided into two branches,
the elder son, Torquil (Norse *Thorkell*, kettle of Thor),
heading the Lewis branch, hence called Siol Torquil (seed
of Torquil), and the younger son, Tormod (Norse *Thor-
modhr*, Thor's wrath), becoming chief of the Harris branch
—the Siol Tormod. From the Siol Torquil came the
MacLeods of Raasay, Assynt and Cadboll, and from the
Siol Tormod, the MacLeods of Dunvegan.

There is a curious old rhyme connecting the MacLeods
with horses. Whether they once thought themselves
to be descended from horses is uncertain; the Clann Ic
Anndai, the MacAndys of Harris and North Uist, held
that the long-tailed ducks were enchanted members of
their clan, even as the MacCodrums were supposed to
have relations among the seals. The MacLeod rhyme is:

Siol nan Leòdach,	(The progeny of Leod,
Siol a'chapuill,	The progeny of the horse,
Bhacaich spògaich,	Lame and awkward,
Bheathaicheadh air	Fed on chaff and
Moll is fòlach,	Rank grass,
Air dubhadan dubh	On the black beard of dried oats
Is golm eòrna.	And singed barley straw.)

Down on the beach beside St. Columba's you will see
cliffs and rocks of the soft red-brown sandstones and
conglomerates (consolidated gravels) which form a small
outcrop in the Stornoway and Gress district. They are
formed by the weathering of the land surface built of the

Lewisian gneiss and all the conglomerate boulders are derived from that rock. Their age is doubtful. Some people maintain that they are of the same age as the Torridon Sandstone of the mainland which built the great red hills of Applecross and Loch Maree, others that they are considerably younger and to be grouped with either the Old or the New Red Sandstone. Whenever they were formed, however, the Lewis gneiss formed a land surface which was probably much more hilly than to-day and the climate was very dry. The conglomerates are the downwash of temporary mountain torrents.

Along the coast you may actually see the junction of the sands and gravels on the ancient gneiss land surface. It is interesting to see how the sandstones and conglomerates wrap around the landward end of the Eye peninsula, as though, in ancient times, it had formed part of a hilly area from whose western slopes the material was weathered off. The gravels become coarser as you go south, suggesting that the high mountains lay to the south, for the biggest boulders would be rolled the shortest distance. This ancient and prehistoric Lewis had mountains to the south and lower country to the north, even as it has to-day.

The district by the old kirk is called Aignish, probably from Norse *egg*, a ridge (Ridge Point), and the Gaelic name of the village there, Knock (*cnoc*, a hillock), suggests the same idea, the land rising from the low spit linking Point to the rest of the island. Knock was the site of an interesting prehistoric find, a stone axe-hammer which was perhaps used in religious ritual. It was very beautifully made, and designed to show the banding of the rock to perfection. The curious thing is that it is made of a rhyolite of a type peculiar to Northmaven in Shetland and is thus an indication of prehistoric traffic.

The seven miles of road to Tiumpan Head from Knock run through undulating country and village after village, new houses mingling with the old black thatched ones. Wherever the land is good, it is cultivated in long narrow strips which pattern the slopes in alternating bands of colour—green oats and the darker foliage of the potatoes, the seed on the hay giving red-brown tints for contrast. They are unfenced, and the cattle are tethered on the pasture strips between the various crops. On the moors I saw big peat cuttings, and everyone was busy (July) getting the peats home, piled in great pyramids upon lorries. Whilst the men and women waited for the return of the lorry they sat and talked, the women knitting the while, the men with their hands folded. The peats home, they were restacked in neat heaps ready for use.

Down at Bayble (Norse, priest's town) I talked with a creel-maker who lived in a black house. He was eager to get a new house, for he said that maintaining the old black house was like painting the Forth Bridge; you no sooner got to one end than you had to start on the other. The rain gets into the walls and they may unexpectedly collapse.

The Point and Harris are the main creel-making districts of the island. The creels are made of cane and Argentine willow, bent round on a special wooden frame set with holes for the cane ends. The material has first to be softened by a three-hour soak in a big tub; the making up of the creel takes a further hour. They are used to carry peats, grass, seaweed and even potatoes, being slung on the shoulders with a webbing band. At Carloway I saw a whole string of men and women, looking like the Seven Dwarfs, bent double against the horizon; each had a full creel of peats and was carrying them to the roadside from the cutting.

Bayble is on the south coast of the Eye peninsula, and a little to the westward is Chicken Head, one of the oddest place names in all the Isles. There was an ancient church upon the headland, a 'cell' of the Celtic monks, and the Norsemen named the headland after it, Headland of the Church. Norse for church is *kirkja*, Lowland Scots kirk. In the mouth of the Gael the *k* softened to a *c*, and turned the name into Rudha na Circ, headland of the hen!

The Tolsta road runs northward along the east coast from Stornoway, as far as North Tolsta village and a bit beyond. Lord Leverhume originally planned a road all the way to the Butt of Lewis along the east coast, and it is hoped to build this road fairly soon. It would open up a good stretch of land for settlement.

The Tolsta road is a pleasant one to travel, if somewhat rough, leading through villages and over open moorlands. First it goes past the red beaches, derived from the red sandstones of Coll, at the back of which is a lovely machair, in summer thick with purple orchis, thrift, bird's foot trefoil, yellow bedstraw, red and white clover. The next bay and township is Gress (our word grass), with a wide spread of machair and good arable land.

Here you will see the narrow strip fields best displayed, a bright banding on the gently sloping hillside.

Coll and Gress were both famous for their whisky stills. Illegal distilling went on openly in the Lews until 1827, and it was quite the thing, if you were treating an Excise officer, to ask him whether he preferred Coll or Gress.

On the machair turf beside the Gress River is the roofless little church of St. Olaf's, the burial place of the MacIvors, and claimed as the only Long Island chapel dedicated to a Norse saint. There was an earth house discovered in the grounds of the nearby Gress Lodge. It was circular, with a central pillar supporting a roof of flagstones. Shells of the large whelk (*Fusus antiquus*) seem to have been used as lamps to light the place.

Now the road begins to climb up over the moorland, before it snakes down to a bridge over the burn in Glen Tolsta, country which recalls some of the Border hills. On the ridges the view is very wide: Stornoway behind, with the hills of Harris and Uig, the Shiant Isles and Skye, and, across the Minch, the Assynt Hills. These mountains, Suilven (the Sugar Loaf), and Canisp, Cul Mor and Ben More Assynt, seem to rise like islands from the sea. When the weather clears, the tooth of Suilven is always the first to show through the thinning cloud.

Near Tolsta a loch was drained in 1874, and in it was found a crannog or artificial island. The structure was built of piles and stones, with heather and moss and an outer covering of earth and gravel. There were the remains of three houses built in drystone on it, and there was a causeway of large stones leading to the shore. Round the island were found mounds of shells (the mussel predominating), bones (deer and the small Highland sheep), ashes and twigs—the rubbish tip of the occupants. Another crannog was found on Stornoway Reservoir— Loch Airidh na Lice.

Beyond the village of North Tolsta the road becomes rougher, winding amongst green hills, with a glimpse of the broad sandy beach of the Traigh Mhor, running north from Tolsta Head. Then it rounds a bend and comes down to the sands of Geiraha, one of the loveliest bays in the Lews. The burn comes down from the moors to a green machair land, backed by craggy hillocks, with a little loch covered with white water-lilies. The sand is soft and white; above it cliffs rise on either side, and from the beach itself rises a group of fantastic rock stacks.

Some of these stacks are mere worn-down stumps, but there are four of fair size. One ends in a pointing finger of rock; the largest has a tunnel right through its base and an old fort upon its top. At high tide they are quite surrounded.

The Lewis townships are all of them placed beside the coast and the good land, the interior being a vast peat bog. Only one village is placed inland, Achmore. Achmore in modern Gaelic means 'big field', but an old spelling has it Athmore ('big ford'), probably in relation to a crossing of a neighbouring loch. Achmore lies on the road which leads westward from Stornoway to Garynahine and Callernish, and eventually to the Butt of Lewis.

But the direct road to the Butt of Lewis, a good tarred road, goes more directly northward, past the Barvas Hills (955 ft.), the highest rise in the bog of Lewis, and through the green valley of the Barvas River with its many shieling huts.

At Barvas itself the main road meets with the route round the coast from Callernish. And though the surface is very poor in places, the longer route is the pleasanter.

You drive across the wide moors with the sparkling lochs and the distant view of the southern mountains to the complicated sea loch, Roag, at Garynahine. There the road divides, one branch to Uig, one to the north. The northward branch leads past the great stone circles of Callernish and the broch of Carloway. It leads under craggy cliffs, spilling great boulders, past the trim village of Carloway with broad slopes divided into strip fields. And there, too, surprisingly out of place, is a fly-over road junction where the principal road is carried over a more direct track from Stornoway.

· The road goes on, over moors, with glimpses of lush fertility down at Dalemore, and never very far away from the Atlantic, which boils angrily against majestic cliffs, cut here and there by a rock arch or a blow hole where a cave roof has collapsed. Inland is a little group of hills, of which the highest, Beinn Bragor, rises to 857 feet.

On the Bragor Hills there is a rough shelter under an overhanging rock, formed by building a wall on the outside of the cave; it is called Both a'Mheirleich, the Robber's Hut.

This particular robber, the story relates, was a very strong man, and when he went down to steal the people's cows he dragged them home by their tails so that the hoof prints would point in the wrong direction. When the owners went calling for their cow, 'Blarach, Blarach', he mocked them, saying, 'Is diomhan dhuibhse bhi'g eibheach Blarach, agus bloigh na Blarach air a ith.' (It is no use calling Blarach when part of Blarach has been eaten.)

However, the people of the coastal townships eventually found the Meirleich's hiding place and surrounded it with men and dogs. The thief rushed out and sprang off a ledge called An Palla Gorm (the Green Ledge), breaking his leg on landing. But such was his strength that he grasped the damaged leg and ran a mile—to Beinn na Cloich—where he was overtaken and hanged.

These villages by the coast, Shawbost, Bragor and Arnol, still retain many old houses and a very primitive appearance. In Bragor the street looks very like an African village with the low thatched roofs of its black houses. Some of the houses are very long, so that carts and beasts may occupy one end and the people the other. Chimneys may be wooden boxes or stove pipes stuck in the middle of the roof; you may even see houses without chimneys and the fire smoking out of the door. Some houses still have hardly any window space. As you walk along the streets of these villages you will hear constantly the clack-clack of the looms making tweed.

Usually the loom is housed in a special hut of its own. Some of the old hand looms are still used but many people have modern treadle-operated machines, which, though expensive to buy, work quickly and surely and with a minimum of effort on the weaver's part. These big looms have to have a perfectly level floor on which to stand, so the Islanders usually lay one of concrete for them. The weavers seem to learn the business from one another, and are always ready to show you how it is done.

There is an amusing story told about an English visitor and the son of one of these Hebridean tweed makers. The visitor had gone out fishing in a boat on one of the lochs but the day was calm and the light bright and conditions hopeless for catching trout. By way of conversation the Englishman asked the ghillie who was with him what his father had been. 'My father,' said the ghillie calmly, 'was a spider.' 'A spider?' exclaimed the visitor in alarm. 'Yes,' answered the ghillie, 'and I'm proud of it.'

The Englishman was now convinced that the ghillie was mad; he asked to be rowed ashore and hurried back to the hotel, where he at once enquired the whereabouts of the nearest doctor. 'That ghillie you sent me out with,' he explained to the hotel proprietor, 'says his father was a spider.' 'Indeed yes and that is right,' was the answer. 'His father was a spider.'

It must have taken a little explaining before the alarmed fisherman was made to realise that weavers (who, after all, do make webs) are called spiders in Highland and Island phraseology.

The west-side villages of Lewis, with the exception of Uig away in the mountains and a law unto itself, have always had a reputation for being backward compared to the east-siders. Captain Thomas, writing in mid-nine-teenth century, heard the expression 'taobh s' iar' (west side), as a term of reproach and contempt. The people living there were held to be a separate race, dark, short men, backward and dirty, who, like the Wiltshire moon-rakers, concealed with foolishness their craft and cunning.

Murdo MacDonald, a very pious man, was sitting at his loom one day in Stornoway when someone came in and asked him, 'Do you think, Murdo, that the west-siders of the Island will go to the same heaven as the enlightened people of Stornoway?' 'I don't think they will,' said Murdo, 'but I think they will go to the same hell.'

I walked through Bragor and down a side road towards

the sea and Loch Ordais, a loch dammed back from the bay by a shingle bank. By the track were the Bragor crofts, a bit untidy-looking—raised lazy beds for oats and potatoes, and a few stone pens to preserve special plants from the sheep. A woman staggered up the path with a creel on her back piled high with cut grass for the cows, the narrow-bladed Hebridean sickle stuck in the side of the load. Probably she would give the grass to the cow at milking time to keep it still, for milking is done out-of-doors, with the animal untethered as often as not.

I climbed over a gate into the jungle of nettles in the graveyard of Teampull Ioin Bragor. St. John's church was almost buried in the vegetation and I could not get near it. It is probably a fifteenth century structure, a little nave and chancel built of local boulders. The walls are more or less complete; it lacks only the thatched roof.

There are a large number of old church sites along the west coast of the Lews from Callernish to the Butt: for instance, Teampull Pheadair (Peter) Shader, Teampull Pheadair Swanibost, Teampull Bhrighid (Bridget) Mid Borve, Teampull nan Cro'Naomh (Church of the Holy Blood, which Martin refers to as Holy Cross) and Teampull Mholuidh (Moluag) Eoropie.

Past Bragor is Arnol, where one house has a whale's jaw bones over a gateway. Between the bones hangs the harpoon imbedded in the dead whale when it was washed ashore in 1922. Oil is said to have oozed from the bones for seven years after they were set up.

Further on, the road joins the main road to the Butt, near the bridge over the Barvas River. Martin relates how the people always sent a man very early to cross the Barvas River on the first of May, thinking that if a woman went across first it would stop the salmon coming up. The people told Martin that they had learned this useful fact from a foreign sailor, but Martin put the responsibility for the idea fair and square on themselves.

'There is on the Northwestten of Lewis ane Logh which is called Logh bervais [Loch More Barvas at the mouth of the Barvas River] and the freshwater river which doth runne out of this Logh is but halff a myll in length, there was thrie thousand bigg salmond slayne in this river in anno 1585' (*MacFarlane's Geographical Collections*).

Barvas itself is a long straggly township with new houses ousting the old black ones; often a part of the old house is left against the new one to serve as cow shed. The road ahead to the Butt and Port of Ness is long and straight, going past Ballantrushal with its great standing stone, over wide moors and past lochs with ruins of duns on their islands, finally through Lionel and Habost to its end at Callicvol (Port of Ness), where there is a little harbour and a sandy beach leading to fine cliffs. From Callicvol there is a broad outlook across the Minch, to the dream-like Assynt Hills, which rise fantastic from the sea.

I followed a big red 'Co-op' van up the road, or rather track, from Port of Ness to the Butt of Lewis. Its large and glittering bulk halted outside the black houses of Five Penny Ness and Eoropie and housewives came hurrying out to buy their supplies. I went on to the ugly red brick lighthouse on the rocks of the Butt.

The cliffs are some 100 feet above the sea at their highest point, and the rock of which they are formed is a banded gneiss thrown into great folds and wrinkles. Seaward, the land ends in a broken group of stacks between which the sea washes with a heavy surge. The cliffs themselves are deeply indented; upon their tops grows a fine short turf with cushions of thrift.

The lighthouse lamp is 170 feet above the sea and can be seen for 17 miles. I sat outside on the edge of the cliff, eating my tea and looking out to sea. Here was the other end of Innis Fhada, the Long Island, a district so different from the cliffs and islands of Barra Head as almost to seem another country. There, in the south, the islands ended in hills and sandy beaches, high cliffs and rock-strewn sounds; here, in the north, in the one cliff and the low bare moors, a motor road leading to the Butt itself instead of a boat on a tossing sea.

Following the Butt of Lewis cliffs round towards the west brings you, after about a mile, to Luchruban, the Pigmies' Isle, of which so much has been written. It is, in fact, a stack off the coast, somewhat difficult of access and with the remains of a building upon it. This building consists of a circular chamber, 10 feet in diameter, which is joined to a rectangular room, 8 feet by 5½ feet, by a passage 9 feet long. The design is similar to that of the bothies of the Clan Macphail in the Flannan Isles, which are related to the beehive huts of the Forests of Uig and Harris. The interest of the island is not so much in the building itself as in the tradition that it was inhabited by pigmies.

One story says that the pigmies were Spaniards, that they came to Lewis in 500 B.C. and that they lived upon 'buffaloes' which they killed by throwing knives at them. In course of time, a St. Frangus who lived on the sands of Lionel was unkind to the little people, so they hanged him on the hill called Bruich Frangus. In A.D. 1, tradition goes on to relate, there came big yellow men out of Argyll who drove the little men out of their cave at Cunndal (south of Luchruben) to the Pigmies' Isle. When their numbers overflowed this rock, they started settlements at Eoropie and Knockaird.

The story may, of course, be a folk memory of one of the many invasions of fresh colonists to the Long Island. But the bones of the pigmies were found in numbers in the building on the stack, and one may suppose that, whatever they were, they were the same sort of small bones that Martin heard of at Nunton, and which were supposed to be those of the children borne by the nuns there. Dean Monro saw the bones for himself and wrote (1549):

> At the north poynt of Lewis there is a little ile, callit the Pigmies ile, with ane little kirk in it of ther awn handey wark. Within this kirk the ancients of that countrey of the Lewis says, that the saids pigmies has been eirded thair. Maney men of divers countreys had delvit up dieplie the flure of the little kirke, and I myself amanges the leave, and hes found in it, deepe under the erthe, certain baines and round heads of wonderful little quantity, allegit to be the baines of the said Pigmies, quhilk may be lykely, according to sundry historys that we reid of the Pigmies; but I leave this far of it to the ancients of Lewis.

There is another curious story about this part of the Lews, given in *MacFarlane's Geographical Collections*, in an account dated about 1630. It says that: 'There is a bigg forrest in that place in the North end of the Lewis being a mountaine called Cadsoill or Cadfeild and the Deir which doeth remaine in this Mountaine or forrest hath two tayles and speciallie the Native and kind of Deir of this Mountaine by all other forrests or mountaines in the Lewes'.

Whether there really was a two-tailed or fork-tailed species of deer in Scotland is open to speculation; the same story is told of a mountain in Reay Forest in Sutherland, where to-day there are many deer and all with normal tails.

The Butt of Lewis is called Rudh 'Eorrapidh, Eoropie Point. Eoropie itself, placed at a point where the cliffs give place to a stretch of sand and machair, was named by the Norse, and means 'Beach town'. But that has not prevented the Butt from sometimes appearing on English maps as Europa Point!

I stopped in the village and went into the shop to get the key of Teampull Mholuidh, the little fourteenth century church of St. Moluag. Translating the Gaelic ('*teampull*') into English ('church'), I asked the girl behind the counter for the key of the old church. She stared wildly for a moment, then brightened and exclaimed, 'Oh, the key of the temple,' and went off to fetch it.

(When I came back with the key I decided that if it came to being bilingual I might try some of it myself, and handed it back with a 'Moran taing' (Many thanks). Even this did not please the lady completely, for she took it back with an English, 'Oh, thank you.')

Grasping the key of the temple, I walked across the flower-spangled strip fields of Eoropie towards the little church. A couple of women in Hebridean dress of dark full skirts and shawls were coming through the fields as I unlocked the door and went inside. It is a simple little rectangular building, restored by having a slated roof put on it. There are narrow lancet windows. Inside you will see a stone font and some old querns and a large earthenware craggan or pot. It was all rather dusty. I stood in the little modern pulpit, a glaring white structure, and looked down at the small floor space in front of me, trying to raise some ghost of the building's curious past, but it had about it that empty, windswept quality that I have often noticed in these deserted island kirks. I saw no visions of the worshippers of Shony.

St. Moluag was a real person. He was an Irish Pict, who came across to Lismore in Loch Linnhe in A.D. 562, the year before Columba came to Iona. He set up his headquarters in Lismore and from there went on missionary journeys to the Outer Isles, the northern Highlands and across to the eastern Lowlands. He died in 592. But Martin Martin's spelling of the name of the saint connected with this church, Malvay, and the curious rite relating to the cure of lunatics, which is so like that of Isle Maree and St. Maelrubha, makes me wonder whether this saint, too, is commemorated at Eoropie. Maelrubha, like Moluag, also travelled widely in the Outer Isles. His dates are A.D. 642-722, and his headquarters were at Applecross, across the Minch on the mainland opposite Raasay.

The Eoropie rite for the cure of lunatics was this: The patient was walked seven times round the building, then sprinkled with water from St. Ronan's Well nearby. The water was brought in a stone cup kept by a particular family said to be descended from the 'clerk of the temple'. The patient was then tied to the altar for the night. If he slept, a cure was expected. If there was a further attack, it was supposed to be useless to try the rite over again. This ritual was being carried out in Lewis in the nineteenth century.

Perhaps odder still is the connexion of Moluag's church with the sea god, Shony. Martin says:

John Morison of Bragir told me that when he was a boy, and going to the Church of St. Malvay (?Maelrubha), he observed the natives to kneel and repeat the Paternoster at four miles distance from the church. The inhabitants of this island had an ancient custom to sacrifice to a sea-god called Shony, at Hallow-tide, in the manner following: The inhabitants round the island came to the Church of St. Malvay, having each man his provision along with him; every family furnished a peck of malt, and this was brewed into ale; one of their number was picked to wade out into the sea up to the middle, and carrying a cup of ale in his hand, standing still in that posture, cried out with a loud voice saying, 'Shony, I give you this cup of ale, hoping that you'll be so kind as to send us plenty sea-ware for enriching our ground for the ensuing year'; and so threw the cup of ale into the sea. This was performed in the night time. At his return to land they all went to church, where there was a candle burning up on the altar; and then standing silent for a little time, one of them gave a signal, at which the candle was put out, and immediately all of them went to the fields, where they fell a-drinking their ale, and spent the remainder of the night in dancing and singing, &c.

Martin wrote about 1695, and when he visited Lewis, the minister told him that he had just managed to stop this sacrifice to Shony. In actual fact, the practice merely seems to have been driven underground, or rather out of the church building, for Captain Thomas, writing in the 1870's, says that a modified version continued almost till that time. The people went out to the end of a long reef and called upon 'Brianuil' to send them plenty of seaweed. This was done in the springtime.

A Captain Dymes, an Englishman who visited the Long Island in 1630 in connexion with Charles I's fishery schemes, gives an even more detailed picture of the people's ideas about Moluag, and perhaps also about Maelrubha and the church at the Butt.

N

He says that the Lewis folk were:

most espetially devoted to one of theire Sts. called St. Mallonuy whose Chappell is seated in the north part of the Ile, whome they have in great veneration to this daie and keepe the Chappell in good repaire. This St. was for cure of all theire wounds and soares and therefore those that were not able to come vnto the Chappell in person they were wont to cut out the proporcion of theire lame armes or leggs in wood wᵗʰ the forme of their sores and wounds thereof and send them to the St. where I have seen them lyinge vpon the Altar in the Chappell. Within the Chappell there is a Sanctum Sanctorum wᶜʰ is soe holy in theire estimation that not anie of their weomen are sufferred to enter therein. Anie woman wᵗʰ child dareth not to enter within the doores of the Chappell, but there are certaine places without where they goe to their devotions.

Dymes goes on to say that there were two big meetings at the chapel, one at Candlemas (perhaps this was part of the Brianuil ceremony of Captain Thomas) and the other at 'Alhollautide', which would be the Shony one. At these meetings they ate and drank, danced, carried lights about and spent the night in the chapel. The minister was then trying to stop the practice.

In this manner, the teaching of the church was welded to the people's old religious ideas, and the saint's kirk used to give authority to the sacrifice to the god of the sea, the first god of every man who lives upon an island.

St. Maelrubha was the patron saint of the Morrisons, Clan Mac Ghillemhuire (Clan of the sons of the servant of Mary), whose headquarters were at nearby Habost. This family were the hereditary judges of Lewis, the judge himself being called the Brieve. He lived at Tigh Mor Thabost (the great house of Habost—Hallstead). For his trouble, he took the eleventh part of the subject in dispute. There was the chance of appeal against his decisions to the Chief Brieve who lived in Islay.

The Morrisons were one of the principal Lewis clans and many are the stories of their quarrels with the MacLeods and with the Uig MacAulays. For time of trouble the Morrisons had a strong fort in Dun Eistean, a stack off the coast to the north of Port of Ness.

The MacAulays, Clann Amhlaeibh (Norse *Olafr*, English *Olave*) claim to be of Norse descent and to have settled in Uig at the same time as the MacLeods came to Lewis. To go to Uig is to go to a different country from the rest of the Lews, to go from the moors into the mountains, to the great massif which, with the Forest of Harris, builds the highest ground in the Outer Hebrides.

It is only 32 miles from Stornoway to Uig, but the single-track road, which is untarred beyond the turn to Bernera, makes the way seem much further. It turns off at Garynahine on the Callernish road and twists over moorland country, with Loch Roag on one hand and the outposts of the Uig mountains on the other.

Great Bernera Island in Loch Roag is reached by a branch road and a ferry, across which it is hoped to build a bridge. The sea loch Loag has a long and narrow branch called Little Loch Roag which runs deep into the hills, its mouth so narrow that, but for the seaweed on its rocks, you would take it for an inland lake as you come down the hill to Morsgail.

Further on are little villages of black houses and fat caterpillars of lazy beds winding down from the townships to the sea loch shore.

Still further on, the road enters Glen Valtos, a straight, narrow ravine whose screes nearly meet across the glen. At the deepest part of the rift the floor of the glen is only 400 yards across and the cliffs on either side rise 250 feet.

At the Loch Roag end of Glen Valtos a road branches off for Valtos itself, a village beside some fine sandy beaches. On the dunes at the head of one of these beaches, Berie sands, were found a skeleton, brass ornaments, the remains of an iron knife, a socketed spearhead and an amber bead. Some of the ornaments had probably been made in Norway or Sweden, and the find seems to have been the grave of a Northman of the ninth century.

In the Valtos area, too, on the Kneep headland at the one end of the Berie sands, has been found a late prehistoric industrial site which manufactured stone implements. Quartz from local veins was used in place of flint, and gneisses were also used. The work was of high quality and the stoneworkers seem to have studied the local rocks very intimately so that they knew exactly how to strike them and thus split and fashion them into the desired shapes.

The Amhuinn a'Ghlinne (stream of the glen) which flows down Glen Valtos to Loch Roag is a small thing, and as you follow it past the young plantations of the Forestry Commission and come out beyond its head at Uig, you see that it could not have made the glen for itself. Valtos Glen, in fact, was cut by water dammed up in a loch where Uig Bay is now. At the end of the Ice Age the boulder clay—the material grubbed up by the moving ice —was left, forming a barrier across the mouth of the bay. Lake terraces—old shore lines high up at Carinish across the bay—indicate that this old lake of Uig was at least 175 feet deep. The water escaped on the Glen Valtos line, trenching that great cutting in the rocks, until the sea broke through the boulder clay dam and Uig Bay came into being.

It is a splendid bay. The green dunes surround it, the clear blue sea runs far out, leaving a great field of white sand, and behind, inland, rise the Uig mountains. They are bare, rocky hills, moulded in smooth curves by the ice and rising to Mealisval, 1,885 feet, the highest mountain in Lewis. There too, a silver flash under the grey rocks of the hills, is Loch Suainaval, a long narrow lake and the deepest in the Lews. Its depth exceeds 200 feet, and it has an average of 108 feet, as against the maximum of the moorland lochs to the north—35 feet.

At Uig the road divides. One way goes northward to Gallan Head, three miles away, the site of an ancient church, Tigh a Bheannaich (the Blessing House), on the windswept cliffs. Southward, the road fades out some ten miles further on, at Mealista, where a sheep fank stands on the site of Tigh nan Cailleachan Dubha. This 'house of the black old women' was a Dominican nunnery, and is associated in Uig tradition with fear and black magic and sorcery.

At Uig itself, set upon the turf beside the bay, among the rank coltsfoot leaves and the orchis and the ragged robin, is the little graveyard of St. Christopher's church. Nothing remains of the old kirk building. Here is one of the places supposed to be the birthplace of Coinnich Odhar, the Brahan Seer. The Uig version relates how his mother, herding cattle, sat spinning at night by the graveyard. During the night the graves opened and all the ghosts flew out, for once a year they were allowed to visit their earthly homes. At cockcrow, back came the ghosts, but one grave remained open after all the others were closed up again. The Uig woman, curious, laid her distaff over it to prevent the spirit getting into it before she could enquire the reason for the delay.

When at last the ghost did come back she told the Uig woman that she was a Norse princess, and that it was because she had so far to go to Norway that she was late in returning.

This was her story. Once the Norsemen were enraged with the Hebrideans for not paying their taxes and the King planned a punitive expedition. Before he set out, he called for the seer to foretell the fate of the voyage. At first the seer would not answer, but under compulsion he told them that they would all be lost at sea. The Norse king was very angry, and was about to thrust his spear into the seer when the king's daughter sprang between them. The seer later gave the princess, in thankfulness for saving his life, the stone into which he looked to see the future. The princess, taking the stone with her, disguised herself as a boy and joined the king's expedition. It happened as the seer foretold; a storm rose up and the whole company was drowned.

The body of the princess was washed into the pool below the churchyard in Uig Bay, and there among the Uig folk she was buried. The stone still remained in the pool, and the ghost of the princess instructed the Uig woman to go and get it. It was this stone with which Coinnich Odhar MacKenzie, Dun Kenneth, used to foretell the future.

The Uig district, being very remote, was one of the last places in the Long Island to give up making its own earthenware pots. It was the coming of good steamer services which introduced cups and saucers, chairs and tables and beds, to every house in the Outer Isles.

The Hebridean pot or, as it was called, craggan, was made of local clay, without a wheel, one hand being kept inside and the other outside, moulding it to shape. They were allowed to dry in the sun and then a peat fire was built round them to bake them. Each pot was filled with milk, and when this was boiling it was smeared on the outside of the pot to give it a similar surface to the inside. The remaining milk was drunk by the maker. The pots frequently cracked when being baked as it was very difficult to get them to heat up evenly.

CHAPTER XIV

HARRIS OF THE HILLS

'Y OU have the nerve,' remarked the Stornoway man, looking at my car, 'to take that low-slung thing into Harris.' And indeed, I believe that they have a proper pride in the bumps of the Harris roads, though, for all that, there are worse tracks on the mainland. But while the other islands' main roads are all tarred now, long stretches in both Harris and the Lews remain untarred, and their cobble-like surface imparts a succession of sharp jolts to anything attempting to travel at speed.

It is some 60 miles by road from Stornoway to Rodil by the west coast of Harris and the head of Loch Seaforth. Leaving Stornoway, the sign-post announces with splendid comprehensiveness UIG, HARRIS, and a little further on, at the turn to Uig, simply, HARRIS.

First the road runs through part of Lewis, past a bog where an attempt has been made to get peat on a commercial scale, and through the long, tenuous string of houses that is Balallan (Allan's town). Below the road is the head of Loch Erisort, a long fiord running deep into the Lews, its green waters and seaweedy rocks strange among the inland moors. This is the district of Lochs, said to have been the last part to be inhabited. In front,

the Harris mountains rise in the proud crest of the
Clisham (2,622 ft.), the highest mountain in the whole
Long Island, the clouds lifting off the summits in the
morning sunlight.

Then Loch Seaforth comes into sight, a splendid and
rather incredible sea loch. It opens into the Atlantic
among the Harris hills, with the Park of the Lews to the
north, runs in a deep gut north-west to Aline, where
Harris marches with the Lews, turns north-east and then
at Ardbruach sharply east, ending at Seaforth Head,
within three miles of the head of Loch Shell, an eastward-
opening fiord on the Lewis coast.

Thus the fiord Seaforth almost converts the mountainous district of Park in the south of the Lews into a
separate island. Park is a deserted land of green pathless
mountains, rising to 1,874 feet in Beinn Mhor. It is
given over to deer forest. Once it was fairly well populated, but the people were turned out to make way for
the deer. One of the Earls of Seaforth built a dyke across
from Loch Erisort to Loch Seaforth to keep the deer in
the peninsula, and probably this gave the idea of the name
Park. Its old name seems to have been Durna, a form of
Deerness, headland of deer.

The only road into Park is the private one leading to
Eishken Lodge on Loch Shell. This road curls round
Seaforth Head, a curious place with the salt water
set entirely amongst green hills, a narrow loch bor-
dered by drying seaware and devoid of any sight of the
open sea. Eishken Lodge itself comes on you as something of a surprise, for here is a fertile little garden, set
around with great trees, pines and copper beeches,
Spanish chestnuts and sycamores, ash and alder, a token

of what can be done in sheltered glens in the Outer Isles.

It was on Eilean Iuvard in the mouth of Loch Shell that Prince Charles spent four days and nights hiding from warships when he and his party were on their way from Stornoway back to Scalpay. Iuvard and Eishken are both names of some interest, the first of them apparently meaning Yew Fiord and the second Cheek of the Yew Tree, and both indicating that woodland once flourished in the Long Island.

Prince Charles had an amusing time on Eilean Iuvard. Local fishermen were drying their fish there when the Prince's boat put in. When they saw the boat and the men-o'-war in the background, the fishermen thought it was a party of pressmen and fled, leaving a good supply of dried fish behind. When the Prince left, he wanted to leave some money in payment for the fish they had taken, but O'Neil and O'Sullivan would on no account permit this, saying that vagabonds and not fishermen might find it.

Edward Burke, who eventually ended his days as a chairman in Edinburgh, acted as cook to the party, with Charles's assistance. When the Prince and Ned were cooking the dried fish they considered that it would be much better if they had some butter to go with it. Then Ned remembered that on leaving the Stornoway district Lady Killdun had given him 'a junt of butter between two fardles of bread'. The bread and butter were, by now, well mixed, but Charles insisted that this did not matter. But when the dish was served, Donald MacLeod exclaimed that not 'a drap of that butter he would take for it was neither good nor clean'. However, it turned out to be excellent eating.

They lived in a miserable hut with the holes in the roof stopped with their sail. The first night they found a craggan and used it to make punch, but the second night it cracked and ended their drinking.

At the Amhainn a'Mhuil, a little stream which cascades down past Aline Lodge to the first bend of Loch Seaforth, the Harris marches with the Lews. Seaward the fiord walls rise sheer from the narrow water, and in the middle of the great loch of Aline is the island of Seaforth, equally divided between Harris and Lewis. The green furrows of old lazy beds are plainly seen about the island's flanks.

Ahead rises the Clisham, rocky ridges intervening, and the road crosses the tumbling Vigadale River and strains upward, as if it meant to climb to the very tops themselves. Few roads give such a surge upward as this road to Harris, such an impression of reaching for the sky. Perhaps it is because it starts from the sea at Loch Seaforth, perhaps because of the craggy rocks, perhaps because the cloud is often on the Clisham so that the road seems to be leading into the mountain mists.

Whatever it is, when you come out in a great glen between the Clisham on the one hand and the terraced rocks of Sgaoth Iosal, the height seems far greater than 616 feet above the sea. A group of burns cascades downward to the beautiful little Loch Maaruig, an inlet of Loch Seaforth, and after you cross the watershed between Seaforth and West Loch Tarbert the mountain glen is floored with a string of little lochs. From this watershed it is an easy matter to walk up over the boggy grass and around the scree patches to the summit of the Clisham, a mile and a half from the road. From that top a ridgeway leads across to the 2,439 feet of the Mulla-fo-dheas, beyond which the land drops dramatically to the great pass which runs north-south from Loch Langavat in the Lews to the shore of West Loch Tarbert. On the other side the mountains rise again, to form a great rocky barrier, the Forest of Harris, running westward to Loch Resort.

Beyond the lochs of the pass the main road south descends steeply to Ardhasig Bridge beside West Loch Tarbert, and between the rugged crags of the mountains on either side one looks down to the sea. Beyond the bright water of West Loch Tarbert are the massive sea cliffs of Harris and Ben Luskentyre and, out to sea, the Island of Taransay.

At Tarbert, Harris is only half a mile across, the West Loch Tarbert cutting in from the west and the East Loch Tarbert from the east in two fiord-like openings. Tarbert itself, the principal port of Harris, is a pleasant group of houses with some trees about and neat gardens. The road thus far is good; it is between Tarbert and Rodil that the jolts begin.

The curious pattern of fiord and mountain which makes North Harris is a result of the wearing down of the land along lines of weakness. In advance of the great eastern thrust plane in the rocks, along which the flinty-crush was developed, faults or breakages developed in the Lewisian gneiss. Along these breakage lines erosion worked more rapidly than on the unbroken rock at each side. These faults thus produced the Tarbert hollow, with the branch valley by Amhuinnsuidhe to Glen Cravadale, and the first part of the Seaforth hollow. This second line of fault can be traced up Seaforth to

Aline and then across country, the course marked by the
rise of the hills to the south, to Little Loch Roag, whose
hollow has also been determined by the fault.

The Tarbert hollow was once a valley, most of which
was drowned when the land sank. Loch Seaforth itself
is the result of the amalgamation of three different
drowned valleys. The head (east-west part) is actually a
drowned portion of the valley which extends right across
beyond Seaforth Head to the fiord Loch Ouirn on the
east coast of Lewis.

The depths of the Seaforth basins are interesting. At
the mouth, the opening into the Minch is crossed by a
rock barrier only 8-20 fathoms below the surface of the
sea, and from which a few skerries rise to the surface.
Inside this barrier there is a basin 54 fathoms deep. Off
Aline, in the middle part, there is a small basin, 9-12
fathoms deep, and then three further basins to the north-
east. The upper (east-west part) has a maximum depth
of only 10 fathoms.

Around Bun Abhainn-eadar ('the mouth of the between river'—perhaps between the two hillsides of its
glen or between two bays) are the ruined piers and
buildings of an old whaling station now being revived.
But long before there was much systematic whaling the
Long Islanders used to go hunting for 'seapork', as they
called it. Martin relates how they used to attack the
whales from a number of boats, hoping that if one
was mortally wounded and came ashore, the others
would follow its blood and likewise come ashore.
Osgood MacKenzie in his *A Hundred Years in the Highlands*
saw for himself one of the last of these whale hunts,
when everyone pursued the animals with all manner of

weapons and succeeded in capturing a number of them.

Captain Dymes says that in 1629 a great many whales came to the Lews, which the people killed with their bows and arrows and swords. Having no salt to preserve the meat which they could not consume fresh, they 'tooke the sea Oare (seaweed) and burned it and then powdered it with the ashes thereof, wch afterwards beinge dryed in the smoake they eate it like Bacon'.

Beyond Tarbert the road winds uphill and then across to the west coast of Harris, a branch route going along the east side by Stockinish (Norse *stokkr*, a chasm separating an island from the mainland). The road to the west side climbs over an interminable moor of glacier-smoothed rocks and peat hags, with a view at the back of it over the Minch to Skye.

I saw this country with the mist drifting low upon the rocks and all their surfaces glowing a lurid pink—a cruel land and desolate. As you come over the watershed into the glen of the Laxdale River, upon either side of the roadside is a line of cairns, big and little. The collection is claimed to be the biggest in Scotland. These cairns each record the halting place of a funeral party, a cairn being built at each place where the coffin was set down. The resting places were usually, as here, at the tops of climbs and watersheds, where the bearers would naturally call a halt.

At the mouth of the Laxdale River the sea runs far out over the sands of the Traigh Luskentyre, and all the salt marsh, in the summer time, is coloured pink with thrift. At the mouth of the bay is a sand bar, the Corran Seilebost, the Sickle of Seilebost, so called from its shape.

There is a track making a short cut from this district

over the ridge of Beinn Luskentyre to Tarbert. It is called the Horse Track and is now difficult to locate. Before the 'Clearances' for deer, the people used to take their horses over this track to the summer pastures in the mountains north of Tarbert.

The main road runs beside the western shore, sandy beaches alternating with rocky headlands. Across a narrow sound is the Island of Taransay, and to the north the line of the Forest of Harris mountains. At Borve (Norse, a fort), the fragment of a broch still stands on a green knoll, and out on a sandy promontory is the great standing stone Clach Mhic Leoid (the Stone of MacLeod).

Ahead, Harris extends north-west to Toe Head, with, rising from the promontory, the conical form of Chapaval (1,201 ft.). Below is Northton with a good stretch of arable machair land and a fine beach, the Traigh an Taoibh Thuath. North, at Seilebost, the sands are white, but here at Northton and Bay Steinigie they are orange and the cliffs are pinkish gneiss. I watched a pale mauve sea coming in, in long breakers, upon these deep yellow sands, the wind blowing the spray off the crests of the waves while the mist shifted on the tops of the mountains to the north. Brown St. Kilda sheep wandered on the narrow road.

Originally the main road ran over the Northton sands, so that you had to regulate your journeys by the tides. The sands have also been used as an aeroplane landing strip.

Southward to Rodil the road goes through wild and rocky country from Northton, along the coast of the Sound of Harris. At Obbe, which Leverhulme rechristened Leverburgh and where he built harbour installations which the people never used, a group of primitive black houses stands by the roadside. Beyond, the road climbs up narrow Glen Strondeval, and then at last the square tower of Rodil kirk is in sight, placed close beside the south-east tip of Harris.

I climbed over a bog behind the church to the ruin of Rodil dun, a rickle of stones on a rocky knoll, the gneiss full of little red garnets. From there I looked down on the cross shape of the little church, with its tower at one end, and the island-strewn Sound of Harris. Beyond the Sound rose the mountains of North and South Uist.

I took the key of Rodil church and went into the churchyard where the big fuchsia bushes overhang an old limestone quarry. As Kiessimul is the chief civil monument in the Outer Isles, so Rodil is the chief ecclesiastical one. Built in the sixteenth century, its style influenced by Iona Cathedral and the freestone of its dressings from the same quarry—Carsaig in Mull—the church was restored in 1873 by the Countess Dunmore and is now under the jurisdiction of the Ministry of Works. 'Within the south pairt of this ile lyes ane monastery with ane steipell, quhilk was foundit and biggit by M'Cloyd of Harrey, callit Roodill,' writes Dean Monro. The date of foundation is unknown, and the building has certainly been reconstructed completely several times. The church is dedicated to St. Clement, and down to eighteenth century times Harris people used to swear by Claiman-moir-a-Rowadill, Great Clement of Rodill.

St. Clement is carved upon the tower, with two men, one wearing the kilt, below him. This particular Clement was probably the Bishop of Dunblane who died between 1258 and 1266.

Inside are three great carved tombs of the MacLeods of Harris, three mailed figures dark and menacing in the black hornblende gneiss of the Lewisian series. There is a distinct family likeness between the three.

One, prepared by Alexander MacLeod of Dunvegan (who was dead by 1547), has over the recumbent figure a panel of carvings in a recess with a further series around the arch of the alcove. These carvings are carried out in the pale sandstone imported from Mull and include some delightful scenes of hunting, a ship and, particularly attractive, the Devil and St. Michael weighing souls.

On the floor of the little kirk is a series of carved slabs with interlace designs. The arch of the north transept, I noticed, was moulded in black gneiss, whilst that of the south one was in the white sandstone.

I wandered up into the little tower, and when I had climbed many stairs found myself looking at an outcrop of rock. The fact is that the whole district of Rodil is uneven rock and that the church was moulded on the country without much attempt at making a level site.

The church itself is empty of any furniture bar a little table with a visitors' book set where the altar once was. The building seemed a shell without a heart, dark with the rain clouds outside, swept clean by the broom in the transept corner.

And yet Rodil has been a place sacred in the Isles for centuries. There is a legend of the church that goes back to Somerled, the first Lord of the Isles.

Somerled had three sons, Reginald, Dugald and Angus, and to each of them he gave a part of his kingdom to govern for him. Angus ruled the Long Island and Skye.

At that time the Northmen were still raiding the Long

o

Island and the people of Uig in Lewis were particularly troubled by their attacks. Angus, however, was amusing himself in Skye and took no steps to protect the Uig people from raids. Eventually the people decided that action must be taken, and agreed to choose a leader who would organise defence. One man among them seemed the ideal choice but he refused the job unless he was formally inducted as chief.

The ritual for the induction of a new chief consisted of the chief-elect placing his foot in a footprint cut in the sacred stone and swearing that he would follow in the footsteps of his illustrious predecessors. Each clan seems to have had its sacred stone; the Kings of Scotland were crowned upon the Stone of Scone; the Constable elected to organise the partly communal activities of Hebridean crofting townships took the oath standing barefoot on the ground.

The stone for the Uig people's use was kept locked up in Rodil church, and as they were acting without the consent of Angus, the problem was how to get it.

They sent a delegation across the mountains, through the passes and southward to Rodil. The purpose seemed simple, merely a renewal of friendships in Rodil and an exchange of news. By Highland custom, each house took it in turn to provide hospitality for the party. But one morning when the Rodil folk asked each other where the Uig party had spent the night, the answer was always 'Not in my house', and eventually it turned out that the Uig men had cleared out without a word.

Rodil was in an uproar. Everyone searched to see if anything was missing, and at last they found the church broken into and the stone gone. Meantime, the Uig party, lugging the stone with them, were hastening back through the passes.

At this moment, a war galley put into Rodil and on board it was Angus. The loss was quickly reported to him and he set off again to intercept the thieves.

It is considerably quicker to sail round to Uig than to walk over the hills carrying a stone and thus when the Uig men came out on a ridge above Mealista, they looked down upon a battle between the local people and Angus. Dropping the stone, they rushed down to join the fight.

There the legend ends. Whether Angus was killed in this conflict, or whether he was, as is generally accepted, killed together with his three sons when fighting the Norse in 1210, the Lewis tradition does not relate. There are four mounds on a Black Point of the Sons of Somerled on Loch Grunavat near Uig which have been suggested to me as the graves of Angus and his sons.

The story has a sequel. There are only three passes leading across the hills to Mealista from the route the Uig men must have taken to Rodil. The Uig keeper, Roderick MacKenzie, came over one of them one day and stood looking down at the wide spread of country below, remembering the old tale. He wondered if this was the pass, glanced down to the ground and found a rough slab of local gneiss with, apparently an entirely natural formation, the faint print of a left bare foot in it! But I fear his find is not the stone of the story, for all the known inaugural slabs have the footprints cut boldly and artificially, and where, as at Dunadd, capital of Dalriada, there is a single print only, it is the right foot, not the left.

The name of Rodil or Rodel is Norse and is perhaps Rauði-dalr, the Red Dale. On the other hand, it may be from hrufa, a rough surface, which seems to fit the landscape better. There is nothing very red about Rodil. It is a pattern of green and grey. The green is intensified where it overlies the Rodil limestone, for the lime improves the grass.

This limestone, which is actually a white marble, is one of the oldest limestones in the world, for it is one of the oldest members of the series of rock types which make up the Lewisian gneiss. It outcrops in two belts, one trending north-west from Rodil, and another parallel to it further north-east and reaching the sea at Bay Steinigie.

In the hills above Rodil the mountain of Roneval (1,506 ft.) is principally built of labradorite (feldspar) rock, and this is quarried to the north of Rodil for use in industry. Roneval's bleak rock-strewn heights are a result of the weathering of this labradorite gneiss. Mac-Culloch, visiting the top in the early nineteenth century, noted how the wind had arranged long tails of rock fragments, each stringing out behind a large sheltering boulder.

The corrie of Roneval, on the north-east side, appears to have nursed a small local glacier in the waning stages of the Ice Age. The Norse name reflects the rough bare nature of the rocks there, for Roneval means 'rough ground fell'.

Although Rodil is the principal church in Harris, the parish church was actually Kilbride, of which there are no remains in the old graveyard at Scarastavore by the Traigh Scarasta near Northton. Beyond Northton, under Chaipaval, is the ruin of another old chapel. The dedication does not seem to be known. Harris also had a church founded by and dedicated to St. Maelrubha, at Maaruig on Loch Seaforth. As well as swearing by St. Clement, the Harris people also used to invoke Maelrubha.

Taransay, off the west coast of Harris, has several chapel sites. There was a curious tradition there, which Martin records, that a man might not be buried in St. Tarran's churchyard or a woman in St. Keith's. If this rule was broken, the corpse would be found dug up again in the morning. However, one Roderick Campbell, whom Martin seems to have known, had a man buried in St. Tarran's without any untoward result. The people abandoned their tradition.

CHAPTER XV

THE CROSS OF CALLANISH

CALLANISH is unique. Of all the world's Megalithic monuments only Callanish in distant Lewis is known to be arranged in the form of the Christian cross—a stone circle and four avenues of stones leading from it. Smaller circles are scattered over the moors around it. It was the great religious centre for the Outer Isles, with a standing equal to Stonehenge or Avebury or Carnac.

And Callanish is unique in another way, for in the Outer Isles the development of the idea of the stone circle can be traced as a logical step from the idea of the great stone cairns. In the cross of Callanish, the cairn and the circle are combined.

The men who built the great stone monuments, the Megalithic people, reached the Outer Isles by the western routes along the coasts of Spain and France and Britain from the Mediterranean. Everywhere that they settled they built cairns and circles and erected monoliths. They lived toward the end of the Neolithic (New Stone Age) period and their culture persisted into the beginning of the Bronze Age. From the number of their monuments, it appears that the Outer Isles were fairly thickly populated in Megalithic times.

These people were hunters but they had also learned farming and the cultivation of cereals. They kept domestic animals, cattle, sheep and pigs. The people themselves were rather slightly built, mostly under 5½ feet tall, and their skulls were long and narrow. As well as hunting and farming, they were seamen and perhaps were the first to develop the trade routes between Britain and the Continent.

'There are,' wrote Martin in 1695 of South Uist, 'several big cairns of stone on the east side of this island, and the vulgar retain the ancient custom of making a religious tour round them on Sundays and holidays.' This of course, is the sunwise, deiseil circle that plays so large a part in many rituals.

The old idea, the Megalithic idea, of religion connected with the stone monuments has lingered to the present day, though the Outer Islanders have pushed their dating of the cairns forward, so that the tradition that I found in South Uist was that they marked the tombs of Norse chieftains.

The cairns are, in fact, communal burying places, though probably only important people were interred in them. The oldest cairns are the long-shaped ones; the round ones are slightly later. Barpa nam Feannag and the cairn at Carinish, both in South Uist, were of the long, 'horned' type. The round cairns number 3 in Barra, 6 in South Uist, 2 in Benbecula, 16 in North Uist, 1 in Harris and 7 in Lewis.

Stand at the North Ford end in North Uist and look northward, and on a low moorland ridge you will see the great mound of Barpa Langass, the most complete of the chambered cairns in the Outer Isles left to us. Even if the chief intention was the burial of the chiefs of its builders, Barpa Langass, like many other cairns, has the secondary function of serving as a landmark. So too, the Megalithic tumuli of Salisbury Plain and the Downs were placed upon the skyline to catch the eye and point the way.

I walked up over the short heather to the cairn. Barpa Langass (*barpa*—cairn, *langass*—of the long ridge) is a tremendous pile of unhewn stones gathered from the neighbouring country and heaped over an internal chamber built of megaliths, or huge slabs. The hillside site has been artificially levelled and the cairn is in a slight hollow, looking down on the pattern of North Uist's lochs. The heap is 14 feet high and 80 feet in diameter. The entrance is towards the east, a passage 19 feet long built of huge uprights roofed with single slabs, leading into an oval chamber, 9¼ feet by 6 feet and up to 7 feet high. This passage and burial chamber fill only a small part of the bulk of the cairn, and Erskine Beveridge, writing in 1911, said he had met a man who had entered a second chamber within the past 30 years. This second chamber opened towards the north, and Beveridge was also told that there was a third chamber.

The only finds from Langass barp seem to have been a barbed arrowhead and some pottery; its builders, of course, operated the pottery kilns at Eilean an Tighe. More interesting is the record of the ruined cairn on Clettraval, North Uist, in which human bones were found that proved to have been cremated. Successive burials were made in these cairns, the earlier bodies being pushed on one side to make way for the latest one. Traces of fire are frequent and it has been suggested that these were

ritual, purificatory fires, but the Clettraval bones had
certainly been cremated deliberately and not merely
scorched.

The small stones making up the bulk of the Megalithic
collective tombs have often been plundered for shielings
and other buildings, and sometimes only the central
chamber of big stones remains. The Coir Fhinn in Harris
on the roadside near Seilebost is such a remnant.

In the Uists, the word for a chambered cairn is barp,
and it is probably to be related to the English word
barrow, meaning the same thing. It is curious that,
though in the Uists the word is still used and understood
in this sense, Lewis forgot the meaning and invented a
Norse prince to explain it.

Thus, a chambered cairn near Gress is called Carn
Bharce Mhic Righ Lochlinn, the cairn of Barc, son of the
king of Lochlann (Scandinavia). Tradition relates that
Barc was killed there whilst hunting and is buried under
the cairn.

But the feature which links the cairns with the stone
circles is found outside the pile of stones—a ring of
retaining uprights. You will see them round the South
Uist barps, and they seem to serve the purpose of acting
as a kerb to the loose stones. They are small, unhewn
slabs set up on edge. But at Langass Barp the retaining
ring is placed outward, away from the cairn, and beginning not to be part of the cairn but to form a stone circle
around it. At Callanish the central cairn is still there,
but the circle has grown bigger so that the cairn is now
a detail in a great scheme of temple building.

Callanish is not one circle but a complex of circles,
the religious metropolis of the Long Island in Megalithic

times. Of the twelve circles remaining in Lewis, seven
are within four miles of it, and of these, three, including
the great circle itself, surrounded burial cairns. Among
our British Megalithic circles Callanish ranks second
only to Stonehenge; it must have formed a centre comparable to Avebury.

Avebury is placed near the junction of the watersheds,
easy of access along the ridgeways which were the chief
routes through a southern England then heavily wooded
in its valleys. Callanish is placed on the shores of Loch
Roag, almost in the middle of Harris and Lewis island,
easy to reach from either north or south and with good
sea communications and a reasonably sheltered anchorage
in Loch Roag itself.

The main circle is placed on a little rocky promontory
of Loch Roag. The best view is obtained from the water,
but even from the road it is impressive—a spiky line of
dragon's teeth along the skyline. If you approach rapidly,
they seem to shift about, giving life to the stories of
petrified men. Inland, the moors lead away to the splend-
did line of the mountains of Harris and Uig. Out to sea,
Loch Roag flashes vivid blue.

Three small circles are in the immediate vicinity.
Two are beside the road as you approach from Garynahine. One on Cnoc Fillibhir Bheag consists of a double
ring of smallish stones; the other, a little closer to the
big circle, is of very big blocks, of which five still stand
and two are fallen. In the middle of this circle is a
ruined cairn.

Standing by the cairn of this circle, one looks down
on the small lazy beds of the Callanish crofters and across
a narrow creek, then up to the ridge beyond with the

great avenue upon it. Inland, on the boggy moors with
their little rocky ridges, was a third circle, between Loch
Baravat and Loch Mhurchaidh. To this third circle I
walked before I went inside the big circle, because it was
from these moors that all the stones are said to have been
gathered.

The third circle has all tumbled down, but it can be
fairly easily found, for it is placed on the crest of a small
rise called Druim nan Eum. Close by are a number of
small crag faces, rounded on the one side and broken on
the other. From the broken faces slabs split off by
weathering and further blocks could be got with little
exertion. This is the traditional quarry for the Callanish
stones, and it is probably the right one. There are also
several big perched blocks dropped by the melting ice
sheets, and these too could have been easily removed.
Others are probably buried under the peat, for, after all,
$5\frac{1}{2}$ feet of peat were cleared from the Callanish circle in
1858, representing a very considerable growth since the
time when it was built.

The stones of all the Long Island circles, cairns and
standing stones are local ones, and there is nothing in the
way of imported stone comparable to the blue stones of
Stonehenge, which came from the Prescelly Mountains
in Wales. Like Avebury, but unlike Stonehenge, the
Hebridean stones are rough and undressed.

You drive down a bumpy track through Callanish
village from the main road, park the car at the road end
and go through a gate into the great avenue of Callanish.
As you walk between the stones to the central circle the
ground rises very slightly, so that, at the further end—
Cnoc an Tursa—you are 100 feet above the sea just below.

The circle itself, enclosing the cairn, consists of 13 stones and has a diameter of 37 feet 4 inches. The avenue which approaches from the north contains 19 stones. It is 27 feet wide and 270 feet long and it forms the long limb of the cross-plan of the design. Southward, there was another shorter avenue of 12 stones and eastward and westward two lines of 4 stones each, thus completing the cross design. The stones range in height from 3 feet 6 inches to 15 feet 7 inches. Each is packed at the base with small stones to keep it firmly in position.

There is a second cairn impinging on the central cairn which seems to be a later addition, and there also seems to have been some idea of making another circle between the west and south limbs of the cross. Callanish, like Stonehenge, shows signs of having been built in stages.

Martin was told by the people that the Callanish stones were 'a place appointed for worship in the time of heathenism, and that the chief druid or priest stood near the big stone in the centre, from whence he addressed himself to the people that surrounded him'.

To the north of the avenue is a field called Buaile an aoin doruis (the field of the one door) and it was in this field that the priest is said to have lived. On the 1st of May every fire in the Island was put out. After three days the priest was supposed to get new fire from a tree in the field where he lived; he gave this to the people to rekindle their fires and addressed them in the circle.

This new fire would be the sacred 'need' fire made by friction, which is supposed to have very special holiness and virtue. It was a common custom in Scotland till comparatively recent times to cure cattle ailments by putting out all the fires in the village and relighting them with the 'need' fire. If any unbeliever refused to put out his fire, the efforts of the rest to kindle the new fire were unavailing. The fire would be carried, sunwise, round the sick animals.

An old lady at Callanish told me that they used to burn children inside these stone circles, and that her father remembered finding ashes there. She also said that the smaller circles were connected to the principal temple by an underground passage.

This tradition of an underground passage is very interesting because it is probably a folk memory of the chambered cairns inside the circles when they were less decayed than they are to-day. The mouths of their passages, when they had fallen in and could no longer be followed into the chambers inside, would very probably suggest an underground passage leaving one circle and coming up inside another.

The burnt remains are, of course, the cremated bones of the men who were buried within the cairns or the ashes of the ritual fires. Why the tradition should hold that children were burned there is less clear; perhaps it may have resulted from the finding of small bones like those of the Pigmies' Island and the vault at Nunton in Benbecula.

The name generally given to these circles is Tursachan. The word may come from the old Norse word *thurs*, a giant; the present feeling about the word's meaning is that it indicates something dreadful or horrible.

Two other Tursachan or circles are just off the road leading to Uig, one mile to the south of Garynahine and forming a part of the Callanish complex. One of these, just off the road to the west, is a well preserved ring of 5 large stones with the remains of a cairn inside it. There is yet another circle at the crossing from the mainland of Lewis at Earshader to Great Bernera in Loch Roag.

All these circles are placed in fairly conspicuous places and near the sea. On the other side of the Lews there is a remnant of a circle at Seaforth near Loch Seaforth head, again close to the water.

The Pobull Fhinn is on the same ridge as Barpa Langass, though not in sight of it. It is a circle of smallish stones numbering some 24 at the present moment which looks over Loch Eport and across to the lovely shape of the mountain Eaval. What is so very striking about this circle is the way is shows up on the hillside when you look across from the other side of Loch Eport, and that it is in sight of two other circles on this southern side of the fiord. It does give the impression of being in some way connected with the sea, even as the Callanish complex seems to hug the waterside.

This brings up the whole question of the meaning of the Megalithic circles. Undoubtedly, one of their main purposes was that of burial. The transition from a chambered burial cairn with a retaining circlet of stones to a stone circle, which is so clearly seen in the Outer Isles, is the final proof. Everywhere that the great monumental circles rise, burial places have been found, as around Stonehenge and at Carnac in Brittany. The ceremonial of the funeral rite must have played a very important part in Megalithic religion.

The Megalithic people were tillers of the soil, and it was essential for them to know when the season was sufficiently advanced for them to sow their crops. A hunter need not worry overmuch about the exact time of the year, he may follow his prey about the country and catch it as best he may, but without some sort of a calendar the farmer might well be misled into sowing far too early or far too late and be faced with starvation.

The business of making a calendar depends on fairly accurate and prolonged observations of the sun, stars and moon. It is a technical business and amongst most early peoples seems to have devolved upon their priesthoods. The priests, supported by the rest of the community, had the necessary time to study the movements of the stars. The making of the calendar could almost become a sort of magic and a fresh source of power for the Megalithic priests.

There is a strong case to be made out for this second use of the Megalithic circles and avenues. Not only were they burial places and temples, they were stone calendars. Stonehenge is orientated on the sun, and this orientation seems to be far too exact to be merely accidental.

Further, it has been detected in many other alignments and circles. Some, however, seem to be aligned on the stars and it has been suggested that Callanish is so orientated, on the Pleiades and Capella. The Pleiades are observed by many peoples because their rising and setting happen to correspond with important times of the year for a farming community. For the Hottentots, they are the Rime Stars, appearing at the beginning of the winter. For us, they rise in midsummer and set in midwinter, both important dates.

There is a third use which the circles may have served, as landmarks. Callanish and the group which includes the Pobull Fhinn would seem to be directed toward the sea. In this sense, they are closely linked with the Megalithic alignments and tumuli at Carnac on the Bay of Quiberon in Brittany. The Carnac monuments seem to concentrate on the river channels which would be used by the Megalithic seamen, and the tumuli are still used as landmarks by sailors. Callanish on Loch Roag is an indication of the sailing ability of Neolithic and Bronze Age men.

That they did serve a purpose of this sort seems to have been handed on by tradition, for Martin writes of North Uist: 'There are three stones erected about five feet high, at a distance of a quarter of a mile from one another, on eminences about a mile from Loch Maddy, to amuse invaders; for which reason they are still called false sentinels'.

There is another story told of Na Fir Bhreige—the three False Men near Loch Maddy—that they are three Skye men who deserted their wives and were petrified by a witch!

Lone standing stones occur throughout the Long Island, and whilst some are on inland ridges, placed to catch the eye from far off, many others are near the sea.

Of the lone standing stones, I remember particularly An Carra (the Pillar Stone) in South Uist below Beinn Mhor, a great slab of gneiss standing 17 feet high, and Clach Mhic Leoid in Harris. An Carra is inland, on a low moorland rise leading up to the flank of Beinn Mhor; the tall spike of MacLeod's Stone rises from a sandy headland close to the sea, looking out over the Sound of Taransay. It is quite close to the denuded cairn ruin of the Coir Fhinn.

But the greatest of the whole series is the Clach an Trushal, the Thrushal Stone at Ballantrushal on the west side of Lewis. This immense megalith is 18 feet 10 inches high, 6 feet wide and 3 feet 9 inches thick at its broadest part. As I walked through the black houses of the village and over to the stone, I saw a girl carrying pails with a wooden yoke and a hoop, and heard the clack-clack of the looms making tweed. The stone itself is on the ridge above, between two parallel stone dykes enclosing fields, which serve to emphasise the height of the great pillar of gneiss.

The tradition that Martin had of these stones was that they were either the monuments of great men killed in battle or that they were men turned into stone by enchantments. They have sometimes served as the place where the old courts of justice were held, some sort of remembered sanctity and authority clinging to them. Ill-luck is supposed to dog those who interfere with them.

These standing stones must have played an important part in the Megalithic cult, though there is no particular reason to suppose that the Long Island specimens are part of a fertility cult. Some standing stones are phallic symbols and, with holed stones, form a part of such a cult.

Other standing stones mark boundaries and routes, and because these lines are important to the people using them, it is considered wrong to remove or interfere with the marking rock. Stones on some desert routes between China and Tibet and India still get their sacrifice of wheel oil given them by travellers. Back in Old Testament times, Jacob, having dreamed of the ladder to heaven whilst sleeping with his head on a stone, 'rose up early in the morning, and took the stone that he had put for

P

his pillows, and set it up for a pillar, and poured oil upon the top of it' (Genesis 28 v. 18).

In the Long Island, the monoliths were almost certainly regarded as holy, but their purpose probably also included the marking of boundaries and the supply of landmarks to a people without made roads or maps.

To visit the Megalithic monuments of the Outer Isles is to traverse the whole of the islands, for the people lived spread over all the country, the peat not having then developed to any great extent. If the exact meaning of the stones in terms of religion is in doubt, at least they are a certain index of a flourishing and widespread Hebridean people in prehistoric times.

CHAPTER XVI

THE DUNS OF THE LONG ISLAND

Dun is the Gaelic word for a fortress or a castle, with a secondary meaning of the knoll on which the castle stands. Now and again in the Outer Isles you will come on a Dun Borve, to be translated Castle Castle, for *borve* is the Norse word for a fort, its roots the same as the Scottish *burgh*, the English *borough* and the archaeologist's *broch*. When the word 'dun' was placed in front of 'borve', the Hebrideans had forgotten the meaning of 'borve' and needed to add the Gaelic 'dun' to indicate that there was a castle there.

There are a great many duns in the Long Island and most of them have been despoiled to make new buildings. For, since the development of the peat over the interior of the Isles, human settlements have been more or less static, and the old buildings have been made over into the new ones put up close beside them.

There are duns upon lonely headlands and duns upon the seashore, duns upon rocks and duns upon islands in lochs. They date from prehistoric times; the round towers or brochs are early Iron Age, and many of the other island duns are also very old and to be dated well before the Norsemen came. Tradition, however, has attributed these duns to the Norse, though the Norse do not seem to have built any castles in stone in the Long Island.

Then there are the medieval duns, usually on islands in lochs. Unlike the pre-Norse ones, the castle does not fill the whole island but only part of it, and there is a wall built round the edge of the island in addition to the fort. There is usually also a harbour for boats. Kiessimul, of course, is the final flowering of this type of fortress. These castles are often called after their former owners or builders, as Dun Aonais, Angus' dun, in North Uist. Dun Aonais is said to be named after Aonghas Fionn, Angus the Fair, who lived in the first quarter of the sixteenth century and who may have built the fort on the island in Loch Aonais.

Most of the duns are over on the west side of the Long Island, for there was the source of their owners' food supply, the fertile machair and the less rocky portion of the coast for fishing.

The duns on islands in lochs are very often reached by a causeway of stones. Traditionally, there was one stone, the rattle stone, so placed that it sounded when stepped upon and alarmed the castle's defenders. The causeways usually had one or two sharp bends in them, so that a stranger might be tripped off into deep water, or again there might be gaps with a similar intent.

The 200 yard long stone causeway leading out to Dun Buidhe in Benbecula follows a curved course. The first 40 yards are made of single blocks of gneiss, the middle part consists of two smaller blocks placed side by side and finally, as the water deepens, it is constructed of small stones heaped to form a causeway 4 feet wide at the top and rising 5 feet from the floor of the loch. In

the shallow Hebridean lochs there were often existing
boulders which could be utilised in the making of a
causeway.

Often the causeways ran underwater as a further pre-
caution. Sometimes they had very sharp zig-zags, and
when an attacker was already wading out over the submerged track he would have great difficulty in finding
these turns or locating the gaps, which are sometimes
about 4 feet across. In some cases, where the level of
the loch water has fallen, a causeway originally under
water is now well above it.

Some of the duns have a network of causeways,
linking them to other islands, on which perhaps cattle
could be kept.

The Early Iron Age brochs are curious structures,
high round towers with only the opening of the door
upon the outside wall. The walls were double, with
passages running round inside and with openings into the
interior from these galleries. The lower passages would
be used by the inhabitants; the upper ones seem to have
been merely a form of internal scaffolding. There is
usually a ledge running round inside the wall of the fort
on which a roof might be supported to cover the circular
space enclosed by the broch which is now open to the
sky. Lewis tradition believes that the brochs tapered
until they could be closed at the top by one flagstone but
this idea is pure fiction.

The Celtic people who lived in the brochs were
farmers and placed their castles beside the rich agricultural land. They seem to have been a fresh influx of
invaders to the Long Island and perhaps they built the
brochs to overawe the people they found already estab-

lished in the Isles. This idea, which has the support of archaeological research, was given form long ago by the old Lewis story of Fionn (Fingal) and the Uig giant.

The broch of Dun Borranish (Dun of the Fort Headland) or Chuithaich (the fort of Cuithuich, the name of the supposed giant) is a mere rickle of stones placed on a rock by the shore of Uig Bay. It is linked to the shore by a causeway, and it would seem that the sea does not now rise so high in Uig Bay as it did when the broch was built, for the way is clear across to the fort at low tide at the present time.

The broch stood about 30 feet high until about 100 years ago, when practically all the stones were carted away for new buildings. The tradition relates how the giant who lived in the broch oppressed the people of Uig to such an extent that they appealed for help to Fionn and his band of heroes, the Feinne.

When the Feinne arrived at Uig, they lined up on the broad Uig sands and challenged the giant to come out and fight. But the giant sat inside the broch and would not show himself. Each day the challenge was repeated, and still the giant would not come out of his castle to give fight.

Oscar, Fionn's nephew, got very tired of this waiting about and asked permission to borrow Fionn's magic sword and go hunting in the hills. This he was allowed to do, provided that he returned as soon as he heard the trumpet blow for battle.

After Oscar had gone, the giant came out to do battle. So dreadful was his appearance that every man of the Feinne stepped back one pace. It is a saying that the Feinne never retreated but for the one step on the sands

of Uig. The Feinne always fought fair, man to man, so
each in turn grappled with the giant. And each in turn
was beaten to his knees, but before the giant could finish
off his man, another stepped in to renew the fight.
Finally, Fionn himself faced the giant, but without his
magic sword he was as helpless as the rest.

Meantime Oscar was hunting, and had given Fionn's
sword to the ghillie that went with him to carry. It is
Highland good manners not to ask for a thing back that
you have given to someone to carry or look after for you;
they must offer to return it themselves. So when Oscar
heard the trumpet sound as the giant came out, he turned
to the ghillie and said, 'There will be a great battle. We
must go back. But what is the use of a man without a
sword?' 'And if you had a sword,' asked the ghillie, 'what
would you do with it?' 'I would kill the third of the
enemy,' said Oscar.

So they went on, and again the trumpet sounded.
Again Oscar said that there would be a battle, but what
was the use of a man without a sword? Again the ghillie
asked him what he would do with the sword and this
time Oscar said that he would kill two thirds of the
enemy.

So they went on and the trumpet called for the third
time. 'There will be a great battle,' exclaimed Oscar.
'We must go back. But what is the use of a man without
a sword?' 'And if you had a sword,' asked the ghillie,
'what would you do with it?' 'I would kill all of the
enemy,' said Oscar. 'Well, then, here is the sword,'
said the ghillie, giving it to him.

So, just as Fionn was about to be overcome by the
giant, Oscar rushed up, and with one blow slashed off the

head of the giant. The body fell back, chipping the rock with its weight; the head rolled and cut a furrow in the turf, both marks still to be pointed out at Uig. The giant is said to have been buried at nearby Croulista, the head and foot of the grave being marked by two stones 11 feet apart.

There were three other giants living in brochs in Lewis at this time, two in Great Berneray and one in Dun Carloway. The Dun Carloway giant followed the Feinne to Skye to avenge the Uig giant's death, and was there killed by them.

Dun Carloway, on the shore of Loch Roag some distance to the north of Callanish, is the most complete broch remaining in the Long Island. The wall is complete all the way round to a height of some 7 feet, and for one half of the circle it rises to a height of 30 feet. In this portion three galleries remain with the stairs leading up into them. Beside the door, there is a little guard chamber in the thickness of the wall.

From this guard chamber an underground passage is said to have led down to a loch some distance away, Loch an Duin. The excavation of such a passage seems very unlikely and it may have been the mouth of a drain which was taken for it. The Lewis story is that a lamb was put down the opening and emerged on the lochside, and I met a man who claimed to have seen the opening of the passage.

These underground passage stories are very common. There is the one of the passage between the smaller circle and the big circles of Callanish, and another of a passage from Dun Borve, on the west side of Lewis, to the sea-shore (*New Statistical Account*). The two brochs, Dun

Telve and Dun Troddan, in Gleann Beag, Glenelg, on
the mainland of Scotland, are also said to be connected
by a passage which was closed up to prevent cattle falling
into it. Furthermore, the wells of Kiessimul Castle are
said to be supplied by an underground pipeline from
Barra, roofed over with flagstones.

These brochs were built entirely in drystone without
mortar, the stones being graded in size from very large
blocks at the base to small ones at the top. Dun Carloway
is said to have been built with stones from the shore of
Loch Roag, which were passed hand to hand by a human
chain up to the site. Probably the rocks are those that
could be collected in the immediate vicinity of the site.

Captain Thomas, writing in 1890, calculated how
long Dun Carloway would have taken to build. He based
his calculations on a good Lewis drystone dyker building
54 cubic feet of walling in a day. Estimating that the
stones of Dun Carloway weighed some 2,028 tons, he
thought 60 men could easily have constructed it in one
summer season.

Dun Loch an Duna at Bragor in Lewis, some eight
miles from Dun Carloway, is another broch, now only
a ruin. It is on an island in the loch reached by a short
causeway. The doorway is still intact and it is noticeable
that it is not placed opposite the causeway to the land
but round on the flank, so that an attacker could not
make a direct rush at it.

Dun Loch an Duna was, according to the *New Statistical Account*, three stories high, tapering toward the
top in 1837. This also seems to be the broch described
by Martin in 1695, who apparently did not visit Dun
Carloway. He describes it as 'of a round form, made

taperwise towards the top, and is three stories high: the wall is double, and hath several doors and stairs, so that one may go round within the wall'. Probably the material went to build some of the houses of the nearby village of Bragor.

The brochs seem to have been used by the Hebrideans over a considerable period of time, and the lengthy story of Donald Cam is probably true enough. This relates to the end of the sixteenth century, when the various sons of old Ruari MacLeod, chief of the Lewis MacLeods, were contending for the succession and when the MacKenzies were already scheming to possess the Lews.

The MacKenzies upheld the claim of Torquil Conanach, son of Ruari by his first wife, Janet MacKenzie, and Conanach was also supported by the Morrisons of Ness, the heriditary Justices of the Lews. But the MacLeods themselves had accepted Torquil Dubh, son of Ruari by his third wife, Janet MacLean, and the MacLeods had the strong support of the Uig MacAulays.

Among the MacAulays of Uig was the mighty fighter Donald Cam MacAulay, and the Morrisons of Ness schemed to do away with him and with Torquil Dubh, knowing that if Donald Cam was out of the way they could readily overcome other opposition.

The Brieve, the hereditary Justice and leader of the Ness Morrisons, captured a Dutch vessel and took her to Ness. He then invited Torquil and Donald Cam and their immediate bodyguard to come to Ness to share in the spoils. This they did, and laying down their arms, joined in the feast. Suddenly they noticed the heaving of the ship and realised that they were at sea. Rushing on deck, they found their arms hidden and a party of the strongest men the Brieve could raise ready to overpower them. Among these was one John Roy MacKay, and he, with the aid of two others, managed to secure the mighty Donald Cam.

The party arrived at Ullapool, where they were imprisoned, chained in pairs and, after a summary trial, executed. The date of the execution of Torquil Dubh is known to have been July 1597, and it is said that at the time of the execution there was an earthquake which rather alarmed the Morrisons, who regarded it as a sign of God's displeasure at their doings. Donald Cam, however, managed to escape. He was chained to one Alister Small Heel, and this man, having one foot smaller than the other and that chained to Donald, managed to slip his foot free. Together they eventually returned to Uig.

Now when Donald Cam came back to Lewis, John Roy MacKay, who had been the means of taking him prisoner, was very frightened indeed. So he went to the broch of Dun Loch an Duna at Bragor and there began to fortify himself.

Donald sent twelve of the strongest Uig men to take John Roy and they attacked him in the dun. But John Roy was so strong that they could not master him. However, John's wife was a niece of Donald Cam and when she saw that her Uig friends were being beaten by her husband she cried, 'What poor fellows! Did you never see a boar libbed?' Acting on the hint, the MacAulays secured John Roy and carried him off to Kirkibost in Bernera, Loch Roag, where he was executed by the order of Donald Cam.

On another occasion, Donald Cam and the Gow Ban, the fair haired Smith of Uig, went to the Flannan Isles, where the Lewis men used to catch numbers of birds, gather eggs, and kill the sheep which flourished there. When they came back, they found that the Ness Morrisons had taken the opportunity of raiding Uig and carrying off a number of cows.

Donald Cam and the Gow Ban at once went in pursuit and soon saw the cows grazing near Dun Carloway, by which sign they knew that the Morrisons would be inside the dun.

The two waited overnight, and in the morning went towards the dun. Outside, a man was cooking one of the cows in a big kettle over a fire. Donald and the Smith were very hungry. The Smith seized the unfortunate Morrison and as soon as Donald had taken the carcase out of the pot, threw the cook in. The Smith went back with the meat to the rest of the MacAulay party, who were some way behind, but Donald went on to study the position.

When the Smith came back, Donald killed the Morrison sentry and posted the Smith at the broch door to keep anyone from escaping. Then, taking two dirks and sticking them alternately into the walls of the dun, Donald climbed to the top of the broch. Meanwhile, the other MacAulays had gathered bundles of heather, and these were pulled up by Donald on a rope and dropped down inside the dun. When he had put in enough, he set the whole alight and suffocated all the Morrisons that were in the dun.

These traditions of the brochs are a good indication of the use to which the old buildings continued to be put. But they also seem to have gathered about them stories of the supernatural, such as that of the fairies who lived in the broch of Dun Borve on the west side of Lewis.

These fairies were often seen in the broch, leading their big black dogs about on iron collars. A fisherman of Borve wanted a mast for his boat but could get no suitable spar. So he took his wooden hand mallet and threw it into the dun with the request that the fairies would turn it into a mast. Wondering how they would manage to do the job, he hid to await events.

Soon the fairies came out and began to discuss the puzzle. One of them exclaimed, 'Nach cruaidh a cheist a chuir am fear a thainig a tir nam fear beo oirrinn!' (What a hard task the man who came from the land of the living has given us!)

However, the fairy tried to make the mallet into a mast. It was very difficult and he was killed in the attempt. His brother, in a fury, cried out, 'Mo bhuilg, m'uird, us m'ionnan; m'ainnis, m'eiginn, us m'aimbeart, crann-bata dheanamh de shimid. Gu ro trom eiginn is cruaidh mhilleadh air an laimh a chuir a steadh an simid, or chuir mo bhrathair a mach ris fuil a chridhe; ach ni mis e.' (My bellows, my hammers and my anvil; my poverty, my distress and my foolishness; to make a mast of a hand mallet. My weightiest violence and my destruction be on the hand that sent in the mallet, for it cost my brother his heart's blood; but I will do it.)

In the morning, the man found a mast in place of his mallet.

The broch of Dun an Sticer (Fort of the Skulker) at Newton in North Uist also appears to have been in use about the same time as John Roy hid in Dun Loch an Duna, Bragor.

About 1601 one Hugh, the son of Archibald the

Clerk, laid claim to a part of North Uist. This claim was resisted and the chief of Clan Huistein, Donald Gorm Mor, sent a force to take him prisoner. Hugh took refuge with his stepmother in Dun an Sticer.

Soon the siege of the dun appeared to be coming to a successful end for the attackers and Hugh swam to another island. He managed to do this without being seen but his movements were betrayed by the stepmother. Hugh was imprisoned in Duntulm Castle in Skye and fed on salt beef until he died of thirst. He nearly made his escape by trying to break down the walls with the beef bones.

Dun an Sticer is still quite a noticeable ruin. It is about 60 feet in diameter and the walls are from 9 to 12 feet in thickness. Inside are the remains of a more recent rectangular building. It is linked to the shore of the loch in which it is placed by a causeway, and has other causeways leading to various nearby islands in the same loch.

Dun Torcuill is the best preserved broch left in North Uist and is also on an island, in Loch an Duin, with a causeway to the shore. It is about the same size as Dun an Sticer, but the walls still rise to a height of 10½ feet.

One of the most interesting broch and causeway systems is that of the dun on the east shore of Loch Hunder under the South Lee in North Uist.

This dun is a small circular drystone building on an island just off the shore of the loch. It is joined to the shore by a good causeway, curved and with two breaks in it. The two breaks appear to be due to decay rather than to the builder's intention.

The little fort, whose walls still rise several feet, fills all the island. In the thickness of its walls there is still

a definite trace of the broch galleries. Another larger
island, without buildings, is close at hand, and a second
causeway leads from the fort to this island, which was
perhaps used to keep cattle on. A third causeway, with a
sharp bend in it, leads back from the big island to the
loch shore.

Many of the Long Island strong places are upon headlands, utilising the sheer cliffs upon either side in place
of walls and leaving only the short neck of the promontory to be defended. Thus Dun Stron Duin on Berneray
(Barra Head) consists of a galleried wall of broch type
built across the headland so as to enclose the end of it.

Another such galleried dun is Dun Ban (the White
Fort) in Barra. The coast under Ben Tangaval is deeply
eaten into by the sea and precipitous geos run far into
the land. A small headland with a long geo inlet on
each side has been made into a dun; a thick wall is built
across the neck, with a circular building inside it. It is
all in ruins now, the fallen stones overgrown with
thrift, the wind blowing fiercely over the narrow rib of
rock and the sea lashing upon either side.

Somewhat similar is Rudha na Berie in Lewis, on
another rocky stretch of coast near Shawbost. Again the
cliff scenery is very fine, high and rocky with a natural
arch cut through an off-shore stack. Nothing remains of
the fort but the ruin of a wall across the headland. It is
a bare rocky place; one looks down upon the sea below,
watching the black skerries appear and disappear as
the clear blue water heaves itself over them toward the
cliffs.

Perhaps one of the most impressive of the headland
forts is Caisteal Odhair, the Grey Castle, near Griminish

Point in North Uist. The defending wall is there placed
not at the narrowest point, but on the further side of it,
where the ground begins to steepen towards the crest of
the headland, a position of some strategic importance.
On either hand the cliffs fall sheerly, on the one side to
a narrow inlet and on the other to a deep geo up which
the tide rushes to cover all the rocks at its head with
white froth.

From headlands to stacks. Many of the rocky stacks
off the Long Island coasts have been fortified. The stacks
on the sandy shore at Geiraha near Tolsta Head in Lewis
are still called Caisteal (Castles) by the local people.
Only one, the biggest, is actually fortified. There is said
to have been a well on the top. Access is by scrambling
up the 100 odd feet of rock to the grassy top, where
there are the remains of a building divided into two
chambers. Broken craggans and some hammer stones,
traces of the inhabitants' fires, are the total of the finds;
the stack had an easy way of getting rid of its rubbish by
throwing it over the side, leaving few remains to be dug
up afterwards by the curious. Caisteal a Mhorfhear, the
Nobleman's Castle, is its name.

In North Uist there are two interesting forts on loch
islands in the Loch Portain district. One, on Loch an

Duin, is called Dun Nighean Righ Lochlainn (the Castle of the daughter of the King of Scandinavia). It is a circular fort, whose walls still rise several feet. It completely fills its little island and it has been suggested that this is an artificial crannog. It is supposed to be joined to the shore by an underwater causeway, 30 yards long, following a slightly curved course. In the rain, with the loch levels high, when I visited the fort, I could not find the start of this causeway and the fort seemed quite isolated in the loch.

On the next loch to Loch an Duin, Loch na Caiginn, is another and probably medieval dun. It is a small building, much ruined, in which some bothies have been constructed, and it fills only a part of the little heathery island on which it stands. The fort is placed near the end of the broad causeway leading back to the shore. At the island end of this causeway are two breastworks which extend out on either side of the entrance so as to form a defensive barrier. These two flanking walls are strongly built in drystone, and are vastly different from the similarly placed, spidery constructions one sometimes sees erected to keep cattle off islands.

The whole island was further strengthened by a drystone wall running right round the shore, broken only by the entrance from the causeway and a small boat harbour. This harbour was made by building out two parallel walls between which a small boat could be drawn up.

Crossing the causeway to the dun on Loch na Caiginn, several stones rattle and rock under one's feet, and it is easy to see how an effective rattle alarm could be devised.

Linking up the series of Long Island forts with their

Q

final flowering in Kiessimul and the MacLeod's castle at Stornoway is Dun Ban (the White Fort) on Loch Caravat in North Uist.

Dun Ban, also on an island, is a medieval castle built with lime-mortar, not drystone, work. Its wall is D-shaped, with the house placed along the straight stroke of the D and the entrance opposite it. Whoever built it seems to have been familiar with the plan of similar mainland castles. The house was roofed with flagstones supported on wooden beams, part of which roof remained until about 1850. Tradition relates that the timbers were Scots firs grown at Knock Cuien on the south shore of Loch Caravat.

CHAPTER XVII

CLISHAM TO MEALISVAL

IT was a ceilidh story that took me on the stravaig from The Clisham, the highest hill in the Long Island, to Mealisval, the highest in the Lewis. Upon the west side of Lewis, south of Uig, there lies a great track of roadless country, mountain to the north, then a middle country of bog and loch, and southward, across the Harris boundary line, the spiky wall of the mountains of the Forest of Harris. It is a country desolate and bleak, wind-swept and lonely, a country of ruined shielings and a few houses still inhabited, with long fiord lochs snaking deep in amongst its crags which face the sea in bulging slabby faces of grey rock. And yet, across the moors, the line of the Harris hills softens the bleakness and turns it into a foreground for one of the grandest mountain skylines in all Scotland.

There is something to be said for setting the ridge of the Harris hills against the ridge of the Skye Cuillin, and giving the Harris hills best. Sailing into Tarbert from the Minch, the mountains seem uninteresting, like grouped sugar loaves, but from the north or south the ridge stands revealed, a clear cut line of arching rock hackles and velvet green flanks from The Clisham (2,622 ft.) in the east to Tirga More (2,227 ft.) in the west, a distance of some seven miles.

I went across these hills and across the moors beyond them, and at last through the rounded mountains of Uig back to the road, for the sake of a fireside story.

About 1831 a cow rubbing herself against a sand dune on the shore of Uig bay uncovered a set of chessmen, some 78 pieces. They are of walrus ivory, wonderfully carved and of Norse workmanship. Probably the Norsemen brought them to the Long Island sometime about 1200, but the story that was told at the winter ceilidhs was very different.

There came, so the tale went, a French ship into the fiord Loch Tealasavay on the west coast of Lewis, her sails torn by a great storm. There she anchored, the high craggy hills on either side of her, the narrow mouth of the fiord leading out into the Atlantic behind her, and a small shingle beach with a shieling on it at the head of the inlet.

Now a man from Uig came over the hills to Tealasavay to look after his master's cattle which were out at the summer grazings. When he saw the ship he sat down and began to watch her. Suddenly a lad came on deck, slipped over the side into a small boat and rowed ashore. The Uig man dodged round the rocks so as to come face to face with the lad, and began to question him.

The boy said they had had to run for shelter into the loch and were mending their sails and repairing damage before setting out again. He himself was sick of the ship and wanted to get home to France as soon as possible. Would the Uig man guide him to the nearest port? The Uig man agreed to do this, but asked how the boy was going to pay for all his trouble and for his passage home. The boy pointed to a bundle under his arm and said that it contained enough and more for all these things.

Together they set off over the hummocky country that lies between the fiord Loch Tealasavay and the fiord Loch Tamanavay. It was slow going, over boggy hollows and up craggy little faces. They came down to the cleft of the Tamanavay River; in front were the grey, rounded masses of the Uig mountains, the great hills of the West of Lewis, cut through by a deep north-south pass, the Bealach Raonasgail. When night was coming, the Uig man pointed to the hills. 'See yonder great mountains,' he exclaimed, 'we cannot cross them in darkness. We must seek shelter here and wait for the morning light.'

The boy was already tired with the rough going and was only too ready to rest. As soon as the Uig man was sure he was asleep, he struck him on the head and killed him, and hastened off with the bundle through the pass to Uig.

When he got there, he was disgusted to find only chessmen in the boy's bundle. He buried them in a dune and went on to Uig to announce to his master that there was a ship ripe for plundering in Loch Tealasavay. Furious at such a suggestion, the master dismissed him, and the man left Uig for Stornoway. After several further crimes, he was caught and hanged on the gallows hill outside Stornoway, but before he died he confessed to the murder of the French lad.

Some versions of this story give the date as seventeenth century, others as 1745-46, when French ships were in Hebridean waters in connexion with Prince Charles. It is a contradictory little tale; how for instance did the French boy and the Uig man manage to talk so easily to each other, and why was the find that the cow unearthed connected with the boy's bundle?

Roderick MacKenzie of Uig was keeper at Tamanavay and discovered there a great series of rock shelters and caves which had obviously once been inhabited. Wandering amongst them one Sunday afternoon, he took shelter under a great rock from a passing shower. Something white attracted his attention; he reached his hand under the rock and drew out a human skull. The story flashed across his mind—the murdered Frenchman!

After MacKenzie had told me his story there was only one possible course. I determined to see the bones for myself.

So, with this end in view, I left Tarbert, Harris, by car and drove to the head of Loch Meavaig, an inlet on the Harris coast at the start of the middle pass through the mountains of the Forest of Harris.

The weather has done everything that it may to me in the Long Island. I have sweltered in a May heat wave on the South Uist mountains, and the following May sat under a boulder of The Clisham with a trickle of melting snow down my back, watching the snow flakes eddy and swirl all about me, the base of the snow cloud a hand's reach above my head.

The morning that I was to cross from Harris into Lewis to stay at the keeper's house at Tamanavay was brighter. The snow line had risen from 600 feet to the summits, where it outlined the crests against a cloudy sky. As we drove along the twisting coast road on the north shore of West Loch Tarbert, I could look back through the Tarbert hollow and across the Minch to Skye, where I saw the white level spread of more snow on the basalt flats of that island. Across West Loch Tarbert the rounded rocky corries of Ben Luskentyre came down to a grey sea. Further south, the sun was shining on the yellow sands at Northton and the sea was blue.

Above us was the massive wall of the Harris hills. First of all The Clisham (2,622 ft.), a great arching back of rock like a tom cat setting at a dog, snow all over its rocks, and then a drop and a lift, a knife edge ridge-walk to Mulla-fo-dheas (2,439 ft.). West from Mulla-fo-dheas was the opening of the three great passes, a deep rift north-south through the hills, the summit of the pass at about 800 feet. Then the mountains rose again, to more craggy backs above green grassy slopes, the group of tops of Uisgnaval (2,392 ft.), ending against the middle pass in the great face of Strone Scourst.

This middle pass, which rises only to 297 feet, is a broad, level through valley leading across the east-west line of the mountains. West of it, more rock edged slopes lift to Oreval (2,165 ft.) and Ullaval (2,153 ft.), beyond which is the cleft of the third pass, again with a summit at about 800 feet. Beyond this pass of Gleann Chliostair stands the massif of Tirga More (2,227 ft.), quite different in form from the other Harris hills. It tends to rounded shapes in contrast to their ragged outlines and narrow ridges. The reason is geological: the eastern tops are carved out of a biotite gneiss of the Lewisian series which weathers into crags and knife edges; Tirga More and the Uig hills to the northward are of a granite gneiss which shapes into more rounded forms, and which is supposed, incidentally, to be the youngest member of the ancient Lewisian series. The granite was intruded into the other older rocks of that series. It forms a great mass covering a wide area along the west side of Lewis and also extends into southern Harris.

As in South Uist, the lower slopes of the Harris hills were smoothed and rounded by the ice sheets, but when one comes out upon the tops, the rock is all rugged and rough, for the tops stood clear above the great glaciers of the Ice Age and were exposed to all the rending action of the frost and bitter cold. On The Clisham, the top 600 feet of the mountain stood clear above the ice, indicating that the ice sheet passing over Harris in this district was some 2,000 feet thick. A few alpine plants seem to have survived the period, living in the crevices of the bare rocks. They still grow up there.

Like The Chisholm, The Pope and The Devil, one always speaks of The Clisham. The name itself is a little puzzling, for the -ham ending is curious, unless it is something to do with the Norse word, *holmi* (a knoll), here applied to a mountain. The prefix is probably Norse *klif* (rocky ascent). MacCulloch wrote it Clisseval, which would mean Rocky Fell.

Oreval perhaps means the Mountain of the Moorcock; Uisgnaval, oxen mountain or fell; and Ullaval is Ulli's Mountain—all Norse names. Tirga More is Gaelic *mor* (big), and perhaps Tirga, the Norse *hörgr* (cairn), big cairn.

I faced the mouth of Glen Meavaig, the middle pass of the Harris hills, and began to walk up a gritty private road leading to some fishing huts on Lochs Scourst and Voshimid. The car turned and rattled back up the hillside towards Tarbert; I watched it go very conscious that I was turning my back upon the hallmark of civilisation, the road. For all the three days that I was to stay at Tamanavay I would neither see nor walk upon a road.

Glen Meavaig is a broad valley, with the River Meavaig flowing in wide curves upon its floor. On either hand the hillsides rise in steep slopes to the snow-flecked rocks of the tops of Uisgnaval and Oreval. In front the craggy bluff of Strone Scourst soars from the glen floor, a rock face rising sheerly for some thousand feet, a litter of bouldery scree at its foot and the blue pool of Loch Scourst cradled in the lap of the pass. The moor, though it was May, was brown and dead looking as though it were mid-winter. Here and there, where a stream dropped down from the heights and debouched upon the glen floor, were the green sites of old shielings, vivid amongst the brown heather. They placed them there, doubtless, to be handy both for the glen pastures and for the fresh supply of water from the heights.

Rather moodily, watching the clouds chase over the tops, I walked up past Strone Scourst. I wondered whether the weather would hold until I reached Tamanavay, whether the Kinloch Resort river would be very full and where I should ford it, whether the boggy, loch-strewn land between the Harris mountains and those of Lewis would take hours to traverse. I rather thought that it would.

Beyond Strone Scourst, but below the top of the pass,

I turned to look back at that tremendous rock. From the northern side it appears a perfect cone, face upon face, separated by narrow grassy pitches, cut by a deep gully, lifting to the tapered summit (1,608 ft.). Looking back, I could trace a ridge of Uisgnaval which links the main mountain massif to the rock bluff and makes a ridgeway back to the snow-flecked craggy crest of the main mountain block. It looked fascinating to walk upon, as do all the Harris ridges, and the linking ridge gave a sort of asymmetry to the Strone itself, so that the cone of dark rock, from one angle, seemed to lean over the valley.

There is another such truncated spur in the Harris hills, at the north end of the most westerly pass (Glens Chliostair and Ulladale). It is called Strone Ulladale and forms the most northerly outpost of Ullaval. Its summit is 1,398 feet; below the sheer rock lies Loch Ulladale at 193 feet. It is a flatter face than Strone Scourst and without the grassy pitches, a great slab of rock presented in defiance to the Lewis bogs. When I had crossed the Kinloch Resort river, I saw the tremendous face at the mouth of the pass, and it and Strone Scourst were in my view from the Tamanavay hills whenever the weather was clear.

Across Glen Meavaig from Strone Scourst I could look up into a high level corrie between the tops of Oreval and Ullaval. A ridge, broken by pinnacles of dark rock, linked the tops and formed the back of the corrie, through which a waterfall poured over ice-smoothed rocks. I was in fact looking at an illustration of the highest levels reached by the ice sheets, the corrie rock smoothed by them, the ridge above frost-riven.

I crossed the watershed, a boggy expanse, and came

to the end of the private road at a fishing hut at Loch Voshimid and Loch an Fheoir—really only one loch with a narrow neck in the middle. Voshimid has a number of small islands upon it. Another rocky nose, the Sron Ard, rose above the loch to the east; when I had rounded it, I could look back to the fine line of crags that front Creag Stulaval. (There are two high hills called Stulaval in the Outer Isles, one in South Uist and one in Harris.) A good path, which runs from the private road, turns up to the east, and, passing under another line of crags, Creag Chleistir, leads over the hills to Vigadale Bay on Loch Seaforth near Aline, on the main road from Lewis to Harris. At this point I had to leave the path and set forth into a maze of morainic hummocks which edge the river from Loch Voshimid and make walking down to the main line of the Kinloch Resort river a plague.

It would have been better to climb on to one of the spurs which form the northern end of the mountains, but the river was a good guide line to follow and I climbed hummock after hummock and plunged through boghole after boghole. Several times I came suddenly upon little groups of deer, the rather undersized variety of these parts, for in this country of little hummocks and soft ground one comes silently and quickly on them.

At last I climbed up a specially large hummock and looked down on the line of the Kinloch Resort river, the green and graceful cone of Stulaval at its head, the ice-rounded hump of Beinn a'Bhoth across the river. From the moors rose a group of three lumpy tops, all coloured uniformly yellow-brown in dead heather and bog grass. The middle one is called, naturally enough, Beinn Mheadhonach (Middle Mountain, summit 1,303 ft.) but that to the west is called Bein a Deas (South Mountain) and that to the east Beinn a Tuath (North Mountain)!

I went down to the Kinloch Resort river, splashed across above its junction with the stream from Voshimid and went slowly on to Kinloch Resort. There is no path of any sort, for too few people use these routes to mark any line at all through the boggy ground.

Loch Resort is a very fine fiord, very narrow, twisting a little so that you do not see the open sea from its head, and with steep rocky flanks, so that it appears a trench in the land surface. At its head is the clachan of Kinloch Resort, a huddle of a few houses and some croft fields, a bridge over the main river replacing the ancient stepping stones; another crosses the stream from Glen Ulladale which here joins the Kinloch Resort river. The folk who live at Kinloch Resort think themselves much more in the world than the keeper and the postman-crofter who stay at Tamanavay, for at Kinloch Resort the postman walks every day five miles across the moors to link up with the Uig bus-route at Morsgail. A mere five miles from a road—indeed they are in the world! Heavy supplies come round by sea from Husinish in Harris.

I took a line up the rock-littered flank of Benisval (624 ft.), past ruined crofts and a sheep fank, behind which a grey, long-haired feral cat vanished into a cairn of stones. From the top I hoped to decide my route through the maze of low rocky hillocks of which Benisval is the highest and the almost countless lochs which make up the country of the Aird Mhor and Aird Bheag.

Three fiord sea lochs enter the land in the country

between the mountains of Harris and those of Uig, Lewis: Resort in the south, Tamanavay in the north, Tealasavay in the middle. Between the lengthy Resort and the shorter Tealasavay is the Aird Mhor (the big headland), and between Tealasavay and Tamanavay is the Aird Bheag (the little headland).

Near the sheep fank on the flank of Benisval there is, so they tell me, a stone commemorating the visit of Lord Campbell, Lord Chief Justice in the 1850's. When I splashed through the Kinloch Resort river, I crossed from Harris into Lewis, and it was Lord Campbell's boundary that I went over.

There was a long dispute concerning the boundary line between Harris and Lewis in this part of the country. Along Loch Seaforth there was no dispute, but here, in the featureless moors, the problem was more difficult.

It all began long ago, when a MacLeod of Lewis married Kintail's daughter. After a year, he grew tired of her and sent her away, and took a MacLeod of Harris' daughter to wife. For her dowry she brought a strip of land upon the borders of Harris in the Kinloch Resort district.

As time went by, this piece of land became a subject for dispute. People from Valtos in Lewis would go to make ready their shielings for the summer season and come back to find the Harris people had destroyed all their work. If the Harris men worked on what they claimed as theirs, the Valtos people destroyed it all again.

Eventually, Seaforth took the case to the courts. Much interesting evidence of old methods of marking the boundary between the two districts was cited. One way was to bury charred peats on the march line. Another, also used in England, was that of beating the bounds. A Harris witness told how his father, who had died twenty years previously at the age of 80, had been whipped on the boundary line by Donald MacAulay of Brenish (himself a descendant of the famous Donald Cam) and Donald Campbell of Scalpa, both of whom gave him five shillings afterwards to salve his wounded feelings.

The case dragged on. Seaforth sold the Lewis to Sir James Matheson, and it was he, after the case had reached the House of Lords, who got Lord Campbell to the actual ground. Up Benisval went the Lord Chief Justice and from the top determined on the boundary line, taking the shortest route from the head of Loch Resort up the Kinloch Resort river and across to Aline on Loch Seaforth.

After his visit it was decided to erect a stone to commemorate the event. A very strong Valtos man got the job of carrying the stone over the hills from Uig. For the work he said he would need two days, and drew two days' pay for it. Then he heaved the stone on his back and walked rapidly over the hills to Benisval in one day.

I saw a cairn on the flank of Benisval, a little below the top, and made for it. From it a line of little cairns and stones set on edge led across the moors and between the lochs. I began to follow them, for they took the direction which I had planned to follow. All the way they led through the peat, which yielded like butter, and over the rocky knolls. Once or twice I saw a vague footprint in the soft ground, but for the most part it was too wet to take any permanent impression, and there was no trace of a path. The stones lead to the postman's house at Aird Bheag—he makes the journey several times a week and brings back, among other things, food supplies ordered by mail from Glasgow. It was the postman who erected the cairns.

I know how this country would look in the height of summer. There would be greens of grass, patches of cotton grass, and everywhere great beds of scented heather. The grey-banded rocks would rise out of a riot of flowers and the numberless little lochs would be very deep blue, and sparkling, while now and again, through a gap, the pale hard blue line of the Atlantic would show. The cloud shadows would dapple the green shapes of the Harris Hills in the south and the grey humps of the Lewis mountains in the north.

I know also how it looked that evening in May when we had December weather. It was brown and colourless, the lochs steely, the wet peat sucking at my boots. A wind came out of the west, so that I had to lean into it to make any headway, and with the wind came a lashing storm of sleety rain. I was blinded by it, floundered deeper in the bogs, lost sight of the cairn lines, realised they were leading to Aird Bheag and not to Tamanavay, plunged round a loch, found a trace of muddy path down a steep cliff slope to the Tamanavay River and a bridge, and so came to the keeper's house.

Tamanavay is a very green little croft at the head of the loch. Loch Tamanavay is a fiord opening in the hills, its rock cliffs giving place to a narrow shingle beach below the house. To the north the ground rises steeply to the rounded grey mountains of Uig, Lewis, while to the south there is the lift to the craggy country of Aird Bheag. Behind the house the hillside rises less steeply to Giura, a low hill which in reality is nothing more or less than a cairn of stones.

If you follow Giura back inland away from the sea, you follow a ridge with rocky outcrops. At the seaward end the rock outcrops give place to a tumble of boulders, huge blocks, some as big as cottages and weighing many tons. The average size is very large; the tumble of rock debris extends from Tamanavay croft up to and over the very top of the hill, which is 275 feet above sea level. I was reminded of the boulder beds on the summit of the Cairngorms, where granite has weathered freely under frost action, and of the great scree spills under some of the bigger crag faces in the Highlands—the Brin Rock in Strath Nairn, for instance.

But Giura is near sea level and not exposed to violent freezing and thawing; no lofty crags spill on it and the rock waste forms the top of the hill itself. There is a very considerable depth of boulders; the whole end of the ridge seems to be built of them. I looked down into deep passages and hollows in which sheep often stick.

The rock of the boulder heap is the local granite gneiss, and it does not appear to be undergoing any intensive weathering at the present time. Turf and heather are growing over the hollows between the blocks. I could think of only one explanation: that the great pile had been formed during the waning phases of the Ice Age. It has been suggested to me by a member of the Geological Survey that the way the rock heap was formed was this: the fiord was filled by a glacier and the ice bumping up against the cliff faces, already exposed to extensive frost action, shattered off this jumble of boulders.

It was amongst these rocks that Roderick MacKenzie found the rock shelters and the human skeleton.

Giura is not the only big scree mass in the district; there are several others of rather similar structure and near the sea, though some appear more normally below higher rock faces. Another big scree and boulder bed is at the head of Loch Tealasavay, where there is a further series of rock shelters.

Giura rocks present far from easy walking, but they make fine caves, after the fashion of the Shelter Stone of the Cairngorms. One crawls under huge blocks to find quite spacious floors on which are a litter of winkle and limpet shells and stones set for a hearth, reddened with the heat. Now and again careful search discovers a piece of rough pottery of the sort the Lewis people made for their craggans.

Some of the overhanging rocks and caves were rather uncomfortable when used as dwellings, and their inhabitants built up drystone walls to block the more awkward and windswept openings. Under one tumble of rocks is a circular cell like a beehive house.

About two thirds of the way up from the Tamanavay River, opposite the first bend of that stream above the junction with the burn from Loch Grunavat, are the human bones. Near by are numerous shelters with walling added to their natural amenities: obviously a place where a good many people lived.

A huge rock overhangs. In front of the overhang a rough wall of big blocks seems to be piled; in the hollow behind it, on a fairly level floor of smaller chips, lies the skeleton. When Roderick found it, he told me, the bones were spread out, full length, with the head towards

R

the west. They have now been shifted into a small pile. The upper half of the skull, the lower jaw, the long bones of the limbs, some ribs and other fragments remain, all very white and friable.

He was a grown man—Roderick MacKenzie would support the theory of his being the Frenchman by supposing that the term 'boy' in the story does not necessarily mean a young man—and he was a big man. The thigh bone is 18 inches long. The skull was long and narrow—it measures at present $7\frac{1}{4}$ inches by 5 inches. The lower jaw, in which practically all the teeth remain —one or two had fallen out and I reclaimed them from the small stones—is virtually intact. The teeth are sound and notable for being worn down quite uniformly, like a horse's, so that their upper surfaces are smooth and polished and no trace of cusps remains. I sat in the heather rubbing my own teeth and wondering what the dead man had lived on to wear down his cusps so evenly.

If ever a Frenchman was murdered at Tamanavay, I cannot think but that his body would have been pitched in a boghole. This skeleton, I think, is much more probably that of one of the rock shelter dwellers deliberately buried here.

And who were the folk who lived in the Giura rock shelters? There is little evidence. They built in drystone, to improve the natural shelters; they ate shell fish in great quantities, mainly limpets and winkles; they made rough pottery—shells and rough pottery of the sort found in kitchen midden sites all over Lewis, roughly dated as Iron Age; that is all we know about them.

I climbed on Cleit na h-Uamha at the head of Loch Tealasavay. This boulder slope rises to 250 feet, and is very similar to Giura, though more overgrown and therefore more difficult to scramble on. Cleit na h-Uamha means the Crag of the Cave. A great cave formed by an underhanging rock attracted me; in front was a green apron of vivid grass. When I climbed up to it I found nettles, the usual aftermath of human habitation, growing in the turf, and the soil was all black ashes from the peat fires. Crawling in, I found the cave extended back some 14 feet under the rock. The fire had been made in the mouth to one side; the other side had been blocked with a drystone wall so as to make the place weather tight. There was the usual litter of winkle and limpet shells, some sheep or deer bones embedded in the black soil, split to extract their marrow, and many fragments of pottery. One of the pieces, which seem to include a lot of grass mixed in the clay, resembles some known pottery from the Antrim coast of the seventh or eighth century A.D., according to Mr. Stevenson of the National Museum of Antiquities of Scotland.

Another plant characteristic of old habitations was growing on the Cleit na h-Uamha crags—the rowan tree. Like Giura, the Cleit seems to have been well populated; during my brief climb I noted many more piles of shells under other boulders on the face. I do not imagine for a moment that Giura and Cleit na h-Uamha were the only inhabited boulder beds in this district; further search would undoubtedly list a number more wherever the rocks were suitable for use as shelters. Cleite nan Uamhannan (Crag of the Caves), above Loch nan Uidhean in the Aird Mhor, would be one of the first places to look next on such a search. Neither the series of shelters at Giura nor that at Cleit na h-Uamha (Loch Tealasavay) has been noted in previous records of the antiquities of Lewis.

From the top of Giura I could look out to sea to St. Kilda, framed in the mouth of Loch Tamanavay, and northward to the grey humps of the Uig hills, of which the nearest, Griomaval (1,600 ft.), is perhaps the best as a view point. It commands all the western coast of Lewis, from Gallan Head down into Harris. A deep and narrow glen traverses the range from north to south; the summit of the pass is at about 800 feet, the hills lifting upon either side steeply, in crags on the north side of the watershed and less rugged shapes on the south.

On the southern, Tamanavay side of the pass, the valley floor is all little hummocky morainic mounds with the green turf plots surrounding old shielings amongst them. The burn down the glen, the Amhuinn Cheann Chuisil, is incredibly clear, every pebble shining on the floor of its pools.

I started up this route in a thick sea haar which came drifting in from the Atlantic, now lessening, now thickening. Objects, rocks and hillocks, appearing suddenly, looked enormous through it, and as quickly were swallowed up. At an old shieling green the line of track marked by the feet of the sheep from Tamanavay when they are driven over to the Uig market can be found and followed to the Uig road; in the mist I failed to strike the line.

I kept near to the stream, for its gurgling was a good guide in the gloom. As I went on, I knew by the stutter of waterfalls down a rock that I must be nearing the top of the pass. The mist thinned; sunlight caught a wet face of rock opposite; little Loch a'Chama, which lies immediately below the watershed, was beside me.

Beyond Loch a'Chama lies the V of the pass summit.
As I reached it the cloud parted, smoking amongst the
crags, showing the lovely lake of Raonasgail below me,
the water steely blue, a yellow line of beach here and
there, rocks submerged in the water aping some water
kelpie. Below me, leading down to the loch, was the
narrow cut of the pass, screes meeting at its head, green
turf slopes between them; above was the castellated line
of crags. There were the vivid moss cushions surrounding little springs of clear, cold water, the castle shapes
of the rocks of Teinnasval, gullies full of green turf edged
with grey rock.

The pass going down to Raonasgail is so deep and
narrow that there is no choice of routes; you must
follow the bouldery line marked out by the sheep. As
the valley widens, as you come down to Raonasgail, you
may take the one side of the loch or the other, though
the east is to be preferred. It is rough going; the haggy
moor below the narrow gut of the pass is all littered with
boulders of every size and shape. Beyond Raonasgail the
moor spreads endless to the Uig road and the sea, a long
plod almost featureless, and hardly a place where you may
set down your foot without first looking to see what
manner of rock or bog you are picking upon.

Mealisval (1,885 ft.), the highest mountain in the
Lewis hills, rises to the west of Loch Raonasgail, and its
northern shoulder, the Mula Mac Sgiathain, lifts from
the level moor in great buttress faces broken by a deep
gully. This rock face, the pass cleft and the shapes of the
hills between Raonasgail and Loch Suainaval to the east,
dominate the moor which leads to Uig. Going from Uig
to Tamanavay, they would urge you on across its expanse;

in the reverse direction you leave them with a sense of anti-climax.

But all things must end, even the moor between Raonasgail and the Uig road, and at last I came out upon the yellow dusty line of the highway, where I stood looking down on the blue sea, the white sands and the green dunes; where a cow, rubbing herself, had uncovered a set of walrus ivory chessmen.

CHAPTER XVIII

NO ROAD HOME

CROSSING the moor between Loch Raonasgail and the yellow road by the sea at Uig, I had plenty of opportunity to consider living without roads. Probably the first thing one notices is the silence. In a roadless community the noises that make up the background of our road-driven civilisation are lacking: the swish of tyres on wet tarred highways, the creak of carts, the echoing horse's hooves, heels tapping on a pavement, boots crunching on gravel.

The second thing that strikes the visitor is the extra effort that is needed to move from one place to another. If you live, as at Tamanavay, upon the roadless bog with no path to your door, you have always to step cunningly from tussock to tussock, rock to rock, not thoughtlessly as on the pavements, never thinking where you place your feet.

Neither of these two aspects is an essential one of living without roads, but both are to some extent symbolic of the difference between communities with roads and those without. What is fundamental is the connexion between the Road and the Wheel. Our civilisation has been built upon the twin inventions of the road and the wheel, and the road came first. In a roadless community the wheel ceases to be of use, and everything must be carried instead of trundled.

The Isles have the whole historical sequence. There are good roads in the main islands, good paths in some of the smaller like Eriskay and Vatersay. On the paths you miss the coup carts and find them replaced by the pony with creels, but it is as easy to move about on Eriskay or Vatersay as in a town, for the paths are good. Then there are the smaller communities, more isolated, mainly dependent on the sea for supplies but still linked to the road by a path, like Rainigadale in Harris. And lastly, there are the true roadless communities, the odd houses placed among the moors like Tamanavay and Aird Bheag, or the cluster at Kinloch Resort.

Tamanavay depends for its rations upon the postman walking along his line of little cairns to link up with the Kinloch Resort postman who walks from Morsgail. The heavy things, like meal, are brought by sea in a small motor boat from Husinish in Harris. At Husinish there is no pier and one has to wade ashore and then wade back carrying whatever is to be loaded.

Tamanavay, being in a rocky country, is outwith the range of the ambulance planes. It is six miles and a thousand foot climb to the nearest telephone and the end of the Uig road; a patient for hospital must wait for a calm sea before he can be shifted.

It is more expensive to live off the road than on it. The sea becomes your roadway. There is the cost of the boat and its fuel, and then the high freight charges of carrying goods to or from the lading place.

In some roadless communities ponies with creels can

be used to carry in peats, cart manure and so forth, but in others, like these amongst the Lewis and Harris hills, there is not enough keep for both them and the cows. Transportation becomes a matter of a creel on your back, for all the seaware for the croft, for all the peats you need to burn, for the potatoes to the clamp. There is no horse traction for a plough; you use a spade or a light two-wheeled tractor—supposing that the fields you have are big enough for it to work and for its cost to be justified.

These roadless communities are a problem both in the Islands and on the Scottish mainland. Many once existed; now they are dwindling rapidly because few people are willing to put up with the difficulties of living off the road. Many of them are in fertile, snug and attractive spots, to which it would be better that the road should come than that the people should leave to seek it. Furthermore, these are the very places that the tourist industry should have an eye to. How many people would visit the Trossachs if the access road was the same that Walter Scott followed on his first visit?

CHAPTER XIX

CROFT AND SHIELING

A CROFTING township is still a community rather than a group of houses, and is linked together by more than mere common interest in a particular sort of work. There is still a tendency to treat one's neighbour as oneself and to regard his property as available for the general service of the hamlet. 'If we want anything, if perhaps we are short of milk, we go and ask someone else for it. Then they, in turn, borrow from us, and so it goes on, without any money payment,' a Sutherland girl told me. Even more is this true of the Long Island crofting townships.

In the Hebrides a form of communism, Run-rig (Gaelic *Roinn Ruith*, division run), existed until something under a hundred years ago, and parts of the system still persist. Run-rig, holding the land in common, meant that any particular strip field passed annually from one man to another until everybody had a turn of it. Similarly, grazing ground was communised, as it still is, and jobs like the cutting and loading of peat and the gathering of seaweed were work for the whole township as a unit. Organisation was in the hands of a constable, who was sometimes appointed by the people and sometimes by the factor; in some instances there were two constables, one representing the people and one the factor. The factor paid his constable in money, the people theirs in kind: 'fiar am beinn, agus peighinn air machair' (grazing on hill and tillage on machair).

Run-rig had some advantages but it meant that the standard for the whole township had to be the standard of the least efficient, since it was no use one man raising the fertility of his strip one year for another to squander the next. Nor was it possible to raise any but standard crops, because the whole system was geared to a particular rotation and the cattle wandered at liberty over the unfenced fields in winter. The cattle still do this, and make it difficult for a crofter to grow winter or out-of-season crops on the open strips.

Run-rig has been abandoned in favour of individual holdings, retaining, however, a strong communal spirit. Two crofters join forces to make up a pair of ponies for ploughing; several club together to put up the money to buy a light two-wheeled tractor; everybody gets together at the peat cutting.

Agriculture in the Long Island not only retained the ancient and once widespread run-rig system until recent times, but also developed some curious techniques of its own. Partly these were due to shortage of wood, partly to the remoteness of the district, partly to the particular problems set by the cultivation of peat land and sandy machair. Many tools once common throughout the Highlands survived longest in the Islands.

Shortage of wood resulted in some curious makeshifts. The St. Kilda people at one time used a light wooden harrow with teeth in front only, the rest of the tines

being replaced by tangle stalks. There was only enough
wood available to make one line of teeth. Lewis tied
bunches of heather behind two rows of teeth. The Isles
are still very fond of using home-made harrows, a square
wooden framework with iron teeth to be dragged either
by man or horse and very well adapted to the soft sand
of the machair lands.

Sheer remoteness allowed the old Highland six-horse
plough to persist. A risteal was obtained at Loch Eport
in North Uist in 1905 that had been in use during the
previous fifty years. The risteal (Norse *ristill*, plough-
share) was a sickle-shaped coulter which was hauled in
front of the main plough by two horses, breaking the
ground for the big plough to turn. The big plough, called
crom nan gad, was drawn by four horses and came behind
the risteal, turning the furrow over. Its place has been
taken by the English mouldboard plough, drawn either by
horses or a tractor, the coulter no longer a separate tool
but a part of the plough itself.

For the smaller plots of ground on which the big
ploughs could not work the Long Islander used his cas
chrom or foot plough. This implement works about
twice as fast as a spade and allows one to dig a tenth of a
Scots acre per day. The handle is some $5\frac{1}{2}$ feet long,
fixed at an angle of 120° with an iron shod footpiece. At
the angle is a peg on which the foot is placed to drive the
tool into the ground. The blade is pressed into the ground
and the soil turned over with a twisting movement, so
that an irregular furrow is produced. The cas chrom
plough was the first tool to be invented to make a furrow
and replaced the digging stick during the late Bronze Age.
A cas chrom type of plough was found in Glastonbury

Lake Village (late Early Iron Age) and the first ox-drawn ploughs were merely a cas chrom hitched to animal traction.

Incidentally, the shape of the field varies with the type of tool one uses to work it. Land dug with a digging stick or a spade may be any shape; once you start to turn a furrow, as with the cas chrom, you start to have rectangular fields. It is interesting to notice that the plan of some of the Hebridean strip fields closely resembles that revealed by air photographs of ancient Celtic ones.

The cas chrom, still to be found in the Hebrides, has been largely replaced by the ordinary spade, by light two-wheeled tractors of 3-6 h.p., and to a certain extent, in the larger fields once hand dug, by the bigger tractors with their ploughs mounted on hydraulic lifts so that they can work right into corners. But the spade remains the only tool for building up a lazy bed, even though the Hebrides have taken the jump from a prehistoric type of foot plough to the latest light tractor in one bound.

The people also had some peculiar customs like plucking their sheep instead of clipping them, a procedure which, the old *Statistical Account* notes (1797), was sometimes fatal if the weather turned cold. The sheep plucked were the small Hebridean variety.

Again, about the same period, they used to pull up their barley by the roots instead of cutting it, so as to take full advantage of the short straw, which they used for thatching. Each year the thatch, impregnated with soot, was removed and used to manure the fields.

In default of imports of manufactured goods, they made sacks, harness mountings and so on from plaited bent grass, and ropes out of twisted heather stems.

Marion M'Innes, in 1829, having no scissors handy at the shieling, laid the material for her new dress on a flat stone and cut it to shape with a sharp stone.

Tobacco was successfully grown in Barra in the seventeenth century. Not only wool was made up into clothing but also flax, which was grown and processed by the islanders. This linen industry was killed by the development of cheap cottons. Had the islanders, like the Irish, managed to maintain their linen making, it might, as in Ireland, have become a valuable high quality export.

For a time kelp burning was an important industry in the Isles. Labour at the burning was part of the agreement between tenant and landlord, the latter scooping most of the profits, which for a short time were high. When the price fell during the middle of the nineteenth century, kelp burning ceased to pay and the industry came to an end; seaweed now has a future in the Hebrides with the new developments of alginate products, and it is again being harvested.

In North Uist the technique of kelp burning was introduced by Hugh MacDonald, tacksman of Baleshare. He got one Rory MacDonald from Ireland to demonstrate the method. Rory's first attempts, about 1735, were unsuccessful and he got the nickname of Rhuary-na-luahigh (Rory, the maker of ashes).

MacCulloch, writing in 1819, at the height of the kelp boom, said that the Western Isles produced some 5,000-6,000 tons each year, of which the Long Island made two-thirds. Loch Maddy alone produced 300 tons, from 7,200 tons of seaweed. The beds were cut every three years, the weed being surrounded with a rope of heather at low water and drawn up as the tide rose. It was next dried and burned in a stone kiln on the seashore. The work went on all through June, July and August; it was hard and continuous, and at the expense of attention to the crofts. The Islanders themselves received very little profit from it.

The potato was introduced in the mid-eighteenth century and grown for the first time with much misgiving by the people. However, it soon became a staple part of their diet and the famine of a hundred years later was caused by the failure of the crop.

Originally everyone had their own quern, but water-powered mills were eventually developed on the Hebridean streams. All these small mills are now defunct. Whilst there is now a move to set up bakeries, many places actually import bread as such from Glasgow, a most unsatisfactory arrangement.

Before the grain could be ground by either hand or water power, it was usually necessary to dry it, and small kilns were constructed for this purpose. Of the little water mills the minister of the parish of Lochs in Lewis, writing in the *New Statistical Account* in 1845, gives an extraordinarily complicated account though they have a very simple structure and principle. He says that:

There is scarcely a stream along the coast, on any part of the island, on which a mill is not to be seen. These mills are of very small size, and of a very simple construction. The water passes through their middle, where the wheel—a solid piece of wood generally, eighteen inches in diameter—stands perpendicularly. A bar of iron runs through the centre of this wheel. This bar of iron or axle rests on a piece of steel, which is fixed on a plank, the one end of which is fixed in the mill wall, the other in the end of a piece of plank, which stands at right angles with the plank on which the wheel rests. The upper end of the axle fits into a cross bar of iron, which is fitted into the upper millstone, the axle passing through the centre of the lower millstone, which is rested upon wooden beams or long stones. There is a purchase upon the end of the said perpendicular beam or plank by which the upper millstone can be raised or lowered. There are nine pieces of board, eight inches broad and a foot and a half long, fitted in the wheel, parallel and at equal distances from each other, upon which the water is brought to bear; which, together with a few sticks for roof, and some heather for thatch, constitutes a Lewis mill.

I examined one of these simple little mills at Tamanavay. It had been in use in the 1890's and is complete except for the roof and the woodwork.

The water from Loch Grunavat falls some 100 feet down a steep valley slope into the Tamanavay river and the mill is situated on a small island in the course of this series of cascades. It is a small rectangular drystone building, about 10 feet by 6 feet inside. The long axis is across the burn, some of the water of which is led through the middle of the island and through the mill house in a carefully built conduit. One millstone has fallen into the stream in this channel, the other lies inside the mill. The stones are of dark hornblende gneiss; I was told that a special band was quarried for the purpose and could be traced across to Loch Resort and The Clisham. At intervals these stones had to be sharpened by chipping out the surfaces with hammer and chisel.

The water-wheel was horizontal in the stream, the lower stone fixed and the upper stone turning with the water-wheel to which it was directly linked on an axle.

I was told that when the Tamanavay mill was last in use there were even then only two houses in the district.

They would carefully save all their corn for milling instead of buying it from outside.

Under the old order every summer, throughout the Highlands, the cattle with the womenfolk and the young folk went up to the hill shielings. The men stayed at home to clean up the homestead and do the necessary work on the crofts, whilst the valley pastures were rested ready for winter.

Up on the hills were the shieling huts beside the rich summer grass, and there the people lived, in apparently idyllic fashion, tending their herds and making butter and cheeses. The sheep walks and the deer forests turned the glens into deserts and the shielings into rickles of stone standing on vivid green mounds of good grass. Only in Lewis does the shieling habit persist, and there, during summer, you will see the cattle out on the moor, the little squat huts smoking and the people tending their beasts.

Most shieling huts were ordinary buildings resembling the usual homestead but built on a smaller scale. On the mainland, where brushwood was available, they might be of timber and wattle; in the treeless Isles they are rectangular huts of undressed stone, roofed with such timber as can be got and thatched with turf, or nowadays roofed with galvanised iron. In the old days the people took their roofs home with them, such was the scarcity of wood in the Long Island.

In the Catholic Islands the start of the shieling season was marked by some little ceremony and the singing of the traditional shieling hymn; the Protestant part of the Long Island had to content themselves with commending their flocks to the shepherd that keepeth Israel. This is the hymn of the Catholic Islanders:

s

A Mhicheil mhin! nan steud geala,
A choisin cios air Dragon fala,
Air ghaol Dia'us Mhic Muire,
Sgaoil do sgiath oirnn dian sinn uile,
Sgaoil do sgiath oirnn dian sinn uile.

A Mhoire ghradhach! Mathair Uain-ghil,
Cobhair oirnne, Oigh na h-uaisle;
A rioghainn uai'reach! a bhuachaille nan tredu!
Cum ar cuallach cuartaich sinn le cheil,
Cum ar cuallach cuartaich sinn le cheil.

A Chalum-Chille! chairdeil, chaoimh,
An ainm Athar, Mic 'us Spioraid Naoimh,
Trid na Trithinn! Trid na Triath!
Comraig sinne, gleidh ar trial,
Comraig sinne, gleidh ar trial.

Athair! A Mhic! A Spioraid Naoimh!
Bi'eadh an Tri-Aon leinn a la's a dh'oidhche!
'S air machair loim, no air rinn nam beann,
Bi'dh an Tri-Aon leinn, 's bi'th A Lamh mu'r ceann,
Bi'dh an Tri-Aon leinn, 's bi'th A Lamh mu'r ceann.

Alexander Carmichael translated this hymn:

Thou, gentle Michael of the white steed,
Who subdued the Dragon of blood,
For love of God and the Son of Mary
Spread over us thy wing, shield us all!
Spread over us thy wing, shield us all!

Mary, beloved! Mother of the White Lamb,
Protect us, thou Virgin of nobleness,
Queen of beauty! Shepherdess of the flocks!
Keep our cattle, surround us together,
Keep our cattle, surround us together.

Thou Columkill, the friendly, the kind,
In the name of the Father, the Son and the Spirit Holy,
Through the Three-in-One, through the Three,
Encompass us, guard our procession,
Encompass us, guard our procession.

Thou Father! Thou Son! Thou Spirit Holy!
Be the Three-One with us day and night,
On the machair plain, on the mountain ridge,
The Three-One is with us, with His arm around our head,
The Three-One is with us, with His arm around our head.

Shieling huts in the Outer Isles might be either of turf (Bothan cheap) or stone (Bothan cloiche). Whilst the rest are all of normal hut architecture, some of the stone ones are of the extremely archaic beehive type, in which the roof is made by progressively overlapping inward large flags until the dome-like roof can be closed by one slab. Furthermore, in some cases these beehive houses are built in groups and remind one of some of the underground prehistoric earth houses of Vallay and other places in North Uist.

The age of these buildings is doubtful. This is the type of hut that the monks of the Celtic church built for themselves, and the beehive houses in the Garvellach Islands are usually claimed to belong to this period. They are there associated with an ancient church site. Elsewhere the shortage of timber for roofing purposes might tend to preserve this ancient method of roofing in stone alone. On the other hand, the Hebrideans have always told enquirers that the beehive shielings are very ancient indeed, merely kept in repair by later generations, and they state categorically that no one, having his own home built in the ordinary way, would make a beehive shieling for himself.

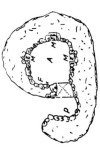

Both an Aird
(First beehive house)
Plate XI

Both Ura near Loch
Tealasavay

0   5   10   15 feet

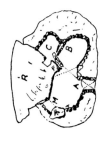

Both an Aird
(Second beehive house
of photograph)
Plate XII

Copies of plans made by Capt. Thomas R. N. of some of
the Lewis beehive houses. In Proceedings of the Society
of Antiquaries of Scotland, Vol. III, 1857-60.

P   porch (Gaelic, *fosgarlan*)
A   main chamber
B   second chamber
M   milk cupboard (G. *cuiltean*)
F   fireplace
C   sleeping place
R   native rock
D   dairy
K   churn room
N   bench

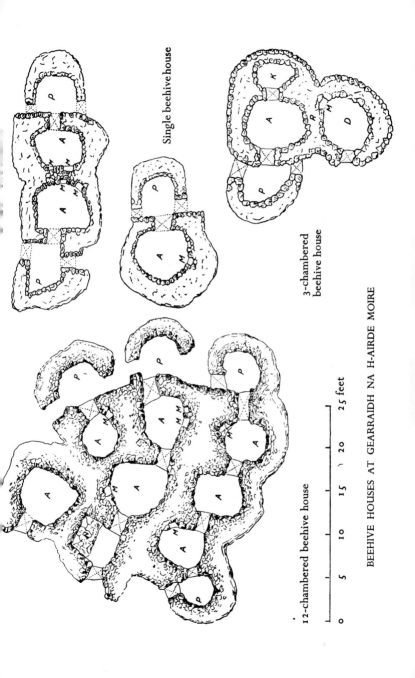

Single beehive house

3-chambered
beehive house

12-chambered beehive house

BEEHIVE HOUSES AT GEARRAIDH NA H-AIRDE MOIRE

0   5   10   15   20   25 feet

The beehive shielings are almost all confined to the mountainous districts of Lewis and Harris. There is a beehive hut in an old fort on the slopes of the South Lee in North Uist, and there were also one or two reported from South Uist and from Benbecula. Outside the Long Island there were the Amazon's House in St. Kilda, the Bothans of the Clan MacPhail in the Flannan Isles and some other beehive chambers in North Rona.

Martin Martin (1695) saw beehive huts in Skye. He tells us: 'There are several little stone houses, built above ground, capable only of one person, and round in form. One of them is to be seen in Portree, another at Lincro, and at Culuknock. They are called Tey-nin-druinich, i.e. Druid's House. Druinich signifies a retired person, much devoted to contemplation.'

Undoubtedly there have probably been many more beehive houses about than are now recorded. Drystone buildings require frequent repair to keep them standing, and a neglected beehive would soon become a heap of stones. It was because they were in regular use and repair that so many have survived in the Lewis-Harris hills.

Captain F. W. L. Thomas, R.N., visited many of the beehive shieling sites in the middle of the nineteenth century and found a number still inhabited. About 1857 some twenty were in use in Uig forest, Lewis. The Bernera crofters used their beehive huts at Beinn a'Chu-ailein near Glen Marstaig until 1872, when they had to be abandoned because the land was given over to deer forest.

The first beehive hut that I visited was the very complete one near Garynahine in Lewis. It stands beside two ruined rectangular shielings on a hillock above the road to Uig and just opposite the Tursachan circle with the central cairn.

It is a beehive-shaped hut built of large slabs of local gneiss, rather bigger than the ordinary run of beehive hut stones. Thus, at a height of 4 feet from the ground, only six slabs are needed to complete the circle, and one of these measures 4 feet 3 inches in length. There are two doorways, opposite one another and facing east and west. I crawled through one—they are only just over 3 feet high—and inside I could stand up easily. The hut has a maximum diameter of 7 feet 9 inches. There are three recesses in the walls for milk bowls and utensils, and a fourth, which leads up into a chimney-like vent which was probably a fireplace. The fireplace is supposed to have been a modern addition. The low doorways I have seen also in rectangular shielings in the Uig district.

This Garynahine beehive was inhabited when Captain Thomas visited it in 1866. The woman who lived in it told him that it was built for a shieling by Dr. MacAulay's grandfather, who was tacksman of Linshader. This would mean about 1780. But another tradition relates that it was built by one Smith of Callanish, and it may be that these people merely repaired an existing hut.

I visited some of the very numerous groups of beehive huts in the Aird Mhor–Tamanavay–Loch na Craobhaig district in Lewis. These sites were studied by Captain Thomas in the 1850's; some at Loch na Craobhaig (Fidigidh) were then inhabited, and he prepared detailed scale plans of the more interesting bothies which were printed in the *Proceedings of Society of Antiquaries of Scotland*. With the aid of these plans, it is still possible to follow the design of the now dilapidated beehive houses at Gearraidh na h-Airde Moire.

There is something very strange about traversing the brown moor and coming upon a little group of bee-hive houses. Originally, they would have looked very much more peculiar, for they were covered over with turfs to make them wind-tight and blended perfectly with their surroundings. Bothan Ruadh, the Red Bothy, at Fidigidh, still retains some of the original turfing, as does the bothy at Garynahine; at Bothan Ruadh I noticed that the upper part of the roof had been mended with timbers instead of stones. As the timbers were still quite in order, the house cannot have been so very long out of use; in fact this group of shielings near Loch na Craobhaig seems to have been in use till just before the 1939 war, though latterly only the rectangular shieling huts there would have been inhabited. One big beehive hut had been squared off and made into a rectangular hut, roofed in the ordinary way. Roderick MacKenzie remembers this being done and says that the original beehive would have held about eleven people.

The beehive houses were, of course, without windows or chimneys (except for Garynahine). Shelving was usu-ally built in to the thickness of the walls—it was easy enough to do this with thin flat stones, and the shelves were useful for bowls of milk and utensils to be stood out of the way. Often there were two doors, they would be closed with wicker frames.

Some beehives have porches outside their doors. Two out of a group of three of the dilapidated Bothan Ura at the head of Loch Tealasavay have porches. These porches are merely a curved wall built out so as to shelter three sides of the entrance. Probably they would be roofed as well. I saw a porch of this type attached to a rectangular shieling on the moor between Loch Raonasgail and the Uig road.

In some cases, a suitable face of rock was used to serve for a side to a bothy. The nearly intact pair of beehive houses at Bothan Ard—high up on Cleit nan Bothan Ard between Lochs Bodavat and Grunavat, south of the Tamanavay, are of this type. One of these beehive houses has two entrances, one of which has an extensive porch. In the other bothy the main chamber opens into an inner sleeping place at the back of the hut against the rock.

Perhaps the most interesting site of all is the village of beehive houses at Gearraidh na h-Airde Moire (pasture of the big headland) on the shore of Loch Resort in the Aird Mhor. The Allt Gleann na h-Airde Moire (Stream of the Big Headland) is a small stream, wandering down a shallow valley to a shingle beach between rocky cliffs near the mouth of Loch Resort. Across the narrow fiord rises the great rocky bluff of Tarran Mor, sheer up from the water, the final word of the line of the Harris hills to the Lewis boundary. On the Lewis side the hills are lower, but they break into rock here and there, and the ground about the stream mouth is all ridged with old lazy beds. To the east side of the opening of the little valley there is a very green ridge with the ruins of three beehive houses on it; to the west, down upon the shingle bank at the back of the beach, is another beehive structure. The sea must have encroached since it was built.

This big beehive house upon the shore consists really of a block of twelve beehive houses joined by passages and with their entrances protected on the outside by porches. One is reminded to some extent of the wheel houses built underground in the early Iron Age; it has been suggested to me that this twelve-chambered beehive was once completely covered over with turf and soil.

Across the way, on the green knoll, is one ordinary single-chambered beehive house with a porch. The other two there are composite. One is a long narrow building, in essence two porched beehives built back to back. It was a semi-detached house for two families. The other is of a circular shape and consists of a main chamber with a churn room opening off it and a second beehive to serve as dairy built alongside. The main chamber has a porch outside the door.

Under the turf of the green mound is a thick kitchen midden layer of winkles and limpet shells, like those of the neighbouring rock shelters. One may also find bits of rough pottery like that of the shelters; it was made in the Lewis from prehistoric times till the regular steamers began to bring manufactured ware up from the south to the remote corners of the Isles.

This then is the pattern of the beehive houses: composite ones down by the shore in the fertile little glens, single-chambered ones up on the shieling pastures. I began to wonder whether the Gearraidh na h-Airde Moire site was really originally a village which has degenerated into a shieling. It was last used as a shieling about 1823 and belonged to the Carnish people. Carnish is near Uig.

If the composite beehives were villages, the single ones may have been their shieling huts. If so, they may be extremely ancient, and have been kept in repair till the present day because of their continued usefulness as shielings. I do not think these bothies in the Long Island are connected with the Celtic Church as many in Ireland are; they are obviously sited either for the summer pastures or, as at Gearraidh na h-Airde Moire, for a small crofting township. The tradition to-day, and as it was given to Captain Thomas a hundred years ago, is that they are very old and that no man knows by whom they were built.

CHAPTER XX

THE OUTPOSTS OF THE LONG ISLAND

ST. KILDA, the Flannans, North Rona and the Shiant Isles—these are the outposts of the Long Island. St. Kilda is ever present on the Hebridean skyline in fine weather, desolate, bird haunted, its great cliffs the highest in the British Isles.

There never was a saint called Kilda. The Norsemen, who brought the little agile brown sheep to St. Kilda, named a well there very simply *kelda*, meaning a well. As the Norse speech died out to be replaced by the Gaelic the meaning of *kelda* was forgotten and the people added the Gaelic word for a well, *tobar*, to *kelda*—Tobar Childa. From which confusion sprang the mythical St. Kilda.

The proper name of St. Kilda is *hirta*, sometimes written *hirt* or *hiort*. *Hirt* possible means death, either because of the dangers of sailing amongst the rocks of this group of stacks and islands, or because it appeared the gateway to the dream islands of Tir-nan-Oig, the land of the ever young.

But the saint of North Rona, a little island forty miles north of the Butt of Lewis, was a real person. He was probably Ronan, abbot of Kingarth in Bute, who died in

737. This same Ronan is the saint of the old Teampull
Ronan at the Butt of Lewis. South Rona off the isle of
Raasay in the Inner Hebrides, however, is named from
the Norse *hraun-ey*, rough island.

No one lives upon North Rona now; like St. Kilda it
was too remote and it was evacuated. Over a thousand
calves of the grey Atlantic seal are reared there every
year; it is their greatest breeding ground. The ruins of
Ronan's little church still stand, a two-chambered building consisting of a little 'chancel', $11\frac{1}{2}$ feet by 7 feet,
roofed with flags originally and possibly of Celtic age,
and a later 'nave', $8\frac{3}{4}$ feet by 14 feet, which had a timber
roof. Nearby are a group of primitive semi-underground
dwellings, some of which have beehive cells in the thickness of their walls.

Even as the St. Kildans were always a race apart,
speaking a different manner of Gaelic and irritated beyond
measure if anyone laughed during the telling of one of
their stories when they came over to the Long Island, so
the Rona folk were distinct in habit and thought. Dean
Monro (1549) speaks of the Rona islanders as 'simple
people, scant of ony religione'. He also says that when
anyone died a spade and shovel were placed overnight
in the chapel, and in the morning the site for the grave
would be marked out for them.

Martin Martin (1695) gives a detailed account of the
customs of Rona at that date. It was one of the Rona
men who gave a sailor a shilling to buy him a wife in
Lewis. The old race died out, according to Martin, when
a swarm of rats arrived from nowhere and ate up all the
corn, added to which misfortune, some sailors landed
and killed the island's bull. This disaster, which was

followed by a new plantation on the island, took place
some 14 years before Martin wrote. The last person to
live on Rona seems to have been one Donald M'Leod,
nicknamed the King of Rona, who left the place in the
1840's.

The old tradition of the coming of St. Ronan to the
island relates how the saint, living at the Butt of Lewis,
grew tired of hearing the Eoropie women scolding one
another, and prayed to be taken out of that place. A
voice told him to go down to the shore, where he found
a great whale which bore him on its back to Rona. When
he arrived, he found the little island full of savage dog-like
beasts, but at the sight of the saint they backed into the
sea and were drowned, their claws scratching the rock
as they went. The marks, it is said, are still to be seen.

Another tradition tells how the Morrisons of Lewis
and the people of Sutherland disputed the ownership of
Rona. Eventually it was decided to race for the island.
The first arrivals would be the owners. The Sutherland
boat drew ahead of the Lewismen's and it seemed that
they would win. But a Morrison shot a burning arrow
and set the island grass on fire, thus getting a prior claim
on the land. This custom of laying claim to a piece of
land by lighting a fire is a Norse one; it seems they considered it sufficient to light a fire at the mouth of a river to
establish a claim to all the country that the river drained.

An exactly similar story of a boat race and a burning
arrow is told of the MacLeods of Harris and the MacDon-
alds of Sleat disputing the ownership of St. Kilda, the
Harrismen getting the island. And there is the story of
St. Moluag and St. Columba racing for the island of
Lismore and St. Moluag outwitting Columba by cutting

off his little finger and throwing it ashore in advance of his rival.

Sheep are still grazed on the Shiant Isles off the east coasts of Lewis and Harris, geologically an outpost of Skye. These also are connected with the old Celtic monks; the name is na h-Eileanan Sianta, the hallowed isles. There appear to have been at least two old chapels on the group.

But for the most fantastic collection of tradition and taboo one must look to the west of Lewis, twenty miles out from Uig, to where the Flannan Isles rise like stumpy teeth from the sea. They form a group of small islands and rocks; even the lighthouse there has a strange story, for at the beginning of the present century the three keepers vanished without trace. It is thought that one must have been swept off by a wave and the other two lost in trying to save him.

The lighthouse, the beehive houses of the Clan Mac-Phail and the little chapel are all upon the largest island of the group, Eilean Mor (Big Island). The rocks and islets round about number perhaps twenty, though the group is often called the Seven Hunters or the Seven Holy Isles. The chapel is only 5 feet by 7¾ feet inside, with drystone walls up to 30 inches thick. At the gables, the roof rises to 8 feet 10 inches. Flannan, the saint of the islands, is perhaps Flannan of Cell da Lua, of whom an account is given in the Book of Leinster. He may have been a contemporary of Brendan, but not much seems to be known about him. The name means 'red'.

John Morisone gives a description of the use the Lewis men made of the Flannans. His account was written between 1678 and 1688. He says that:

There are seven Islands 15 myles Westward from the Lews, called the Isles of Sant Flannan, lying closs together; wherin there a cheaple, where Sant Flandan himself lived ane heremit. To those in the summertyme some countriemen goes; and bringeth home great store of seafouls and feathers. The way they kill the fowls is, one goeth and taketh a road 10 or 12 foot long, and setts his back to a rock or craig, and as the fouls flieth by, he smitheth them continuallie, and he hes ane other attending to catch all that falls to the ground; for the fouls flee there so thick that those who are beneath them cannot see the firmament. These Isles are not inhabited, but containeth a quantitie of wilde sheep verie fatt and weel fleeced. When the people goe there, they use everie two men to be Comerads. They hold it a breach of the sanctitie of the place (for they count it holier than anie other) if any man take a drink of water unknown to his comerade or eat ane egg or legg of ane foull, yea take a snuff of tobacco: It is for certaintie that upon a tyme a Countriefellow being sent there and left in it, be reason he could not be keept from theft and robberie and so on a time the fyre went out with him, without which he could not live, and so despaired of lyfe and since he saw that there was no remead, he betook him to pray both to God and the Sainct of the Island as they term'd it and by night being fallen in a deep sleep, he sees a man come to him well clade saying aryse, betake thee unto the Altar and there thou shall find a peate in fyre, for the Lord hath heard they prayer. So he arose and accordingly found the fyre, which he preserved untill he was taken home, and henceforth he proved as honest a man as was in the Countrie.

Rona, too, has a story of the miraculous rekindling of a fire which had gone out. In these places fire had to be carefully preserved by smooring the peats each night. On the main islands a lighted peat used to be carried up to the shielings to start the fires.

The taboos of the Flannans were very complicated. Obviously the islands were held in very great veneration; equally obviously they were held in this veneration long before Saint Flannan arrived there. Martin Martin (1695) relates how the Lewismen would make towards the islands with an east wind; but if before or at landing the wind turn westerly, they hoist up sail, and steer directly home again. If any of their crew is a novice, and not versed in the customs of the place, he must be instructed perfectly in all the punctilioes observed here before landing; and to prevent inconveniences that they think may ensue upon the transgression of the least nicety observed here, every novice is always joined with another, that can instruct him all the time of their fowling: so that all the boat's crew are matched in this manner. After their landing, they fasten the boat to the sides of a rock, and then fix a wooden ladder, by laying a stone at the foot of it, to prevent its falling into the sea; and when they are got up into the island, all of them uncover their heads, and make a turn sun-ways round, thanking God for their safety. The first injunction given after landing, is not to ease nature in that place where the boat lies, for that they reckon a crime of the highest nature, and of dangerous consequence to all their crew; for they have a great regard to that very piece of rock upon which they first set their feet, after escaping the danger of the ocean.

The biggest of these islands is called Island-More; it has the ruins of a chapel dedicated to St. Flannan, from whom the island derives its name. When they are come within about 20 paces of the altar, they all strip themselves of their upper garments at once; and their upper clothes being laid upon a stone, which stands there on purpose for that use, all the crew pray three times before they begin fowling: the first day they say the first prayer, advancing towards the chapel upon their knees; the second prayer is said as they go round the chapel; the third is said hard by or at the chapel; and this is their morning service. Their vespers are performed with the like number of prayers. Another rule is that it is absolutely unlawful to kill a fowl with a stone, for that they reckon a great barbarity, and directly contrary to ancient custom.

It is also unlawful to kill a fowl before they ascend by the ladder. It is absolutely unlawful to call the island of St. Kilda (which lies thirty leagues southward) by its proper Irish name Hirt, but only the high country. They must not so much as once name the islands in which they are following by the ordinary name Flannan, but only the country. There are several other things that must not be called by their common names, e.g., Visk, which in the language of the natives

T

signifies Water, they called Burn; a Rock, which in their language is Creg, must here be called Cruey, i.e., hard; Shore in their language, expressed by Claddach, must here be called Vah, i.e., a Cave; Sour in their language is expressed Gort, but must be here called Gaire, i.e., Sharp; Slippery, which is expressed Bog, must be called Soft; and several other things to this purpose. They account it also unlawful to kill a fowl after evening-prayers. There is an ancient custom by which the crew is obliged not to carry home any sheep-suet, let them kill ever so many sheep in these islands. One of their principal customs is not to steal or eat anything unknown to their partner, else the transgressor (they say) will certainly vomit it up; which they reckon a just judgment. When they have loaded their boat sufficiently with sheep, fowls, eggs, down, fish, &c., they make the best of their way homeward. It is observed of the sheep of these islands that they are exceeding fat, and have long horns.

Martin was sceptic enough to ask one of the Lewismen if he prayed as often and as fervently at home as he did on the Flannans. The man said no, he did not, but that the islands were so holy that a man became more disposed to devotion there.

CHAPTER XXI

CHURCH SITE AND SCULPTURED STONE

THROUGHOUT the Hebrides, from the most populated islands to the remote outposts like Flannan and Shiant, one comes constantly upon ancient church sites, with or without actual ruins, and, less frequently, upon sculptured slabs and crosses. Their story is part of that of the history of the Outer Isles, and many of the sites date back to the early days of the Celtic Church in Scotland.

To understand the carved stones and ruined chapels of the Long Island in their proper historical setting, one needs to look outside the Hebrides, not only to Scotland but to Europe and to Ireland. The story began in southern Scotland when a young Briton of the name of Ninian went southward to Rome in the days when the Empire was breaking up.

When Ninian had finished his education in Europe he came back to the north to preach the Gospel. But before he returned to Scotland he spent some time with St. Martin of Tours and from him learned the monastic ideas which were to permeate the whole of the Celtic Church.

In A.D. 397 St. Ninian was building his first church,

Candida Casa (the White House), at Whithorn in Galloway. From this centre Ninian travelled the length of Scotland. His routes can still be followed because of the rather clannish habit of the Celtic Church of naming new foundations after the particular saint who founded them. There are many Kilninians, Ninian's Church (Gaelic, *cille*, spelt '*Kil*' in English, a church), scattered up the east coast of Scotland.

The Venerable Bede records that Ninian converted the southern Picts, Columba (Columcille) the northern, but Bede was thinking in terms of Ptolemy's geography, which twists all Scotland round at right angles to England. His south is our east. Ninian did not stop short at the Highland line, he bypassed it by the eastern lowlands.

This was the line which the Roman legions took on their expedition to the shores of the Moray Firth. It avoids the one great barrier to movement about the Highlands, the north-south mountain range called Drum Albyn (the Ridge of Scotland) which extends from Cape Wrath to Loch Lomond, as well as the lesser barrier of the Mounth (commonly called to-day the Grampians) which juts out from the line of Drum Albyn toward Aberdeen.

Ninian's foundations can be traced along this line: Stirling, Arbirlot, Dunnottar, Methlick, Glen Urquhart on Loch Ness-side, Navidale and then across the sea to Orkney and even Shetland. Dunrossness in Shetland has an ancient graveyard known as St. Ringan's Isle—Ringan is ordinary Scots for Ninian. At Dunrossness was found an Ogam inscription which is supposed to read ' . . . the enclosure of the son (or family) of Nan the Baptiser'. Nan is a British form of Ninian.

This lowland route up the eastern seaboard of Scotland was to become the high road of the Celtic missionaries from Candida Casa. Already Ninian had turned towards the Hebrides. There is no doubt that Kilninian on Loch Ness in Glen Urquhart is one of his foundations, and it lies on the great through valley, the Great Glen, which is the main crossing of Drum Albyn from east to west. Off this great pass, other glens like those of Garry and Moriston provide further easy access through the mountains to the west coast and the Isles.

Did Ninian reach the Hebrides? I rather think he may have done. There is a Kilninian in Mull on the shore of Loch na Keal which appears to me to be an ancient site. It is placed snugly near the sea, upon fairly good land and with a fine spring of water beside it, called St. Ninian's Well.

Candida Casa also sent missions to Wales and across the sea to Ireland. Caranoc, the first martyr of Ireland, was one of Ninian's companions. He travelled as far north as Turriff in Aberdeenshire, then crossed to Ireland, where he is said by tradition to have baptised St. Patrick.

The Hebrides thus received the faith from two directions, from Candida Casa by the east coast route and the Great Glen and its branches, and by the sea route from Ireland. The Saint Donnan of the Kildonnans in South Uist and Lewis who was martyred in Eigg was the leader of the last big mission from Candida Casa in c. A.D. 580 Donnan's route was by the east coast and then up the Great Glen and Glen Garry to the west.

The country now known as Scotland was not then inhabited by Scots. In the north were the Picts, speaking a species of Gaelic allied to Welsh, in the south, around

Strath Clyde and Whithorn, the Britons; upon the east
coast, in what is now East Lothian and Berwick, the
pagan Angles were settling.

Across in Ireland there seem to have been Picts also,
and the Scots, who spoke a different species of Gaelic.
The Scots took ship across to what is now Argyll, the
land west of Drum Albyn (Bede's 'northern' Scotland)
and founded the little kingdom of Dalriada.

The settling by the Scots in Argyll did not meet with
approval by the Picts, who attempted to push the colonists back into the sea, or at least to make them acknowledge Pictish overlordship. It is a curious quirk of fate
that this small settlement of Scots eventually gave their
name to the whole of the country now called Scotland,
imposing their nationality upon it, while the once widespread and powerful Picts seem to have vanished like a
dream. Only traces of the Pictish variety of Gaelic occur
in place names along the eastern shores of Scotland; the
Gaelic of the Highlands and of most of the place names
is all of the Scottish variety.

It may well be that the little Scottish colony was saved
by one man's genius. That man was Columcille, Columba
of Iona. In A.D. 563, when he came first to Iona, the
small settlement of Dalriada was in a very poor way. Its
king, Gabhran MacDomongart, had been killed in battle
with the Picts, and his successor, Conall MacComgall,
forced to abandon the title of king for that of toshach
(vassal) to the Pictish king.

Columba was a Scot and a politician. From his monastery on Iona he seems to have kept a hold on Scottish
affairs, consolidating the colony's position and going up
the Great Glen to Inverness to treat with the Pictish

king Brude and obtain recognition of Dalriada as an independent kingdom.

But because Columba was a Scot, his missionary efforts were confined to Dalriada, to Argyllshire, to Mull and its adjacent islands. He did not even speak the Pictish sort of Gaelic. The Outer Hebrides were outside the Scottish area of influence and it seems fairly certain that all the dedications to Columba out there are later and not foundations of the saint himself. He does, however, seem to have visited Skye and Canna.

The political relations between Pict and Scot were reflected in a similar division in the Celtic Church. Irish Picts also sailed across to the Western Highlands and Islands and there seems to have been little love lost between them and the Scots. The story of how Columba raced St. Moluag for Lismore and was outwitted by Moluag's trick may not be strictly true, but Columba's temper and curses upon the occasion are probably an accurate gauge of the spirit of the times.

Moluag of Lismore was a remarkable man. He settled there a year before Columba came to Iona, and, being a Pict, was able to move much more freely about Scotland than Columba. His foundations, traced by place names, lead up the Great Glen and then north and south along the eastern lowlands. In the other direction, he sailed the Minch and founded churches in the Outer Hebrides, of which that at the Butt of Lewis is the most famous. He also visited Skye and Raasay. He died in Nairnshire in A.D. 592.

It is interesting to compare the sites of Iona and Lismore, both fertile Hebridean islands off the west coast. Lismore is, I think, the better from the agricultural point of view, and it is quite probable that Columba would have liked to have had it rather than Iona. It is also more sheltered and less likely to be storm-bound.

Both islands, however, have the same strategic position. Both are at the mouth of the Great Glen, the main east-west route across the Highlands, and both are set on the main sea routes serving the Western Highlands and Isles as well as on the route to Ireland.

One of the most interesting islands in this connexion is Tiree. Tiree is a very fertile island, almost all level land with good spreads of the sandy machair which was ideal for growing corn. Iona had a settlement there and it served as their main home farm. So, too, had Moluag from Lismore a holding on fertile Tiree. The sites of old churches are scattered throughout the island, upon all the fertile stretches, and if relations were strained between Columba and Moluag when they were in their separate islands, it seems more than likely that there was a certain amount of rivalry in Tiree, parcelled out between Pict and Scot. Adamnan, in his life of Columba, relates how the Iona settlement at Soroby in Tiree alone escaped from an outbreak of plague which ravaged all the other monasteries there. Perhaps it was less Columba's prayers that saved the Soroby folk than their normal habit of avoiding their Pictish neighbours!

Another saint who travelled widely in the Hebrides was Maelrubha, who came across from Ireland in A.D. 671, founding his great monastery at Applecross in A.D. 673. He journeyed all over the Highlands and was also a great sailor, making many journeys to Skye and to the Outer Isles, founding churches in a number of places there.

The Norse invasions carried fire and sword into the Celtic monasteries; Iona was ravaged time and again. However, even in the Outer Isles, where the effect of the pagan Norse invasion was most pronounced, the memory of the churches founded by the Celtic saints still lived, and as the Norse themselves became Christian a Norseman could set up his memorial stone at the ancient church of Kilbarr in Barra. Even if the Northmen killed off most of the Celtic inhabitants of the Outer Isles, they did not do it thoroughly enough for the early Celtic Church sites to be lost sight of, as might have been expected.

The sculptured stones tell the same story of the divide between Pict and Scot. The early carved stones of Scotland fall into two groups, one of Irish affinity and related to Dalriada, the other Pictish and connected with the Candida Casa routes.

Round about Candida Casa the Roman influence was still strong and the earliest monuments of that district include ones with Latin inscriptions. The cross is not the typical symbol but the Chi-Rho monogram. East of Drum Albyn this Chi-Rho monogram was slowly developed into the wheel cross. This wheel cross also appears in Raasay, at Moluag's church, and of course in the area of Pictish influence. Ireland meantime developed the elaborate Celtic cross, and this was brought across to Dalriada, where it is the typical design; from Iona it spread through the Western Highlands.

The art of the Picts east of Drum Albyn, the people to whom the Candida Casa missions mainly went, consisted till about A.D. 800 of carvings upon natural, undressed boulders. The carvings include lively portraits of animals, bulls, boars, horses, stags, tigers, wolves, eagles, serpents and fishes. There are also the mysterious Pictish symbols. These include designs which have been called for convenience the crescent, the mirror, the comb, the double disc. There is also a curious beast with long jaws and scroll feet. Obviously these symbols must have had a meaning; very probably they are a sort of picture language telling of the person whom the stone commemorates. But their meaning is entirely lost and it is impossible to make any definite guess. The mirror and comb might be feminine symbols.

Originally the symbols may have been purely pagan, but they are found combined with the cross, as, for instance, on the elaborate stone at Rosemarkie said to mark St. Moluag's grave, so that many of them belong to Christian times. The symbol stones are found entirely east of Drum Albyn, with the exception of one or two outliers west of Drum Albyn but outside the influence of Dalriada. Thus one has been found in Skye, and in the Outer Isles two have been discovered—on Pabbay, south of Barra, and in Benbecula.

The Picts began to trim their stones after A.D. 800, and from then till about A.D. 1000 the cross was carved on a trimmed slab, surrounded with the symbols and groups of figures and animals, all intervening spaces being filled up with elaborate fret and interlace designs. The Moluag cross at Rosemarkie belongs to this period. Some of the carvings are of scenes from the Bible; others seem to be inspired by stories from the old bestiaries.

Scotland at last became a united country, and the Pictish symbols and language vanished. From A.D. 1000 to the twelfth and thirteenth centuries the art of the carved stones is Irish and Scottish, represented by the great standing crosses of Iona, of Soroby in Tiree, of Keills in Knapdale. The Outer Isles seem to have no notable examples of these Irish-Scottish High Crosses, though one should remember the Kilpheader cross in North Uist. Probably others existed but have been lost or destroyed.

These standing crosses are carved all over with figure groups and interlace work. The idea was to divide the object to be decorated into panels and cover each one with some form of ornament. Spaces not filled with figure groups have designs of interlace, fret, spirals and intertwining foliage, together with ribbon animals, creatures whose bodies and legs are immensely long and interlaced and criss-crossed in imitation of wicker work.

Most of the carved stones of the Outer Isles belong to the period between the twelfth century and the Reformation. The country of the Lordship of the Isles, carrying on the traditions both political and artistic of Dalriada, was the scene of the flowering of West Highland Celtic art. There are many notable crosses of this period, though not in the Outer Isles, and also recumbent slabs, of which a few remain in the old graveyards of the Long Island.

These recumbent slabs commemorate local chieftains and ecclesiastics and fall into two groups. Some have the figure of the person commemorated carved upon them, life size. In the Outer Isles there are the MacLeod slab at St. Columba's at Eye in Lewis and the monuments in Rodil church. Others have a sword surrounded by foliage. Or the slab may have a purely formal design of interlacing foliage and strapwork. The sword design is perhaps the commonest, and it is supposed that the swords, which have a strong individuality, are portraits of their owners' real weapons. There may be panels with very attractive carvings of Highland galleys or hunting scenes. Inscriptions are rather rare.

It is a curious commentary on lowland ideas of Highland savagery at this period of history that the Western Highlands and Islands could and did produce such a highly finished and civilised art form. It was not even a matter of stones being carved in one or two centres like Iona; it was an art known generally, and local trends and differences can readily be seen on the stones which still remain in Highland graveyards.

The Reformation put an end to the making of these crosses and slabs. However, in Inchkenneth, an island off the coast of Mull with a ruined chapel on a site originally chosen by St. Kenneth, a contemporary and friend of St. Columba, there is a curious survival of the style. This is a slab carved in the typical West Highland manner, with a life size figure. The attitude is medieval, but the figure is seventeenth century and wears a steel bonnet, a breastplate and the kilt. Instead of holding a spear, he grasps a cannon ball in his right hand.

If the rocks of the West Highlands and the Hebrides were very suitable for the carving of crosses and slabs, they were not so suitable for the quarrying of large amounts of stone to make large or elaborate church buildings, nor indeed were the Hebridean resources of labour and money probably ever equal to such an undertaking. The typical ruined chapel of the Hebrides is very small, built of undressed boulders as often as not, and originally covered with a roof of thatch. The only stone vaulting

to be found in the Outer Isles in a church building is at
Teampull na Trionaid. Iona Cathedral itself is a fairly
small building, like Rodil in Harris, which was modelled
on Iona's design. The only two buildings of any size
in the Outer Isles besides Rodil are St. Columba's, at
Eye in Lewis, and Teampull na Trionaid in North Uist.
St. Columba's and Teampull na Trionaid were monastic
churches and both belonged to the parent monastery of
Inchaffray near Crieff in Perthshire. Inchaffray's own
foundation, incidentally, dates back to the days of the
Celtic Church. Rodil is also described as having been a
monastery.

As in Ireland, the small churches and chapels are
sometimes grouped together. There is a group of old
chapels at Howmore in South Uist, another at Kilbarr
in Barra. There is another very interesting group, now
of two, but originally of three, at Kirkapoll in Tiree.
But although these buildings are very primitive and
simple in appearance, they are of medieval date and none
can be traced back to the early days of the Celtic Church.
Authentic ruins of the Celtic Church are to be found only
in North Rona and on the Garvellach Islands in the Firth
of Lorne.

Most of the Celtic Church buildings would be of
timber, small and of simple construction. In the Isles
timber was not always available, and so the people turned
to stone, building themselves beehive huts like those of
the Lewis and Harris shielings, and small beehive vaulted
churches.

I doubt that any of the beehive shielings of the
Hebrides date back to the Celtic Church, though
they are undoubtedly very old. They are, however, of

the same type as the buildings put up by the early saints.

The small stone vaulted chapel on North Rona can with fair certainty be dated from the times of the Celtic Church, and the chapel on Eileach an Naoimh in the Garvellach group can definitely be dated so. Here it is interesting to recall that Ninian's first church at Whithorn was called Candida Casa, 'White House', because it was a substantial stone and lime building. To this day in the Hebrides, White House means a stone and lime slated building in distinction to the Black House of drystone masonry.

The Celtic chapel on Eileach an Naoimh in the Firth of Lorne, a site which had associations with St. Brendan and St. Columba as well as other saints, is a small rectangular drystone building measuring 21 feet 6 inches by 11 feet 3 inches. The walls are beautifully built of flaggy schists and are 3 feet thick. They now stand just about 6 feet 6 inches high, enough to show the beginning of the convergence which made a stone beehive vaulted roof. There is a single doorway at the west end and a single window in the east wall. This window is very tiny, but has both an inside and an outside splay, so that it admits the maximum of light. It is possible that this may be the very same building, or at least the site of it, in which the Mass of the saints as related by Adamnan was celebrated. Saints Comgall, Cormac and Brendan were present, and Columba, who said the Mass, was, so the story goes, seen by Brendan with a ball of fire rising from his head.

The site of the Celtic monastery on Eileach an Naoimh is very interesting. Though rocky, the little island is very fertile, and all available ground has been cultivated

in the past in lazy beds amongst the little crags. The
monastery is placed in a sheltered hollow in the middle
of the island, with a landing place on the rocky coast
just below, and a good spring of water, St. Columba's
Well, close by. Beside the chapel there is an underground
house, of beehive type but roofed with large flags, which
reminded me of the dairies attached to the beehive
houses in the Lewis hills and which was probably used
for some such purpose. There are some rickles of stones
which may be collapsed beehive houses, and a structure
called the monastery but latterly used and reconstructed
for a cattle fank. It has, however, fairly obviously been
some large house or group of houses in the past. In
addition there is a kiln for drying grain and a winnowing
house—these may be fairly recent and belong to the not
so very distant period when people still crofted on the
island.

Some way off from the sheltered hollow of the chapel
and monastery is a very large double beehive house.
This building, of which about half remains, consists of
two big beehive houses built side by side with a com-
municating door between them. Each has a door to the
outside; the bigger of the two also appears to have had
a window through its wall. They are much larger beehives than any I explored in Lewis and one can stand
upright anywhere inside.

It is tempting to date the beehive houses with the
little chapel and suppose them part of the Celtic Church
settlement. However, the facts are that they are some
little way off from the group of buildings round the
church, and may belong to a slightly later period.

The graveyard beside the monastery had, when the

island was visited by MacCulloch, the geologist, early in the nineteenth century, many sculptured stones of West Highland type. Only one of these, very much worn and now lying beside the little chapel, is still to be seen, though many may be buried under the luxuriant growth of meadow sweet and rush. The island has a second old burial ground in which stone coffins of an early type were discovered.

The Garvellach remains give one some idea of the sort of structures which once existed throughout the Hebrides during the period of the Celtic Church.

These communities would be self-supporting, and the early church sites were usually on good land for this reason. They were also usually situated near existing townships, which would be similarly placed for the same purpose. In the Outer Isles most of the church sites are near the sea, for the Christian period does not ante-date the formation of the central peat mosses, amongst which only the Megalithic monuments are to be found.

There remain the Long Island outposts and their connexion with the Celtic saints: rocky islets like Shiant and Flannan. These got their connexion with the saints from the latters' custom of withdrawing to lonely islets, either for a time or permanently, for prayer and meditation. To me, landing on some sun-drenched rock in the Atlantic, or picturing the snugness of a beehive house with the winter gale screaming over it, there has always seemed to be a lot to be said for the idea!

The old church sites and burial grounds in the Long Island fall into two groups: those still connected by their name and dedication with a saint of the Celtic Church who actually founded the original church, and those of the post-Norse, post-Celtic Church period, when the custom of dedicating churches to the saints had been introduced. Some of these may be re-dedications on old sites.

Of the later dedications, there are several to St. Michael in the Long Island, on whose day the horse races were held. I noted that several of these churches of St. Michael are placed upon similar sites, upon windswept headlands facing the Atlantic.

There are also a number of dedications to St. Columba in the Long Island. Perhaps some of Columba's fame had a political motive. He became the saint of Dalriada because the Scots when they became the dominant element in the Scottish scene were eager to commemorate their own national hero rather than any of the Pictish saints. Columba himself never seems to have penetrated to the Outer Isles, but nearly all the Hebridean prayers and hymns seem to include a petition to 'kind Columcille'.

BIBLIOGRAPHY

THE following is a list of books and papers which I found useful in compiling this book. In them will be found detailed accounts of the archaeology, geology, history, etc., summarised in the present text.

Abbreviations: *P.S.A.S.* Proceedings of the Society of Antiquaries of Scotland.

Trans. Inver. Gael. Soc., Transactions of the Inverness Gaelic Society.

Anderson, Joseph. 'Notice of Dun Stron Duin, Bernera, Barra Head.' *P.S.A.S.* Vol. 27, pp. 341-346. 1892-93.

Baden-Powell, Donald and Elton, Charles. 'On the Relation between a Raised Beach and an Iron Age Midden on the Island of Lewis.' *P.S.A.S.* Vol. 71, pp. 347-365. 1936-37.

Bathymetrical Survey of the Fresh Water Lochs of Scotland. Edinburgh, 1910. Vol. 1, Part 2. Lochs of Lewis, Benbecula and North Uist.

Beveridge, Erskine. 'Earth-Houses at Garry Iochdrach and Bac Mhic Connain in North Uist.' *P.S.A.S.* Vol. 66, pp. 32-66. 1931-32. 'Excavation of an Earth-House at Foshigarry, and a Fort, Dun Thomaidh, in North Uist.' *P.S.A.S.* Vol. 65, pp. 299-357. 1930-31. *North Uist*, William Brown, Edinburgh, 1911.

Blaikie, W. Biggar. *Itinerary of Prince Charles Edward Stuart, 1745-46.* Scottish History Society.

Blundel, Odo. *The Catholic Highlands of Scotland*, Vol. 2. Edinburgh, 1917.

Book of Barra. Compiled by various authors. Routledge, London, 1936.

Carmichael, Alexander. 'Grazing and Agrestic Customs of the Outer Hebrides.' *Crofter Royal Commission Report*, pp. 451-482. Edinburgh, 1884.

Childe, V. Gordon. *The Prehistory of Scotland.* London, 1935. *Scotland before the Scots.* London, 1946.

Curwen, E. Cecil. 'Prehistoric Agriculture in Britain.' *Antiquity*, Vol. 1, pp. 261-289. 1927.

Edwards, Arthur J. H. 'Report on the Excavation of an Earth-House at Galston, Borve, Lewis.' *P.S.A.S.* Vol. 58, pp. 185-203. 1923-24.

Fraser Darling, F. *Crofting Agriculture.* Edinburgh, 1945.

Fraser, G. K. 'Peat Deposits of Scotland.' Part 1, Wartime Pamphlet No. 36. Geological Survey and Museum, London, 1943.

Gregory, Donald. *History of the Western Highlands and Isles of Scotland.* Edinburgh, 1836.

Gregory, J. W. *The Nature and Origin of Fiords.* London, 1913.

Harrison, J. W. Heslop. 'A Preliminary Flora of the Outer Hebrides.' *Proc. Univ. Durham Phil. Soc.* Vol. 10, Part 4, pp. 228-273. December, 1941.

Henderson, George. *The Norse Influence on Celtic Scotland.* Glasgow, 1910. *Survivals in Belief Among the Celts.* Glasgow, 1911.

Jehu, T. J. and Craig, R. M. 'The Geology of the Outer Hebrides.' In five parts, published in Vols. 53, 54, 55 and 57 of the *Transactions of the Royal Society of Edinburgh.*

Lacaille, A. D. 'A Stone Industry, Potsherds and a Bronze Pin from Valtos, Uig, Lewis.' *P.S.A.S.* Vol. 71, pp. 279-296. 1936-37.

Liddel, Peter. 'Note of an Underground Structure at Gress, near Stornoway, and other Ancient Remains in the Island of Lewis.' *P.S.A.S.* Vol. 10, pp. 741-744. 1872-74.

Lindsay Scott, W. and Phemister, J. 'Local Manufacture of Neolithic Pottery.' *P.S.A.S.* Vol. 76, pp. 130-132. 1941-42.

Lindsay Scott, W. 'Neolithic Pottery Kilns in the Hebrides.' *Man*, Vol. 39, p. 25. 1939.

Lyon in Mourning. Bishop Forbes' Collection of Documents relating to Prince Charles and the Forty-Five. Scottish History Society.

MacFarlane, A. M. 'Sea Myths and Lore of the Hebrides.' *Trans. Inverness Scientific Society and Field Club.* Vol. 9, pp. 360-309. 1918-25.

MacFarlane's Geographical Collections. Vol. 2. Scottish History Society.

MacKellar, Mary. 'The Shieling: Its Traditions and Songs.' In two parts. *Trans. Inver. Gael. Soc.* Vol. 14, pp. 135-153, and Vol. 15, pp. 151-171.

MacKenzie, Donald A. *Scottish Folk-Lore and Folk-Life.* London, 1935.

MacKenzie, Kenneth S. 'An Economical History of the Hebrides or Western Islands of Scotland.' *Trans. Inver. Gael. Soc.* Vol. 24, pp. 120-139. 1899-1901.

MacKenzie, W. C. *The Book of the Lews.* Paisley, 1919. *History of the Outer Hebrides.* Paisley, 1903. *The Western Isles.* Paisley, 1932.

MacKenzie, W. M. 'Notes on Certain Structures of Archaic Type in the Island of Lewis—Beehive Houses, Duns and Stone Circles.' *P.S.A.S.* Vol. 38, pp. 173-204. 1903-4.

MacKenzie, W. 'The Gaelic Incantations and Charms of the Hebrides.' *Trans. Inver. Gael. Soc.* Vol. 18, pp. 97-182. 1891-92.

MacLeod, D. J. 'An Account of a Find of Ornaments of the Viking Time from Valtos, Uig, in the Island of Lewis.' *P.S.A.S.* Vol. 50, pp. 181-189. 1915-16.

Martin, Martin. *A Description of the Western Islands of Scotland.* c. 1695. Edition of MacKay, Stirling, 1934.

Mitchell, Arthur. 'On Various Superstitions in the North-West Highlands and Islands of Scotland, especially in relation to Lunacy. *P.S.A.S.* Vol. 4, pp. 251-288. 1860-62.

Monro, Sir Donald. *A Description of the Western Isles of Scotland called Hybrides.* c. 1549. Edition of MacKay, Stirling, 1934.

Muir, T. S. *Ecclesiological Notes on Some of the Islands of Scotland.* Edinburgh, 1885.

Munro, Neil. *Children of Tempest.*

New Naturalist. A Journal of British Natural History. Section on the Western Isles in first volume (1948). Edited by James Fisher.

New Statistical Account of Scotland. Vol. 14. Ross and Cromarty: Inverness-shire, 1845.

Origines Parochiales Scotiae. Vol. 2, Part 1. Bannatyne Club, Edinburgh, 1854.

Parker, J. A. 'The Outer Hebrides.' In *Scottish Mountaineering Club Guide*, The Islands of Scotland (excluding Skye). Edinburgh, 1934.

Phemister, J. 'The Northern Highlands.' *British Regional Geology.* H.M. Stationery Office, Edinburgh, 1936.

Robertson, J. L. 'Log of the *Dutillet*.' *Trans. Inver. Gael. Soc.* Vol. 26, pp. 11-30. 1904-07.

Royal Commission on the Ancient and Historical Monuments of Scotland. 9th Report. 'The Outer Hebrides, Skye and the Small Isles.' Edinburgh, 1928.

Scott, W. Lindsay. 'The Chambered Cairn of Clettraval, North Uist.' *P.S.A.S.* Vol. 69, pp. 480-536. 1934-35.

Statistical Account of Scotland. Volumes 19 (1797), 13 (1794) and 10 (1794).

Thomas, F. W. L. 'On the Duns of the Outer Hebrides.' *Archaeologica Scotica.* Vol. 5, Part III, pp. 365-415. 1890.

'Notice of Beehive Houses in Harris and Lewis; with Traditions of the "Each Uisge", or Water Horse, connected therewith.' *P.S.A.S.* Vol. 3, pp. 127-144. 1857-60.

'On the Primitive Dwellings and Hypogea of the Outer Hebrides.' *P.S.A.S.* Vol. 7, pp. 153-195. 1866-68.

'Traditions of the MacAulays of Lewis.' *P.S.A.S.* Vol. 14, pp. 363-431. 1879-80.

'Traditions of the Morrisons (Clan MacGhillemhuire), Hereditary Judges of Lewis.' *P.S.A.S.* Vol. 12, pp. 503-556. 1876-78.

Watson, W. J. *Place Names of Ross and Cromarty.* Inverness, 1904. *The History of the Celtic Place-Names of Scotland.* Edinburgh, 1926.

INDEX OF PLACE NAMES

Achmore, 167

Aignish, 163

Aird Mhor, 237, 263, 265

An Carra, 100, 208

Ard a' Mhòrain, 140

Aurora Borealis, 25

Baleshare, 147

Balivanish, 113

Barpa Langass, 199

Barra, 22, 94, 254

Barvas, 167, 171

Bealach a'Chaolais, 95

Beehive Huts, 259, 269, 285

Beinn a'Bhaile, 146

Beinn Bragor, 168

Beinn Eoligarry, 28

Beinn Mhor (South Uist), 92, 99

Beinn Ruigh Choinnich, 92

Benbecula, 110, 262, 282

Berneray (Barra Head), 61, 223

Berneray (North Uist), 137

Borve (Benbecula), 113

Bragor, 169, 217

Brochs, 213

Bun Abhainn-Eadar, 189

Butt of Lewis, 172, 269

Caisteal a'Mhorfhear, 224

Caisteal Bheagram, 76

Caisteal Odhair, 223

Callanish, 198, 216

Calvay Castle, 76

Carinish, 133

Cas Chrom, 252

Chicken Head, 165

Cille-Bharra (Kilbarr), 25, 30, 281, 285

Cille Bhrianain (Vatersay), 47

Cille Donnan (Kildonnan), 74

Cill Mhoire, 147

Clach an Trushal, 209

Clach Mhic Leoid, 191, 208

Clettraval, 200

Clisham, 187, 227

Coir Fhinn, 201, 208

Corodale, 107

Crannogs, 166, 225

Duns of the Outer Hebrides, 211

Dun an Sticer, 137, 221

Dun Ban (Barra), 223

Dun Ban (North Uist), 226

Dun Borve, 221

Dun Buidhe (Benbecula), 112, 212

Dun Carloway, 216, 220

Dun Loch an Duna, 217

Dun Nighean Righ Lochlainn, 225

Dun Raouill, 77

Dun Torcuill, 136, 222

Earth Houses, 96, 105, 147, 166
Eaval, 125, 129
Eilean an Tighe, 138, 200
Eriskay, 78, 94, 136, 248
Eye (Lewis), 160, 283

Feaveallach, 92, 105
Fife Adventurers, 18
Flannan Islands, 262, 271, 288
Foshigarry, 149
Frith, 122

Gallan Head, 181
Garvellach Islands, 285
Garynahine, 262
Gearraidh na h-Airdhe Moire, 264, 265
Geiraha, 167, 224
Giura, 240
Glen Meavaig, 233
Gress, 165, 201
Griminish Point, 143, 149, 223
Gulf Stream, 86, 156

Habost, 178
Harlaw, 16
Harris, 184, 231, 237, 262
Heaval, 38
Hecla (Mingulay), 56
Hecla (South Uist), 92, 99, 106
Howmore, 73, 285

Innse Gall, 2, 14
Inverlochy, 17
Iona, 113, 161, 192, 278, 285

Kelp, 254
Kiessimul Castle, 36, 40, 212, 217, 226
Kinloch Resort, 236, 248

Kintail, Mackenzie of, 18, 218

Leum MacNicol, 105
Lewis, 94, 157, 237, 257, 262
Lewisian gneiss, 9, 93, 188, 232
Liniquie, 70, 93
Loch Bee, 93
Loch Boisdale, 91
Loch Caravat, 226
Loch Eport, 125, 128, 206, 252
Loch Eynort, 92, 97, 98
Loch Hacklett, 151
Loch Hunder, 130, 222
Loch Maddy, 127, 132
Loch na Caiginn, 225
Loch na Craobhaig, 263
Loch na Geireann, 138
Loch Portain, 150, 224
Loch Raonasgail, 245, 265
Loch Resort, 236, 265
Loch Scadavay, 127
Loch Seaforth, 185
Loch Skiport, 92
Loch Snigisclett, 97
Loch Suainaval, 181
Loch Tamanavay, 229, 237, 263
Loch Tealasavay, 228, 237, 241, 242, 264
Lordship of the Isles, 13, 283
Luchruban, 173

Machair Leathann, 138, 139, 148
MacLeods of Lewis, 161
Mealista, 181, 195
Mealisval, 181, 227, 245
Megalithic culture, 11, 198
Mills, 255
Mingary, 99
Mingulay, 54

Monach Islands, 147
Muldoanich, 50

North Lee, 125
North Rona, 262, 268, 285
North Uist, 94, 125, 132, 262
Nunton, 113

Ormaclett Castle, 74, 94
Orosay, 39

Pabbay (Barra), 52, 282
Park, 185
Pobull Fhinn, 206, 208
Port na Copa, 144
Port nan Long, 137
Prince Charles in the Outer Hebrides, 63, 79, 107, 114, 186

Rainigadale, 248
Risteal, 252
Rocabarra, 41
Rodil, 192, 283, 285
Roneval, 196
Rueval, 110, 112, 118
Run Rig, 250

Saint Barr, 25
Saint Bridget, 103, 120, 140
Saint Catan, 160
Saint Clement, 192
Saint Columba, 88, 103, 120, 124, 270, 278, 286
Saint Donnan, 74, 277
Saint Flannan, 271
Saint Maelrubha, 176, 178, 197, 280
Saint Moluag, 176, 270, 279
Saint Ninian, 275
Saint Olaf, 166

Saint Ronan, 268
St. Kilda, 101, 156, 251, 262, 268
Sandray, 51, 94
Shiant Islands, 5, 271, 288
Shielings, 257
Sloc-a-Choire, 143
Sloc Roe, 143
Smooring prayer, 123
South Lee, 125, 262
South Uist, 64, 94, 262
Stornoway, 157
Strone Scourst, 233
Strone Ulladale, 234
Stulaval (Harris), 235
Stulaval (South Uist), 92, 95, 150
Stuley Island, 94, 96

Tamanavay, 239, 247, 256
Taransay, 197
Tarbert (Harris), 188
Teampull Ioin Bragor, 171
Teampull Mholuidh, 175
Teampull na Trionaid, 134, 285
Tertiary rocks, 9
Tigh Talamhant, 150
Tolsta, 166, 224
Traigh Mhor (Barra), 26
Triuirebheinn, 92, 94, 95
Tursachan, 205

Udal, 141
Uig, 179, 214, 218, 228

Vallay, 138, 148, 259
Valtos, 180, 237
Vatersay, 44, 248
Vikings, 12
Virgin nut (Molucca Bean), 86

Weaver's Castle, 89